D1601079

Public Sector Ethics

Finding and Implementing Values

ROUTLEDGE STUDIES IN GOVERNANCE AND PUBLIC POLICY

Public Sector Ethics

Finding and Implementing Values

Edited by Charles Sampford and Noel Preston
with C-A Bois

THE FEDERATION PRESS | ROUTLEDGE
1998

Published in Australia, New Zealand and
Papua New Guinea by
  The Federation Press
  71 John St, Leichhardt, NSW, 2040
  PO Box 45, Annandale, NSW, 2038
  Australia
  Ph: 61 (02) 9552 2200
  Fax: 61 (02) 9552 1681

Published in the United Kingdom and the
rest of the world by
  Routledge
  11 New Fetter Lane
  London EC4P 4EE
Simultaneously published in the USA and
Canada by
  Routledge
  29 West 38th Street
  New York, NY 10001

National Library of Australia Cataloguing-in-Publication data:

Public sector ethics: finding and implementing values.

Includes index.
ISBN 1 86287 298 8

1. Civil service ethics. 2. Public administration – Moral and ethical aspects. 3. Public
officers – Professional ethics. I. Sampford, CJG (Charles JG). II. Preston, Noel. III. Bois,
C-B. (Series: Routledge studies in governance and public policy).

172.2

British Library Cataloguing in Publication Data
A catalogue record for this book is available from the British Library
Library of Congress Cataloging in Publication Data
ISBN 0-415-19482-2

Individual © 1998 Individual contributors
Editorial and volume © 1998 National Institute for Law, Ethics and Public Affairs

Typeset by The Federation Press, Leichhardt, NSW.
  Printed by Ligare Pty Ltd, Riverwood, NSW.

Contents

ABOUT THE CONTRIBUTORS

ROSALIE BERNIER is a former Manager, Defence Ethics and Conflict of Interest at the National Defence Headquarters, Canada. She is responsible for the continuing development and implementation of the Defence Ethics Program within the Canadian Forces and the Department of National Defence and for the administration of the Conflict of Interest and Post-Employment Codes. A graduate of Laval University, Québec, with a degree in Education, she has held teaching positions and has extensive experience in human resource management, including recruitment, labour relations and training as well as audit.

C-A BOIS is currently working in academic publishing. With degrees from the United Kingdom, the United States and Japan, her teaching experience has included political studies and social and economic history. She has undertaken research in government-industry relations, the notion of rights in Asian constitutions and degrees of corruption and partiality in Japanese colonial rule. Since moving to publishing, she has edited works on public sector and legislative ethics, human rights, democracy, postmodern and feminist legal theory, constitutional interpretation and cross-cultural awareness in education.

DAVID CORBETT is an Emeritus Professor of Political Theory and Institutions, Flinders University, Adelaide, and Visiting Fellow at the Centre for Public Policy, University of Melbourne. A former Commissioner of the Public Service Board in South Australia, he is the author of *Australian Public Sector Management* (Allen & Unwin, 2nd edn, 1996).

ROGER DOUGLAS is a graduate of Melbourne, Yale and La Trobe Universities and a Barrister and Solicitor of the Supreme Court of Victoria. He is currently a Senior Lecturer at the School of Law and Legal Studies at La Trobe University, Melbourne, where he lectures in administrative law, equity and civil procedure. His publications include *Administrative Law: Commentary and Materials* (co-author, 2nd edn, Federation Press, 1996) and *Guilty, Your Worship. A Study of Victoria's Magistrates' Courts* (co-author, La Trobe University Legal Studies Department, 1981).

MEL DUBNICK is currently Professor of Public Administration and Political Science at Rutgers University – Newark, USA. Managing editor of *Public Administration Review* and former co-editor in chief of *Policy Studies Journal*, his publications include *American Public Administration* (co-author, Macmillan, 1991) and *Thinking About Public Policy* (co-author, John Wiley, 1983). An active member of both the American Society for Public Administration and the American Political Science Association, he was recently appointed to a task force to improve the role of civic education in America's colleges and universities.

COLIN HICKS is a senior adviser in the State Sector Development Branch of the State Services Commission, New Zealand. He has a background in social work, industrial relations and criminal justice policy development. In recent years, he has focused on ethics in the Public Service. Colin has published a number of articles on the subject, and is asked regularly to participate in seminars and workshops on ethics. He is involved currently in developing ways of managing and promoting ethical values and standards, and in ethics education and training.

HENDRIK KAPTEIN is a Lecturer in Jurisprudence in the University of Amsterdam Faculty of Law, and an adviser to REOB, the national organisation for research in legal and political sciences in The Netherlands. A regular contributor to the two leading newspapers in The Netherlands, mainly on criminal law and the bar, he has published a book on methods in ethics as well as articles on ethics, theory of argumentation in law, criminal law and public solidarity.

YOUNG JONG KIM is a Professor in the Department of Public Administration, Soong-Sil University, Seoul. He is currently the Chairman of the Korean Association for Corruption Studies and Dean of General Affairs of the University. A ACUCA lecturer in 1991, he was a Visiting Professor at the University of Washington, Seattle Pacific University and University of British Columbia between 1994 and 1995. He has published widely in the field of public ethics and corruption, with over 100 journal articles and more than 20 books, including *Korean Public Administration and Corruption Studies* (Hak Mun, 1996) and *Development Administration* (Bom Mun Sa, 2nd edn, 1997).

ALAN LAWTON is a Lecturer in Public Services Management at the Open University Business School, UK. He has taught at a number of UK universities, specialising in public sector management, ethics and management and policy analysis. His research interests focus upon public services organisations and their managers and include performance management, strategic change and ethics and the public service ethos. His publications have appeared in numerous journals and at conferences and include *Case Studies in Public Service Management* (co-editor, Blackwell, 1996) and *Organisation and Management in the Public Sector* (co-editor, Pitman, 1991). He is also editing a series on public services management and authoring its first book, *Ethics and Public Services* (forthcoming).

SEUMAS MILLER is Professor of Social Philosophy and Head, School of Humanities and Social Sciences, Charles Sturt University, New South Wales. He has undertaken research in the areas of public morality, violence and police culture and ethical principles underlying law enforcement. The author of four books and over 100 refereed articles, book chapters and other academic papers, he has published in a large number of international journals, including *Mind, Synthese, Philosophical Studies, Nous, Australasian Journal of Philosophy, Journal of Applied Philosophy, Professional Ethics* and *Public Affairs Quarterly*. His recent publications include *Rethinking Theory* (Cambridge University Press, 1992) and *Police Ethics* (Allen & Unwin, 1997).

STEPHEN D POTTS is the Director of the US Office of Government Ethics. A qualified lawyer who formerly was a partner for almost 30 years in a large law firm and who served in the US Army's Judge Advocate General's Corps, he is also a member of the Administrative Conference of the United States and the President's Council on Integrity and Efficiency and a voting delegate to the Judicial Conference of the District of Columbia.

NOEL PRESTON is the Director of the Centre for Ethics in Government, the Market and the Professions, Queensland University of Technology, Brisbane. Former president of the Australian Association of Professional and Applied Ethics, he has held consultancies with the Queensland Electoral and Administrative Review Commission and the Western Australia government commission on codes of conduct. He is a regular commentator on ethics and political practice in the print and electronic media. His extensive publications include *Understanding Ethics* (Federation Press, 1996) and *Ethics for the Public Sector* (editor, Federation Press, 1994).

CHARLES SAMPFORD was the Foundation Professor of Law and is the Foundation Director of the National Institute for Law, Ethics and Public Affairs, Griffith University, Brisbane. He has written widely on constitutional law and theory, jurisprudence, applied ethics, human rights, and legal education, including *The Disorder of Law* (Blackwell, 1989) and *Legal Ethics and Legal Practice* (co-editor, Clarendon Press, 1995). He has undertaken consultancy work on codes of ethics and legal education in both Australia and internationally, including the Nolan Committee in Britain in 1995, and is currently the legal advisor for the Queensland Parliament's Scrutiny of Legislation Committee.

GERALD SCANLAN is a senior adviser in the State Sector Development Branch of the State Services Commission, New Zealand. Gerald's areas of specialty include strategic management, governance, managing the government's interests as owner of departments, and performance management. He holds an MBA from Otago University, New Zealand, and has had articles published in several journals, including *Long Range Planning*. His current research interest concerns the applications of complexity theory to the task of governing the government management system.

TOM SHERMAN's career has been substantially in public law in the Australian Federal Attorney-General's Department. A former Commonwealth Crown Solicitor and Australian Government Solicitor, he was appointed Chairman of the Queensland Electoral and Administrative Review Commission in 1989. Currently a Visiting Fellow at the Centre for International and Public Law, Australia National University, Canberra, he is also Chairman of the National Crime Authority and a former President of the international Financial Action Task Force on Money Laundering.

ADRIENNE TAYLOR is the former Asia Pacific Regional Secretary for Public Services International (PSI), responsible for more than 100 unions in 23 countries, ranging from Palestine to the Pacific. With a BA in Sociology and a Diploma in Criminology, she has been involved with trade unions for over 15 years, including a number of international trade unions. She is also the Women's Secretary for PSI with a global responsibility.

MIKE WAGHORNE is currently the Assistant General Secretary of Public Services International (PSI). He is responsible for PSI's research and policy development work on public sector issues and other professional and political issues-oriented work, such as the environment and equal opportunities.

INTRODUCTION

Over the past three decades, serious questions have been asked about the performance of public institutions in most liberal democracies. The confidence produced by success in war of the few democracies that survived the 1930s and the remarkable economic and social progress of old and new democracies during the 1950s and 1960s was chastened by the apparent inability of the United States to win the Vietnam war and its internal war against poverty. Scandals and ethical failures took on greater significance. In many Western democracies, the stock market crashes of 1987 and property crashes of the early 1990s exposed weaknesses in business and in some governments whose 'business-like' approach led senior ministers into activities which were all too much like those of the failed businessmen (whose business empires were as ephemeral as the lies and accountants' statistics that had appeared to support them). In the United Kingdom, the unravelling of the conservative government exposed personal venality that earned the nickname 'sleaze'. In Western Australia, the government's involvement in ultimately failed businesses (most spectacularly Bond Corporation) was first praised and then vilified as 'WA Inc'. In Queensland, the long tolerated corruption of police and some political circles were exposed by the Fitzgerald Enquiry into police corruption from 1987 to 1989. The sudden decline in the fortunes of East Asian tigers in 1997 and 1998 led to widespread recognition of governmental corruption.

The public reaction to concerns about entrepreneurs, public servants and politicians tends to follow a similar pattern. It begins with outrage at outcomes (eg the squandering of money by business in takeover booms or by corrupt governments). Then follows the search for culprits and calls for tougher sanctions enforceable by law. When the limitations of the enforcement of such laws becomes apparent, there is a call for improved ethics. This is generally assumed to involve the writing of a code of ethics. These are often criticised unless they include tough penalties on the unethical. It is rarely appreciated that such penalties essentially involve a return to legal regulation and enforcement without legal safeguards, a system which has in any case been found to be wanting. Finally, it is, often dimly, appreciated that the problems are not solely a matter of individual conduct and the sanctions (legal or otherwise) that can be applied. We would argue in this volume that the problems and solutions are as much institutional as they are individual. Improving ethics must be linked to institutional and management reform. Indeed, we argue that the solutions to the problems identified by the ethical crises and occasional 'ethical meltdowns' can only be addressed by a co-ordinated programme of ethical standard setting, legal regulation and institutional reform (Sampford, 1994; Sampford and Preston, forthcoming).

Government efforts have not generally got beyond the first or second stage of enacting codes of conduct, with or without legal sanctions. Institutional reform is generally driven by other, potentially conflicting agendas concerning privatisation, corporatisation, competition, cost-cutting and the retreat of the state.

This book seeks to contribute to the task of understanding the processes by which ethical standards can be identified and institutionalised in the public agencies of liberal democracies. It forms part of a collaborative project on Public Sector Ethics led by the National Institute for Law, Ethics and Public Affairs and funded by the Australian Research Council and the Queensland Office of the Public Service (whose generous support is hereby most gratefully acknowledged).[1]

An important aspect of such work is the creation of dialogue and collaboration between two kinds of contributors: 'engaged academics' and 'reflective practitioners'. The 'engaged academics' are researchers in law, ethics, public administration, management and business studies who wish to 'road test' their theories in the complex and complicated bureaucratic environments and the fact situations those environments throw up. The 'reflective practitioners' are public officials and ethics consultants who are keen to explore the philosophical foundations of their work and its implications. To assist this dialogue and to enable academics and practitioners to share each others' perspectives, the National Institute hosted a workshop timed to coincide with the 5th International Ethics in the Public Sector Conference in Brisbane in August 1996. Papers were delivered at the conference, then subjected to intense debate, discussion and comparison at the workshop. The papers were not delivered a second time but introduced by those with differing perspectives to the authors (generally with a practitioner introducing an academic's paper and vice versa).

The reflective practitioners included: Rosalie Bernier, Dr Brian Grainger, Colin Hicks, Stephen Potts, Adrienne Taylor and Tom Sherman. The engaged academics included: Prof James Bowman, Dr Roger Douglas, Prof Mel Dubnick, Prof Leo Huberts, Prof Hendrik Kaptein, Dr Robert Kelso, Prof Alan Lawton, Dr Carol Lewis, Prof Seumas Miller, Assoc Prof Noel Preston and Prof Charles Sampford. Some were both, including Professor Young Jong Kim and Professor David Corbett.

The intention is that, after the workshops, the academic work will be far better informed than it could have otherwise been with a consequent improvement in the quality of the research output. Policy advice on the construction and implementation of ethics regimes can be improved. Those involved in those ethics regimes can have a deeper understanding of the issues with which they must grapple. Finally, ethics education in the public sector can be improved.

It is hoped that it also produces a book that provides a balance between theoretical perspectives on public sector ethics, experiences of implementation and suggestions of ways forward. While not a 'how to' guide *per se*, it does offer guidelines based on theoretical consideration and practical experience that will be of use to those teaching ethics within the public sector, structuring ethics programs or codes or implementing such activities.

The central focus of the following discussions may be found in the first chapter in the general list of common values and methods for their implementation found in ethics programs today. Subsequent chapters expand on and analyse each value or method individually, with the benefit of case studies from various sectors of the public service (including the police, defence forces, the legal profession and trade unions). Further, the broad geographical spread of the chapters (covering the United Kingdom, the Netherlands, the United States, Canada, Australia, New Zealand, South and North Korea, Russia and China) allows for the international comparison that is essential in today's global environment. In sum, each chapter builds upon the previous one, creating a thorough and provocative examination of ethics in the public sector.

These chapters make clear that there is no single approach or method that will work in all jurisdictions, let alone in all liberal democracies. Instead, each jurisdiction (and in some cases, each agency) needs to employ a variety of methods co-ordinated into an ethics regime (Sampford, 1996) attuned to the particular goals of the institutions, their culture, history and context. Motivation for ethical conduct is a theme running throughout the chapters, as is the concern for accountability. Freedom of Information Acts and the increasing level of public awareness (most often via the very powerful media) have made the demand for accountability unavoidable. While all of the contributors applaud this development, they question, in various ways, what constitutes accountability and how it should be manifested.

VALUES

Tom Sherman opens the discussion with his consideration of the need for core ethical values, underpinned by codes of conduct and other mechanisms, to promote and reinforce ethical behaviour and attitudes in the public sector. Sherman offers as a guideline a compilation of common values drawn from a number of codes and ethics programmes:

- honesty and integrity
- impartiality
- respect for the law
- respect for persons
- diligence
- economy and efficiency
- responsiveness
- accountability

While Sherman notes that such a list (with certain variations according to context or culture) is crucial, he emphasises that such values alone will have little impact. Codes of conduct, administrative law mechanisms, whistleblower protection legislation, effective enforcement of criminal law, effective auditing and monitoring regimes and training and support of ethical standards must also be implemented in order to create the infrastructure upon which the ethical environment can prosper.

But the public service is not a world in isolation; it faces external pressures and these too must be taken into account. Factors such as the politicisation of the public service (with the spectrum ranging from the United States on the high end and the United Kingdom on the low), the influence of the media, the pressures of economic rationalisation (with its privatisation and commercialisation of public services), arbitrary appointments to the public service and the influence of interest groups affect the public service to varying degrees and must be addressed in attempting to develop and protect an ethical mindset in the public service.

In short, Sherman advocates the development of an underlying rationale for a government system in which ethical conduct can flourish. Only then will these lists and mechanisms function effectively.

Hendrik Kaptein picks up on several of Sherman's values in his examination of professional ethics among the legal profession. **Honesty and integrity, respect for the law, respect for persons, impartiality** and **accountability** all play a part in his discussion the notion of autonomous morality within the law.

It is this autonomy which Kaptein examines, countering the notion that professional morality rests not upon artificial codes and procedures but upon individual notions of what is right and wrong. Rather, Kaptein asserts that it is what the legal and public service professional *do* and who they *are* that configures the nature of their professional ethics. For those in the legal profession, it is their duty to realise the rights rather than the interests of their clients (or themselves). Hence, the above values should be foremost in directing their actions. However, as Kaptein sees it, there is in the Bar another set of values which seem to receive more attention: confidentiality, independence and confraternality. While these values do not necessarily conflict with those found in Sherman's list, they can lead to a profession more intent on serving itself rather than those it is meant to serve.

Similar to Sherman, Kaptein's conclusion emphasises the need for an integrated approach, an integrity of 'understanding and acting upon the proper role of the profession in the legal order and in society'. Values, be they from Sherman's list or some other guideline, must be considered with the underlying principles of a profession as well as the role to be played in the community.

Community is central to Seamus Miller's consideration of autonomy, discretion and **accountability** in the police. What Kaptein termed 'confraternality' is here called 'institutional culture'. And it is the discretionary powers at different levels and of varying strengths as well as inter-institutional relationships within this culture which Miller examines within the context of accountability as responsibility and autonomy in the police force.

Miller uses four case studies to illustrate the varying aspects of authority and discretion in policing. Sherman's value of **respect for the law** comes into play here, as Miller identifies four aspects of police discretion (concrete interpretation and application of law; law is not exhaustive but often open-ended ('reasonable cause'); balancing law with the maintenance of social calm and preservation of life; and the need for on-the-spot solutions). The potential conflict between 'original authority' (the law) and delegated authority (human (ie police) directives) reveals how an institutional culture, with its notions of responsibility and accountability, can be at odds with those of the individual or of the community at large. Further, Miller emphasises that while accountability, be it legal, moral or administrative, does not equal liability, it most often implies it. This creates an individual liability in a situation where the individual may not have been acting upon his or her own discretion, further bringing individual and institutional values into conflict.

While admitting that moral vulnerability in policing is an occupational hazard (similar to the views of Potts below in a different context), Miller feels that there must be an integration of the individual, institutional and communal to help ensure accountability among the police. Joint institutional and community mechanisms (including peer accountability and a just system of rewards and penalties), together with training and supervision, can be of great use in inculcating the desire to act ethically. Once again, it is the underlying principles and motivation to act ethically which are of central importance.

Alan Lawton takes a conceptual approach in his appraisal of the utilisation of business practices in the public service. It is the economic rationalism, referred to by Sherman, which has brought many business methods and approaches into the public service arena, often with overwhelming (but not necessarily positive) force.

Lawton takes up the argument of the genericists and differentialists, siding with the latter. It is essential, Lawton feels, that the individual political, social and economic conditions under which a public service organisation or institution exists be taken into account in determining which, if any, practices from the commercial world are to be applied in the public sector. Much like Kaptein, Lawton acknowledges that the goals of the organisation must be considered in addressing any restructuring or refocusing. And with the institution's goals are the people, with their skills (reiterating Sherman's value of **respect for persons**). The drive for **economy and efficiency** does not necessarily come with a wholesale absorption of indiscriminately chosen 'business' practices.

Further, a number of other factors must be considered: the role of management in changing organisations (and with that, changing responsibility and **accountability**, discretion and authority); the relationship between the different stakeholders (internal and external); the potential conflict between long and short-term approaches to service (itself relating back to the goals of the organisation). By referring to examples from the United Kingdom, the United States and Canada, Lawton demonstrates the merit of adapting management prescriptions to a culture or specific organisation. Overriding these differences with across-the-board precepts, priorities and procedures not only stagnates creativity and wastes existing intellectual property but can also impose an ethos inimical to the actual goal of the service.

Mel Dubnick's chapter closes the first section of the book with its in-depth analysis of **accountability**. A value referred to throughout the book, accountability is considered here in detail. To Dubnick, accountability is *the* crucial value in public sector ethics. Yet it is a term overused and little contemplated, with few real attempts to define or delineate its meaning. Dubnick first considers the term in English, highlighting its particularly anglican nature and contrasting it with comparable but not equivalent terms in French, Spanish, Portuguese, Italian, Japanese, Hebrew and Russian. In short, cultural context (be it geographical, institutional or situational) is crucial in understanding the meaning and implications of accountability.

Moving from linguistics to ethical theory, Dubnick refers to the various schools of thought which have considered accountability (eg Freudians, Marxists, behaviourists, social action theorists) and have been utilised within the field of public administration. Yet it is Nozick's notion of moral push versus moral pull which Dubnick finds most useful. Utilising this overall approach, he develops a framework for accountability which encompasses the moral 'pulls' of liabilities, answerability, responsibility and **responsiveness** and the 'pushes' of obligations, obedience, fidelity and amenability. This framework, used with the four institutional contexts of legal, organisational, professional and political structures, allows one to consider what Dubnick sees as the duality of accountability: the accountability of conduct (the moral pushes) and the conduct of accountability (the moral pulls). By taking both elements into account as well as the context, it may be possible to construct an ethical framework which is both effective and feasible.

IMPLEMENTING VALUES

Having considered the central values of public sector ethics and their role within varying contexts, the book then moves onto discussions of the 'practical' means for implementing and institutionalising them.

Stephen Potts addresses the issue of corruption in the public service and its high economic, social and political costs. By implementing strong and appropriate preventative mechanisms, public service can not only cut these often very substantial costs but focus on fulfilling its purpose: to serve the public, rather than the selfish and pecuniary interests of public servants. **Codes of conduct**, a system of disclosure of financial interests and **training** are crucial mechanisms in an effective ethics programme but must be coupled with **monitoring** and enforcement measures as well.

Potts then outlines the approach to public sector ethics taken in the United States, which has the longest history of institutionalised attempts to enhance ethics. Methods such as **legislation**, setting aspirational goals for employees and telling employees what to and what not to do are considered. He then addresses efforts on the international front (eg UN and OECD codes of conduct, the Inter-American Convention against Corruption). Throughout, he reiterates the importance of implementation and enforcement of the aforementioned mechanisms. For Potts, prevention is the key both against corruption and for an ethical and efficiently functioning public service.

Corruption takes centre stage in Young Jong Kim's comparison of the phenomenon in socialist and capitalist states. After examining what the term means within various cultural contexts, Kim then goes on to assess the potential causes for corruption: organisational or socio-cultural. While opting for the former, Kim acknowledges that although the latter may not be the cause *per se*, it is such a central factor in corruption's perpetuation that it must be taken into account in the attempt to eradicate it. Equally, the stage of economic development can be seen to play a part in both the level and breadth of corruption.

Kim then offers a guided tour through the corrupt corridors of China, Russia, North Korea and South Korea. He considers the factors of delivery systems of goods (a prime target for corruption); anti-corruption campaigns, bodies and legislation; the level of exposure of corruption; centralisation and excessive hierarchical bureaucracies with lack of accountability; individual subsystems within bureaucracies; lack of respect for the law; and the role of nepotism and authoritarian structures.

As this list reveals, the elements of corruption in the two political systems are not vastly different. Rather, it is the level and expanse of it which may vary. In either case, Kim concurs with many of the contributors in saying that an integrated approach is the most feasible way forward for a less corrupt and more ethical public service. Kim integrated approach envisages a service based upon common goals and values, a degree of decentralisation with autonomy but also **accountability**, **legislation** (anti-corruption, whistleblower, ombudsmen) and transparency.

Colin Hicks and Gerald Scanlan support Kim's focus on an integrated approach. A country with an extremely low level of corruption, New Zealand has undertaken a radical managerial reform of its public service in what the authors term an 'integrated' approach. This integration entails the use of mutually reinforcing initiatives consistent with a devolved management system. These initiatives are 'supportive of the government's priorities and reflective of the values of the wider political context'. Using the slogan 'direction, autonomy, control', the focus is on managerial performance, driven by clear goals and an understanding of the distinction between government purchase and ownership interests (and the importance of both).

Through its process of managerial reform, New Zealand has developed clear-cut goals twinned with incentives, compliance-based procedures with clear lines of **accountability**, **legislation** and on-going monitoring systems. But successful as the system is, it has become clear with time that it is easy for codes at one level to conflict with incentives at another. Departmental allegiances can develop, hindering inter-departmental relationships. People joining the public service do not automatically absorb (or are even aware of) the underlying principles and values of the institution. Thus, the authors stress the need for mutually reinforcing methods, a combination of standards, guidance, education and recognition of good practice and, not surprisingly, clear and constant communication.

Rosalie Bernier provides an insight into developing an ethics programme for a particular sector of the public service: here, the military. In 1994, the Canadian Forces and Department of National Defence implemented a Defence Ethics programme in response to both internal pressures (fiscal restraints, downsizing and a greater awareness of rights following the implementation of Charter of Rights and Freedoms) and external developments (Canada's increasing involvement in international peacekeeping efforts).

The Canadian programme is value-based, working at both the managerial and employee level, seeking to foster a certain agreed set of values and encourage an 'ethical mindset' rather than implementing a strong compliance-reward/penalty based structure. This is in contrast to the stronger suggestions for prevention and monitoring put forth in other contributions, such as Kim, Potts and, to a certain degree, Sherman. Yet the principles and obligations central to the programme reiterate those mentioned throughout the book. Again, the values of **respect for the law**, **respect for persons**, **honesty**, **impartiality** (here, fairness) and **diligence** are noted, in addition to loyalty, courage and obedience.

Bernier outlines the structure of the programme, how it has developed and how it is changing. Players such as the Senior Ethics Coordinator and the Ethics Resource and Assistance Centre support the internal structure, along with ongoing training and **monitoring**. Like Corbett (see below), this programme advocates case-driven training over pure abstraction. Further, the programme works within the *Conflict of Interest and Post-Employment Code for the Public Service* 1987, thus ensuring that the ethical structure developed in this sector of the public service is not at odds with other sectors.[2]

This link between codes, law and good government are explored by Roger Douglas. Focusing on the particular mechanism of administrative law, Douglas looks at its function in general and then homes in on legislature and judicial decisions.

Douglas perceives administrative law as a regulator of the relationship between the citizen and the executive branch of government. While it has taken its values from the politicians and judges who created it against a backdrop of 'responsible government', it can act as compensation for the limits of this responsible government, offering the citizen more input into their government and public service. Indeed, Douglas highlights the irony of the executive-dominated legislature passing executive-constraining legislation. Statutory bodies, such as the ombudsman and review tribunals, offer the investigative authority and monitoring ability referred to in Sherman, among others. And while their power is, respectively, informal and formal, Douglas is clear that this does not necessarily make the impact of one greater than another. Judicial administrative law can further be seen as a counterbalance to the executive.

Once again, the centrality of the values upon which a structure (here, administrative law) is built are emphasised. Douglas takes Sherman's list and assesses its application to this tool, finding each present but in varying degrees of theory versus practice and their implicit or explicit expression. Even so, Douglas admits that administrative law, while a useful tool for helping to ensure an ethical structure, will not necessarily contribute to the achievement of these values for their own merit. Rather, it may merely be a case of adhering to the values for the sake of good administration.

While notions of institutional culture and departmental or sectoral allegiance have been addressed so far, the factor of inter-departmental or institutional links has not. Adrienne Taylor and Mike Waghorne address that imbalance with their focus on public sector trade unions. The rationalisation and commercialisation of the public service, referred to in Sherman, Lawton and Hicks, has yielded a new kind of 'management', involving greater use of consultants, short-term appointments and supposedly cost-effective staffing. Such managers are often unaware of their responsibilities either to their staff or to the goals and values of the service as a whole. In response to this, Taylor and Waghorne advocate a recognised code of management to ensure fair treatment for workers and long-term success for the service and to bring management practice into line with public sector values. The power of the role is not be overlooked, a point repeated by Sherman, Dubnick, Potts and Corbett.

Like other codes discussed in this volume, the one suggested here must be integrated and not conflict with existing codes and legislature nor with employment contracts. It must explicitly articulate the key goals, standards and values of the service and of the manager's role itself in the organisation. Enforceability is a must, as is supportive training and monitoring. And in addition to such a code, the authors, not surprisingly, emphasise the need for strong and effective whistleblower legislation, for the protection of both management and staff, and consumer charters. But to ensure that any and all of these mechanisms work as more than ethical window dressing, they must articulate, advocate and perpetuate a core set of values repeatedly and consistently across departments, across institutions and even across nations.

David Corbett concludes the book with an insightful piece on the central importance and inevitable difficulty of training in ethics. In his three central points (public sector ethics is not separate from ethics in society as a whole, segments of community or individual sectors of the public service; teaching can be limited by a teacher with limited experience to draw upon; and ethical public service means virtuous public service), he draws together many of the points made throughout the volume. The importance of integrity between community and the public service, the recognition of context, the essential need for personal motivation to act ethically, the need for mechanisms of encouragement and enforcement; all these factors must be expressed in the context of training, for if it does not occur at this level, it is difficult for it to be perpetuated on any sort of coherent and consistent basis.

Corbett, like many of the other contributors, is a great believer in the concrete joined to the abstract. For that reason, he advocates the use of storytelling (using here the tales of death of Captain Cook and Daniel and Belshazzar) to demonstrate how something concrete and experiential can be utilised to teach abstract values such as those listed by Sherman. While it is best to avoid too many in-house horror stories and 'war' stories, there are any number of stories (be they mythological or historical) which can impart a knowledge and understanding of ethical behaviour far more effectively than any flowchart or abstract list of values. Taking into account context, Corbett asserts that even if a story has a particular cultural context (as do his two examples), they can still be effective through their dramatic content and cast of characters. Ethics is not a theoretical construct but the active debate over 'how we should live our lives'. It is part of the life of a public servant and is about that life. As we ask ourselves the questions about the values such lives should realise and the means of implementing those values, exemplary tales of those who have succeeded and failed to achieve those values are one of the most powerful tools for considering how we may live our lives. We hope that this book will assist public sector ethicists and managers to assist public servants to enjoy more fulfilling lives by furthering the values outlined by Sherman and in so doing, live up to the term 'public service'.

NOTES

1   Other works generated by the project include Preston et al (eds) (1998) and Sampford and Preston (forthcoming).
2   This code covers ethical standards, public scrutiny, private interests, public interest, gifts and benefits, preferential treatment, government property and post-employment.

PART I

FINDING VALUES

1

PUBLIC SECTOR ETHICS
Prospects and Challenges

Tom Sherman

INTRODUCTION

The recognition and exposition of ethics in the public sector have made considerable progress in the last decade. Whether or not this has produced higher standards of ethical conduct in public administration is harder to measure. Progress is also evident in the private sector, both in the business and professional areas.

It is equally difficult to assess progress at the political level.[1] For example, a code of conduct for federal members of the Australian parliament and their staff was recommended in 1978 by the Report of the Committee of Inquiry into Public Duty and Private Interest (the Bowen Report) (Bowen, 1979). Although registers of interests have now been established in the House of Representatives and the Senate, no general code of ethics has been established applying to all members of parliament. A similar situation applies in most of Australia's State and Territory legislatures.[2]

Australian Prime Minister Howard's *Guide on Key Elements of Ministerial Responsibility* (April 1996) represents another evolution of a practice which commenced in 1983, whereby prime ministers advise their ministers of appropriate standards of conduct based on the recommendations in the Bowen Report (Office of the Prime Minister and Cabinet, 1996). These guidelines developed a sting very quickly. In October 1996, two members of the Howard Ministry resigned because of breaches of the guidelines relating to the holding of shares in companies in respect of which they had made favourable ministerial decisions. Subsequently, several others have followed suit for a variety of other reasons.

As attested to throughout this volume, these developments are not particular to Australia. However, they do demonstrate the growing concern with public sector ethics and developments which seek to address this concern.

This increased awareness of the importance of public sector ethics has several sources. First, there have been a number of inquiries into scandals in recent years which demonstrated a less than desirable state of affairs in public sector conduct. The cash for questions scandal in the United Kingdom, the Gingrich and Wright affairs in the United States and the repeated prime ministerial corruption scandals in Japan are to name but a few. Notable among those in Australia were the Fitzgerald Report on police corruption and related matters in Queensland (1989) and the report of the WA Inc Royal Commission in Western Australia (1993).[3] Both reports exposed quite high levels of official corruption in those jurisdictions. Such scandals diminish confidence in public administration and often have adverse electoral consequences for the governments perceived as responsible.

The recent Royal Commission into Police Corruption in New South Wales reinforces this trend. Further, the Independent Commission Against Corruption (ICAC) in New South Wales and the Criminal Justice Commission in Queensland (CJC) are now in the process of conducting inquiries into the conduct of ministers and officials in those States.

As elsewhere, there have also been a number of other inquiries and controversies in Australia over the last few decades which have examined allegations of improper conduct particularly by federal ministers. Examples of these are:

- the Finnane inquiry in 1979 in relation to dealings in Ian Sinclair's family companies;

- the Senate Standing Committee on Finance and Government Operations inquiry in 1981 into the Australian Dairy Corporation and its Asian subsidiaries which examined Ian Sinclair's involvement in the activities of the corporation and its subsidiaries;

- the Colour TV affair in 1982 involving conduct by Federal ministers John Moore and Michael MacKellar;

- the Combe-Ivanov affair where the Hope Royal Commission in 1983 found that federal minister Mick Young made improper or unauthorised disclosures of official information to journalists Eric Walsh and Rod Cameron; and

- the Black inquiry in 1984 into the Paddington Bear affair relating to the conduct of federal minister Mick Young concerning customs documentation.

In fairness to some of the ministers concerned, not all inquiries found that ministers engaged in improper conduct.[4]

These problems in relation to unethical conduct in the public sector demonstrate quite effectively that such behaviour occurs quite regularly and at all levels of government.

Another source of increased awareness of the need for proper standards of ethical conduct in the Australian public sector has arisen from the work of a number of bodies (in some cases, following on from inquiries such as those noted above) which has led to the establishment of frameworks and principles to encourage more ethical conduct. In Australia, such bodies include the Independent Commission Against Corruption, the Criminal Justice Commission and the Electoral and

Administrative Review Commission (EARC) in Queensland, as well as the Commission on Government in Western Australia. More recently at the federal level, there has been the publication of a report on ethics in the Australian public service by the Management Advisory Board (Management Advisory Board, 1996).

The third source has been the growing public demand (expressed principally through the media) for more openness and accountability in public administration. The work of a number of academics has also contributed to this process (see, eg, Harman, 1994, p 8; Jackson and Smith, 1996 p 23; Kernaghan, 1996; Mancuso, 1995; Rosenthal, 1996; and Thompson, 1995).

CORE ETHICAL VALUES

Increasingly, a number of jurisdictions have put in place codes or guidelines relating to ethical conduct particularly for public servants on both state/provincial and national levels. In some instances, those standards are finding expression in legislation.[5]

These codes and guidelines refer to a number of core ethical values to shape public sector conduct. What follows is a composite listing of the more common values included.[6]

- honesty and integrity
- impartiality
- respect for the law
- respect for persons
- diligence
- economy and efficiency
- responsiveness
- accountability

This listing is intended to be illustrative, not exhaustive. There are other values which might be added, such as 'courage' and 'neutrality'. On the other hand, some may question the relevance of 'economy and efficiency' and 'responsiveness' in a statement of core ethical values.

Some of these tensions concerning which values are 'essential' go to the heart of the debate about the role of the public sector in a democratic society. There is a discernible trend in many countries at all levels of government to see the public sector increasingly as utterly loyal instruments of the government of the day. Proponents of this view would give greater emphasis to the values of 'responsiveness' and 'economy and efficiency'.

Others would argue that the public sector has a more fundamental role than simply to serve the government of the day. They contend that public officials (including elected officials) are holders of a public trust and ethical values have to be considered in the context of the official's ultimate objective to serve the public interest. Proponents of this view would give greater emphasis to values such as integrity and impartiality.

These views raise complex issues which cannot be further developed within the constraints of this single chapter. However, the tensions need to be recognised and accounted for when developing and implementing codes or guidelines for ethical conduct.

By way of comparison, it is worth noting the core principles developed by the Nolan Committee in its Report on Standards in Public Life in the United Kingdom (Committee on Standards in Public Life, 1995). The important work of this committee originated in the cash for parliamentary questions scandals in the UK Parliament in the early 1990s. The seven principles of public life developed by the Nolan Committee were:

- selflessness;
- integrity;
- objectivity;
- accountability;
- openness;
- honesty; and
- leadership.

These two lists of values illustrate the point that ethical values will vary from country to country and they will also vary between the categories of public officials to whom they are intended to apply. The Nolan Committee principles are intended to apply to members of the UK Parliament. The composite Australian list is drawn from codes and guidelines which apply principally to public servants. Nevertheless, it is significant that both lists contain the important values of integrity, honesty and accountability.

Support Mechanisms for Core Values

Before leaving the area of core ethical values, it is relevant to consider the negative side of these values which serves to emphasise their importance. Clearly, developing positive values aims to deter negative conduct, such as dishonesty, secretiveness, partiality, nepotism, unfairness and, at the base line, criminal conduct.

Yet it is generally recognised that the mere promulgation of legislative standards or codes and guidelines is not enough. They must be supplemented and supported by measures, legislative and otherwise, to create a climate where ethical conduct is more likely to prosper. Such measures can include:

- administrative law mechanisms, such as freedom of information and merits and judicial review of administrative decisions (see Douglas, Chapter 10);
- whistleblower protection legislation (see Taylor and Waghorne, Chapter 11);

- effective enforcement of the criminal law, particularly in the areas of serious misconduct and corruption;
- establishment of effective auditing and monitoring regimes; and
- training in, and systemic support of, the application of ethical standards (see Corbett, Chapter 12).

While measures such as these are in place in one form or another in many jurisdictions concerned with public sector ethics, the challenges for the future will be their continuous improvement in the light of experience and greater harmony amongst domestic jurisdictions, in the case of multilevel or federal states.

The issue of harmony has particular relevance to federal structures, where the unwillingness of some jurisdictions to implement reform has a debilitating and deleterious effect on the whole federation. Unitary systems of government generally do not have this problem. Once again, it is essential to bear in mind the particular institutional, cultural and social characteristics of a state and its public sector when developing and implementing a program of ethics (Mancuso (1998) specifically addresses the institutional element of the ethics formula).

Another important but often overlooked mechanism is that of training in ethics (see Corbett, Chapter 12; also see Preston, 1994). Formal training in ethics, both in educational institutions and as part of 'on the job' personal development training, is essential to fostering good ethical conduct. Unless ethical codes and guidelines are supported by appropriate training, they will quickly gather dust and lose vitality as well as relevance.

Another important aspect of ethical training is the example showed by leaders and managers to those for whom they are responsible. Training by example has two important aspects. First, there is the negative aspect. If leaders and senior managers are not themselves ethical, then their staff will quickly see ethical codes and guidelines as an essentially hypocritical exercise. Secondly, there is the positive aspect. Good managers who are seen to be ethical will have a much greater and lasting impact on ethical standards than any other form of training.[7] It is not necessary for them to articulate core ethical values; simply demonstrating them by their own actions can inspire others to do the same. The power of the role model should not be overlooked, even in these cynical times.

It is also important that elected officials, such as ministers, lead by example. It makes little sense for public servants to try to conduct themselves ethically when their elected masters in many cases have not as yet developed their own ethical standards and where they have encounter difficulty in abiding by them.

International Mechanisms

There are of course some relevant developments at the international level. Notable amongst these are the 1991 Harare Declaration on Good Governance from the Commonwealth Heads of Government meeting in Harare, Zimbabwe and the 1995 Millbrook Commonwealth Action Programme, developed following the Harare Declaration. The Harare Declaration addresses democratic characteristics of good governance, such as respect for human rights, as well as the rule of law and the independence of the judiciary. The declaration also refers to the importance of just and honest government. The Millbrook Action Programme includes the development of an integrity in public office code. The Harare Declaration is particularly significant because it is an expression of political commitment at the highest level by 52 countries, covering a third of the world's population.

International initiatives are particularly important because they reflect transnational standards. These initiatives will, in the context of the global village, influence developments in each country. The consequent challenge is for each nation to then make an effective contribution to these developments.[8]

THE CHALLENGES

The future for public sector ethics must be concerned with dealing with a number of significant challenges rather than with resting on past achievements. Systems change as do the players involved on both domestic and international levels and ethics structures must change with them to varying degrees.

The five principal challenges considered here are:

- the need to extend the application of ethical standards to other holders of public office, namely, ministers, parliamentarians, members of the judiciary and holders of statutory office;
- the growing politicisation of the public service;
- economic rationalism encompassing privatisation and commercialisation;
- arbitrariness in public sector appointments; and
- undue influence of interest groups in decision-making.

Before examining each challenge, two general points need to made clear. First, each challenge is a substantial topic in its own right and only some general observations that have relevance to public sector ethics can be made here. Secondly, describing these areas as challenges does not suggest that they are all necessarily undesirable developments. Rather, they constitute some potentially difficult issues for public sector ethics that must be worked through.

While many of the issues raised here are not easily solved, that shouldn't be an impediment to discussing them. Indeed, we owe it to our forebears and future generations to keep them squarely on the agenda.

Extending Public Sector Ethics to Other Holders of Public Office

This proposal may not be palatable to many of our politicians. One of the paradoxes of the evolution of public sector ethics is that, while public servants are expected to observe the highest ethical standards, there doesn't seem to be the same interest or progress in the development of ethical standards for ministers and other members of parliament. (See Preston et al (eds) (1998) on legislative codes of conduct.) Similar arguments could be put in relation to other important categories of public office, namely, members of the judiciary and statutory office holders.

Some may contend that it is unrealistic to expect politicians to observe ethical standards in their political activity because it is an inherently competitive business and politics is essentially about winning and holding office. I believe that this is an impoverished view of democracy. Politics should surely be pre-occupied with serving the public interest and delivering good government to the community. Ethical conduct is not an optional appendage to public office; it is an essential part of its exercise.

Further, it is generally recognised that the whole political process and those who participate in it are held in low regard in the community. The cynicism is well expressed in the old joke 'Don't tell Mum I'm a politician. She thinks I'm a piano player in a bordello'. There is a growing disillusionment in many countries with the standard of political conduct. Part of the reason for this might be that the ethical values such as honesty, integrity and accountability are not rigorously applied in public life. Indeed, much political activity seems to have more to do with dishonesty, broken promises and a diminution of ministerial responsibility to the legislative body. The test of conduct seems to be 'Will I get caught?' rather than 'Is it right?'.

The time is fast approaching where political leadership must start articulating and applying standards of proper ethical conduct in political life. In Australia, the recent Commonwealth guidelines on ministerial responsibility are an important development but they are limited to Commonwealth ministers in their ministerial capacity and, to a lesser extent, their staff (Office of the Prime Minister and Cabinet, 1996). Registers of interest and codes of conduct are slowly, but perhaps far too slowly, making ethical inroads into this important but still reluctant segment of the public sector.

Judges should not be considered in any special position as public officials; mere adherence to the law in such areas as conflict of interest is far from enough. For example, there have been calls for gender awareness training for Australian judges following some quite remarkable statements from members of its judiciary about women in rape cases.[9] In the UK, the outrageous comments of Judge Pickles have elicited similar demands. Indeed, the problem is wider than gender awareness. Such statements also reflect a lack of appropriate ethical values, such as respect for persons.

Another area concerning the judiciary is that of nepotism. For example, in my early years of practice in the law in the late 1960s, I was struck by the number of associates to judges who had the same surname as the judge. This may not be simply an historical problem. For example, a current telephone listing in Queensland shows four Supreme Court and six District Court associates bearing the same surname as the judge they serve. It might all be coincidence but it might also suggest nepotism. Any judge who sees no problem engaging his or her children and relatives as an associate (which is a public office) is in desperate need of ethical enlightenment. Needless to say, this is an issue that potentially cuts across all parts of the public sector.

Some may argue that judges have no need for codes of conduct because they have practised with professional ethics as barristers and solicitors. (Professional ethics amongst the legal profession is critically assessed in Kaptein, Chapter 2.) Without diminishing the importance of professional ethics, some points should be made about this argument. First, judicial office is a high public office and calls for the application of different and higher standards of ethics than applies in legal professional practice. Secondly, although professional rules are currently undergoing revision in this regard, legal professional ethical rules have traditionally been more preoccupied with protecting members of the profession from the chill winds of competition. Thirdly, there has been an increasing incidence of appointing non-practising lawyers to the Bench who may have had little or no experience of working on a daily basis under professional ethical rules.

It needs to be stressed that judges are generally highly ethical individuals who often accept significant restrictions on their personal lives and the company they keep in order to maintain high standards of conduct. Nevertheless, there are always persons in any group in society whose standards are lower than their peers. Further, ethical guidelines may assist even the most ethical of judges in making decisions in difficult grey areas.[10] It is interesting to note that the United States has had codes of judicial ethics in place since 1924. In fact, the 1990 revision to the Model Code of Judicial Conduct requires judges to report on serious misconduct of other judges and lawyers (Shaman et al, 1990, p 23).

If codes of judicial ethics are to be developed further, they will have to be developed by the judges themselves. Practical and constitutional reasons make it inappropriate for others to carry out this task.

Finally, it should be noted that many holders of statutory office are generally not subject to public service ethical guidelines unless they are employed under the various Public Service Acts. Whilst some statutory officers may be subject to their own agency specific ethical guidelines, there are no general guidelines applicable to them. This category covers some very significant public offices, such as reserve banks, securities commissions and even crime and 'defense' commissions (eg the FBI and CIA in the United States). Many countries boast hundreds of statutory authorities and a significant portion of the public sector is employed within them. It is essential that ethical codes of conduct and the programmes to support them be developed to ensure good governance.

Growing Politicisation in the Public Service

The second challenge is that of politicisation in the public service. In spite of all the commentaries on this matter, it appears we are still searching for a proper balance between the merit principle and ministerial control over those for whom they are responsible.[11] Even those from the Westminster and Washington systems seem to be looking for a more feasible cross-breed.

This is perhaps a reflection of the deficiencies in each of the systems. The permanency of civil service heads in the United Kingdom is seen as too rigid and inflexible. The Washington system unapologetically involves political patronage and is seen as extending politicisation too far into the lower levels of the federal civil service as well as producing discontinuity of expertise and experience when presidents change office. It obviously has drastic implications for long-term impartiality in the public service, which some see as one of the strengths of the Westminster system.

Nevertheless, in producing greater flexibility in senior public service appointments, we must be careful not to throw the baby out with the bathwater if the public service is to retain its custodianship of national experience for the benefit of future governments and the people (Hasluck, 1968, p 93).

We now seem to be entering a period of substantial erosion of the merit principle without any clear justification other than pragmatic political convenience. Even so, the more 'political' US system does have its merits. It operates in an environment of congressional checks on appointments of senior public officials; it also involves a much greater movement between the public and private sectors than exists in some other countries.

Another aspect of politicisation is the increasing and sometimes undue influence of ministerial staff. While the basic role of the ministerial staffer as an alternative source of advice to the minister particularly on political issues is not under question, ministers should be able to obtain advice from a *variety* of sources. It would be unhealthy if the public service had a monopoly on the provision of that advice. Ministerial staff should not however act as barriers to keep out public service advice or as censors of that advice. Problems usually arise in this area when the minister is a weak one or does not have an understanding of proper processes.

Often too there are no real accountability mechanisms for the actions of ministerial staff. In some countries, they may not be called before legislative committees to account for their actions or advice. Their actions and decisions are not generally subject to administrative or judicial review.[12]

A number of these issues are not debated because public servants, particularly those who are incumbents, are reluctant to take issue with governments. Also, this is one area where the media (with some notable exceptions) is not particularly concerned. This is possibly because the media doesn't see any real difference between the major political parties and so there is, in the media's view, no news value in the issue.

Economic Rationalism

The recent developments in the area of economic rationalism also raise ethical issues as we move towards more commercialisation and privatisation of significant areas of the public service. The major issue is: what ethical standards and accountability mechanisms are going to apply in these privatised/commercialised areas? (Lawton, Chapter 4, considers the shift from public to private and the pitfalls encompassed therein.)

In the case of privatisation, it is clearly inadequate to leave these matters to the law of contract, particularly when the contracts themselves may be confidential. Are decisions going to be made subject to judicial and merit reviews and other accountability mechanisms? One of the paradoxes here is that we are striving to achieve greater accountability and higher ethics in the public sector when whole parts of that sector are leaving it. Although regulators are frequently proposed in a number of these privatised areas, they are generally limited to ensuring market outcomes are achieved.

An interesting example of how far privatisation has extended is provided by Gary Sturgess, the former head of the Cabinet Office in New South Wales.

> The Commonwealth government under Labor, for example, has contracted with the private sector to carry out some of our most sensitive security functions. It is well known that the US/Australian defence facility near Woomera in South Australia played a key role in monitoring SCUD launches during the Gulf War. What is not so well known is that the men and women who took those signals off the satellites and who conveyed the data to the Patriot missile batteries were private contractors. Moreover, they received a Presidential citation for it. (Sturgess, 1993, pp 87–8)

Commercialisation is potentially less troublesome. It makes obvious sense to introduce appropriate commercial practices into public service areas where they are likely to produce greater accountability and efficiency. Nevertheless, commercialisation can create ethical tensions particularly between the interests of clients and the public interest. A number of commercialised organisations in the public sector are now dealing with ethical issues in the new environment.

Appointment of Public Officials

Many jurisdictions have legislation which enshrines the merit principle in public service appointments. This is an enduring legacy of the Northcote Trevelyan reforms of the 19th century.[13] However there are many, and in some cases, very significant public offices where appointments are not subject to merit principle processes of selection. Statutory office holders (in contrast to the staff of those authorities) and judicial appointments are decided made on ministerial or some other high official's recommendation. It is in this area that a political patronage system is quite free to operate.

I am of course not suggesting for one moment that all appointee to public office are beneficiaries of political patronage. In most cases, those appointed to public offices are generally the best available persons. Nevertheless, the appointments process is open to abuse.

Perhaps the only real check which presently exists in this area is the media. Thus, we see or hear major public appointments being speculated upon in the media from time to time, with potential candidates are praised or criticised. While this speculation can be beneficial in that it may expose potential nepotism or 'giving jobs to the boys', it sometimes has a comical element, as when an individual identified as a candidate has not and will not be approached or if the position itself is non-existent.

Some would advocate that governments should be free to appoint persons who are best suited to carry out the duties of the relevant public office. These same individuals would also argue that informality is the key to effectiveness in this area;

for example, many persons of ability, particularly those in the private sector, will not apply for public office and allow themselves to be subject to a selection process. Further, some would argue (perhaps justifiably) that subjecting these appointments to full merit selection processes would be too cumbersome.

There is force in these arguments. Even so, there is considerable inconsistency and potential for abuse in the present system. For example, much often relies on informal networking at ministerial and senior bureaucratic levels. Where there are genuine endeavours to find the best available person, the system works moderately well. The abuses occur where persons are appointed simply for political reward or where competent people are excluded for political and other unrelated reasons. In addition, women and members of other groups who have experienced systemic discrimination can and often do suffer in this process.

The challenge here then is to devise consistent principles and processes of appointment which protect the merit principle and avoid political abuse.

Undue Influence of Interest Groups

Public sector ethics can come under strain when strong interest groups in the community have undue interest over government policy and decision making. By their nature, lobbyists are not necessarily concerned with the wider public interest. They are paid to advance the interests of those whom they represent. However, while lobbyists and interest groups do play an important part in the democratic process, care should be taken to avoid situations where other competing voices are cut out or where the regulator becomes the captive of the regulated.

Difficulties more often arise where processes of decision-making are secretive and arbitrary. It is in this environment that undue influence can occur. One protection against undue influence is in open and consultative processes of decision-making. If the public has access to information on the content of lobbyists' arguments, those critical of those interests can have a greater chance of meeting the arguments.[14]

The experience of the EARC in Queensland, in which I was involved, is relevant here. In all of our reviews, we made public all material furnished to us and entrenched into the review process opportunities for persons to comment on the submissions of others. The process not only gave greater credibility to our reports but the comments process also enabled others to expose deficiencies in arguments which we might have missed. This is real consultation, not just token consultation for the sake of saying it had been done.

In short, secretiveness is not conducive to good decision-making and much more needs to be done to make government decision-making more open and consultative, even if decisions take a little longer to reach. There will always be occasions when governments have to make decisions quickly and full consultative processes are not practical. On the other hand there are many decisions which are conducive to consultation but are not reached in that manner.

CONCLUSION

It is more than clear that the application of sound ethical principles is fundamental to good government. It is equally important that we have sound structures and processes to underpin government decisions. The challenge now is to develop an underlying rationale for our governmental system which will create an environment in which ethical conduct can flourish.

NOTES

1   Preston et al (eds) (1998) provides an insightful overview of ethics in the legislative arena.

2   A brief history of the battle to develop and implement a general code of conduct in both Australian federal houses is related in Kernot (1998).

3   The latter was an investigation of illegal business dealings which resulted in several former state premiers and other high ranking party figures being gaoled.

4   A concise summary of these and a number of other incidents involving allegations of improper conduct by federal ministers is contained in Codd (1995) pp 83–110.

5   For example, in Australia there is the *Public Sector Ethics Act* 1994 in Queensland. At the Commonwealth level, the new Public Service Bill is expected to contain a code of ethical conduct for federal public servants. See Management Advisory Board, 1996, p 11. In Canada, there is the *Conflict of Interest and Post-Employment Code of Public Office Holders* (1994) and the *Code of Conduct for Members of Parliament* (1996) in the United Kingdom.

6   This particular list is drawn from various Australian codes and guidelines.

7   My own experience has been that working for highly professional and ethical persons, particularly in the early stages of my career, had a significant influence on my own ethical values in public service.

8   For example, I believe that Australia can make a particular contribution in the Asia/Pacific region. In this regard, I should mention the work of the Asia-Australia Institute's ethics seminar programme. See Potts, ch 6, who expands upon this issue of international initiatives.

9   For example, Justice O'Bryan of the Victorian Supreme Court (*R v Stanbrook*, unreported, 16 March 1993); Justice Bollen of the South Australian Supreme Court (*R v David Norman Jones*, unreported, 26 August 1992); and Judge Jones of the County Court of Victoria (*R v Hakopian,* unreported, 8 August 1991).

10 There have been some positive developments at the judicial level in Australia in particular. The Australian Institute of Judicial Administration has issued a lengthy discussion paper on judicial ethics and has called for comment on it (Wood, 1996). The Queensland Magistrates Court has implemented a code of ethical conduct and the federal Immigration Review Tribunal has also established codes of conduct.

11 I would define the merit principle as 'the selection of the best available person in accordance with a fair selection process and objective selection criteria'.

12 An example of undue influence by a ministerial staffer was given by Vince Fitzgerald, a former Commonwealth departmental head, when he referred to a statement by the former head of Treasury, Tony Cole, to the effect that a ministerial staffer changed economic forecasts which the government was going to present (Fitzgerald, 1996). This a disturbing example because official economic forecasts should be seen as objective if they are to have credibility. The example also violated another principle and that is changing public service advice simply because it does not suit the interests of the

government is dishonest and violates the purpose of the advice. Rejecting advice is quite proper but changing it is another issue altogether.

13 These reforms occurred as a result of the 1857 Northcote Trevelyan Report in the United Kingdom. The main result of the reforms was the abolition of rampant political patronage in relation to appointments to public office in the United Kingdom (jobs could actually be purchased up until the reforms) and the commencement of a merit system of appointment.

14 Canada established a *Lobbyists Code of Conduct* in March 1997 (see http://strategis. ic.gc.ca/sc_mrksv/engdoc/homepage.html). Ironically, Australia has recently abolished its Registry of Lobbyists.

2

AGAINST PROFESSIONAL ETHICS

Hendrik Kaptein

PROFESSIONAL PHILOSOPHERS AND LEGAL PROFESSIONALS

From time to time, philosophers and legal professionals convene to discuss legal ethics, that is, professional morality in the law. More often than not, such conversation displays strange contrasts between general friendliness on the one hand and complete lack of common ground and understanding on the other.[1] After discussion, there is chat over a few drinks, friendly farewells and ...? Nothing much changes for the better, it seems.

At one such an occasion, lengthy expositions by professional philosophers were met, again, by growing lack of interest and occasional unrest in the audience, stirring the speakers to even higher levels of abstraction. At the end of the long afternoon, a prominent lawyer tried to save the day by stating that professional morality in the law is a matter of plain hunch and common sense and that it is better left at that. According to him, personal conscience plays no major role in professional practice.

While the public sighed with relief, the academics thought: such a shame that the importance of scholarly insights is reduced to personal opinion and belittled to such a degree. To top this already disappointing conclusion, a prominent (and most polite) member of the Supreme Court of The Netherlands told the academics that she found (professional) morality 'quite interesting' but 'really rather difficult' (as if she had been listening to an explanation of advanced computer technology).

Why, then, one more scholarly contribution to legal ethics? It has been done before, to no good effect, it seems.[2] Still, there is the pertinent feeling that not all is well in the practice of law. Though many popular moral criticisms and condemnations of the Bar and the legal profession may be misplaced, it is not very likely that late 20th century legal professionalism has surpassed the dreary state so vividly depicted by the artist Daumier in the 19th century (see Cain, 1954).

The lack of relevance of legal ethics may have an unexpected background. Attempts to morally edify legal practice generally take for granted an unholy tripartition. First, there is the law, a complex entity in which and with which good as well as bad can be done. Secondly, ethical or moral standards are suggested in order to keep legal conduct within bounds. Thirdly, individuals are to pick and choose from motives from either of these standpoints, or even from both, not forgetting their own best interests. Small wonder that explanations of professional morality couched in such terms, however implicitly, fail to catch attention, let alone compliance.

Here, then, a rather different approach will be sketched. The Bar is the main example here, not just because many legal ethics problems emanate from it but also because explanation of its contested role within the modern legal order may serve to show the redundancy of autonomous legal ethics.[3] Conclusions to be drawn from that sector of the profession may hold good for other legal and public service professions as well.

A cursory criticism of 'autonomous' morality and law as a complex of 'instruments' will be followed by an attempt to explain what the Bar is or, what amounts to the same thing, what the Bar is good for, as an indispensable part of the modern legal order. Confidentiality, independence and confraternity regain their proper meaning here. Still, imperfect procedural and material justice may qualify lawyers' duties to realise rights and not all the interests of clients, revealing the impact of the separation of morals and the law.

Individuals acting within the law appear to derive part of their identity from their understanding of the meaning of their profession. In the end, what matters in professional morality is motivation, not by any doubtful and incomprehensible factors from outside but by a better understanding of what legal and public service professionals are doing and who they are. That is what constitutes a professional approach to the problem of legal ethics. (See Corbett, Chapter 12, for a view of professional ethics in general.)

'AUTONOMOUS' ETHICS:
DOUBTFUL STATUS AND PRACTICAL INSIGNIFICANCE

Abstract (philosophical) approaches to professional ethics generally suffer from a lack of practical relevance. Professional ethics is almost invariably expounded in terms of a contrast between abstract ethical or moral considerations on the one hand and more or less complicated facts about professions on the other. Such approaches are fatally hampered by at least two problems. First, too much is expected from both the epistemological status and practical effect of abstract morality. Secondly, the wrong kind of professional facts are focused on, suggesting a neutral complex to be acted upon by moral standards.

Explanation or even codification of moral maxims like 'treat people as equals' or 'respect the human rights of all individuals' or 'do not cause unnecessary suffering' are undoubtedly plausible but not always clear in their implications in ever-changing specific circumstances. Even if lawyers were willing to stick to such principles, not many problems would be solved by such abstractions. Further, the tendency of abstract moral principles to conflict (at least in principle) may lead to the search for a single basic principle, with all the attendant problems of such simplifications.[4] Persistent doubts on the status of general ethical or moral principles do nothing to encourage professionals' confidence in abstract approaches to professional morality. More than a few lawyers turn amateur relativist and scepticist philosopher if they can ward off professional ethics in such a way.

It comes as no surprise, then, that such abstract philosophy is largely incomprehensible to outsiders, be they legal professionals or just ordinary informed citizens. Even if abstract moral philosophy could be rescued from relativist doubts and was applicable in practice, the problem of understanding and motivation would remain. The influence on human conduct of explicit moral conceptions, be they material or epistemological, is not to be overestimated. In that sense, not only moral relativisms and noncognitivisms but also many other academic moral philosophies may be relegated to the playgrounds of philosophy.[5]

PROFESSIONAL ETHICS AND INSTRUMENTALISM IN THE LAW

Instrumentalism completes this brief sketch of contemporary professional ethics and practical scepticism. In a 'tool kit' conception of law, the legal order is no more than a set of complex hindrances and instruments on the way to the realisation of any number of interests. With few exceptions, such interests will be of a self-regarding nature at the expense of others. Thus, limits are set not by any kind of benevolent interpretation and application of the law in terms of basic principles and goals but solely by calculation of risks of apprehension and its costs.[6]

Methods used to reach or maintain these interests may range from flooding other parties with documents or forging them to not informing other parties that a case may be lost in private law just by inadvertently skipping a formal time limit. It can even reach the level of cheating the public prosecution and/or the court or putting pressure upon unwelcome witnesses. The Bar offers particularly favourable conditions for such instrumentalism. Predominant here is the prerogative of confidentiality. There can be no Bar without it; on the other hand, such confidentiality may hide misdemeanours which cannot be legally brought to light.

The existence of a basic relationship between such instrumentalism and varieties of moral noncognitivism is clear. If there are no moral limits to what may be done in general, there can be no such limits in the use of the law either. To put it another way, any notion of misuse of the law presupposes some standard or standards which are deemed to be absent.

A still more fundamental relationship may be found in 'externalisation' of the law. The law and the legal order are no more than parts of a complex outer world, in which and with which individuals can do no more than fight for their survival and (perceived) well-being. In such a reality, lone individuals are at a moral loss, as there seems to be no foothold for any moral conception outside their own subjectivity and self-interest.

All notions of the law and the legal order as exemplifying basic human relationships can then be considered as lost. Something like a state of nature is reinstated after all, a most ironical paradox, to say the least. Legal orders protecting rights and furthering reasonable interests are acted upon as a complex of hindrances and helps in realising those same multiple interests without regard to the legal and moral quality of such interests or the deterioration of the legal order by such instrumentalism. Of course, such free riders flourish by the labours of a majority abiding by and contributing to the law and the legal order.

In fact, relationships between moral noncognitivism and instrumentalism may be represented by another tripartition. Individuals confront the outside world as a complex of neutral facts, to be acted upon according to moral standards from some unknown third realm. No wonder noncognitivisms fit such conceptions of individuals, law and morals. Morals and morality can be no more than some other-wordly authority, be it a religious or some other authority. Why seek guidance by such inchoate (to some) entities over concrete and immediate self-interest?

Unattractive and implausible as such an instrumentalist and opportunist conception of the Bar and legal practice may seem, it has gained some predominance in practice. Both tendencies to commercialism and popular 'partisan' conceptions of the Bar tend to foster this instrumentalism or even to condone it as probably slightly adverse to public morals and its misunderstandings but still being the essence of the life of lawyers, *miles togati* for their clients, and, not to be forgotten, for themselves.

WHY DO WE HAVE LAWYERS?

Criticism of the alliance of between noncognitivism and instrumentalism is probably too moralistic to be effective. Even if its theoretical untenability could be proven beyond doubt, there will surely be few conscious or subconscious adherents of this tool-kit conception of law and morals to be convinced by such proof, let alone be brought to a change of conduct. Still, an important practical disadvantage should be noted here. Instrumentalist behaviour leads to a lack of confidence in lawyers by the courts. Apart from many other disadvantages, lawyers' self-interest and the interests of their clients may suffer from such behaviour as well.

A radical change of perspective may be brought about by a better understanding of what the Bar is and of what it is good for. Why is there something like a Bar at all? Such a return to the facts may lead to results more acceptable to people prone to shy from matters ethical. It is notable that this question is seldom put forward in an explicit fashion, let alone answered adequately. When faced with the question of what the Bar is, most lawyers try to answer it by offering more or less detailed descriptions of their (sometimes not so) daily activities, without being able to state in clear and succinct terms why their profession is there at all. In such a way, roads to instrumentalisms are wide open, as professional contexts are again reduced to complexes of specific facts to be acted upon on the basis of motives independent from any inner value or worth of such legal facts.

The Bar is a product, a cause and, above all, an indispensable part of the inevitable complexity of law. Lawyers derive their reason for being from a tragic paradox, if not even from an outright contradiction. Simple and comprehensible law cannot be just; just law must be complex and incomprehensible (a classic statement of this is to be found in Fuller, 1969).

Thus, lawyers exist because people cannot secure their rights on their own. Few people are experienced in the law and the legal process to a degree sufficient to serve their own interests before court. There is no just and effective legal order without lawyers. There may even be legal obstacles against appearing in court without a lawyer. In most civil law systems, parties may not appear on their own in court at all; lawyers must represent them. Though this seems to be in complete contrast to the basic right to appear in person before court in common law systems, the main role of lawyers remains the same.

Given this fundamental role of lawyers, important conclusions follow naturally. Lawyers are to see to it that if their clients are 'right', their rights will be realised. It is to be kept in mind here that it is a primary purpose of law to realise contested rights and that lawyers play a main role in the realisation of that purpose.[7] Impressions are that this is not always the case.[8]

Lawyers are to state in terms as legally favourable as possible the claims of their clients, both to other parties or the public prosecution and to the courts. In principle, it is not the duty of lawyers to further the interests of clients by whatever means. If it were so, there would in principle be no limits to furthering clients' interests against other parties and/or legal authorities and the law. Anything would go, hidden behind confidentiality as a veil of ignorance for the rest of the world. Yet it is the courts which are to determine who is to win or lose, *not* lawyers using all kinds of tricks in order to let their clients (and their own purses) win against the purpose of the law in the realisation of justice and fairness.

This belief in the service of justice is also expressed by oaths taken by lawyers upon entering the Bar (on the seemingly old-fashioned and secret subject of oaths and the Bar, see Kaptein, 1996, pp 295–9). In most such promissory oaths, lawyers state that they will not further a cause that they cannot believe to be just. This excludes furthering claims based on factual falsities, however hidden to other parties. Also, procedure is not to be misused in advancing (or thwarting) clients' interests. Material justice of clients' cases may be more contestable, of course.

An important advantage of this kind of 'factual' approach is confrontation of instrumentalist lawyers on their own terms. They occasionally react to professional morals by stressing that it is positive law that matters and nothing more, be it morals, religion or whatever people may believe in. Yet when it is asked what the law is with regards to the purposes of one of its main professional roles, represented by the Bar, the dishonesty of such an appeal to the law comes to light.

PRINCIPLES OF THE BAR CLARIFIED

The classical principles of the Bar need to be reiterated here. Confidentiality comes first. As clients are unable to determine the legal importance of facts, it is in their best interest 'to tell everything' in order to enable lawyers to present their cases as based upon all possibly relevant facts.[9] Such facts are not be related to third parties, as the position of clients would then be (much) worse than in legal conflicts without lawyers at all.

On the other hand, this may lead to problems concerning confidential facts unavailable to other parties and threatening to their legal position. Confidentiality creates the common cause of lawyer and client. Lawyers' independence from clients' interests is most important as well. Although lawyers are to listen to their clients' stories (or may be necessitated to do their best to bring them to light), they are not to comply with all and anything their clients may want to happen. It is their role to secure clients' *rights*, not clients' *interests*, whatever they may be.[10]

Confraternality is the consequence of this. In principle, lawyers are to stand not only by their clients but also by the legal order and its justice and fairness. This implies that procedures are not to be frustrated in ways which have nothing to do with the merits of the cases of clients. Thus, confraternality may imply that lawyers inform each other and even the public prosecution of hindrances to outcomes acceptable from a material point of view.

LAWYERS' JUSTICE IN CRIMINAL LAW

This conception of the Bar holds good in criminal law as well. But what is a rightful cause in criminal law? According to the conception just sketched, it would seem that no criminal case can be defended by lawyers, just as a lawyer may not act on behalf of a patently unjust civil cause. However, criminal defence does not concern facts of charges (apart from exceptions) but the safeguarding of defendants' rights, concerning adequacy of proof, observance of due process and so on.

Lawyers' insistence upon due process in criminal law may have earned them more popular moral criticism than anything else. Criminal lawyers face special problems of illegally obtained evidence and other faults in criminal procedure. In many modern legal orders, such violations of defendants' rights lead to barring the public prosecution or acquittal of the defendant. Material proof of the facts of charges may still be overwhelming in such cases. Lawyers who succeed in having their clients go free on such grounds are often looked upon as accomplices in crime.

However, responsibility for this behaviour is not to be allotted to the Bar. The legislature and the courts created defendants' protection to cover such eventualities. Also, the question arises whether lawyers are to rectify errors committed by the public prosecution. In many cases, there is nothing to be repaired at all. Factors like undue violence of privacy in obtaining evidence or undue pressure during interrogation cannot be made good afterwards. But what if lawyers learn that the public prosecution is bound to violate a deadline? According to lawyers' roles in realising justice, they should inform the appropriate authorities about this, as in principle they should do in a civil procedure.

The standard argument against such action stresses the inequality of parties in criminal procedure. Lawyers may use any means in defending their powerless clients against the almighty state in order to more or less restore such disturbed balance of powers. However, this scenario may be far from the reality of the situation. In more than a few cases, criminal defendants may hire armies of 'top' lawyers, accountants and other specialists in their battle against often ill-equipped public prosecution offices.

Such an argument cannot rest on the assumption of an imbalance of power alone. It also assumes the imbalance is utilised through misuse of power against criminal defendants, for example, by illegally obtaining evidence. Though such things happen, they are not the rule in most legal orders. Yet this still leaves open the question of whether lawyers may use illegal means to make good public prosecution's errors which would otherwise lead to unjust conviction of their clients.

In any case, the basic distinction between rights of clients and interests of clients and lawyers holds good in criminal law as in other areas of law. Criminal lawyers are not there to let criminal defendants go free by whatever means.[11] Unfortunately, quite a few criminal lawyers seem to have lost a grasp of this distinction, as they act as if they are fighting for survival of their clients and their own interests in the new state of nature.[12]

PRINCIPLED PROFESSION IN THE REAL WORLD

At least two serious and deeply related objections may be raised against this principled conception of the Bar. First, lawyers are simply to serve their clients, not to realise justice and fairness on their own.[13] Secondly, this conception relies heavily upon the quality of the legal order and the wisdom of the courts.

The first objection emerges from sensitive areas, such as deadlines. Lawyers or public prosecution officers may neglect deadlines, with fatal consequences for their cases. Are lawyers representing other parties to sound warning notes against such negligence? If lawyers do act accordingly, clients may consider that their interests were ill served. If clients with a fair case to be heard go on to lose their cases by some or other mishap, they may well try to put their lawyers before (disciplinary) court.

On the other hand, lawyers disclosing errors of procedure to other parties or the public prosecution may consider that cases should not be won in ways which do not depend on their legal merits alone. Difficult problems pop up here as well, aggravated by the apparently natural tendency of lawyers to wage war on other parties by all means, as victory is all that counts in practice.[14] Again, pride of place for clients' (and, of course, lawyers') interests cannot be the principle of the Bar. Such priority implies no limits to lawyers' conduct in principle. Anything may be done, then, from 'cooking the books' to threatening unwelcome witnesses.

Against that, clients may argue that the rule of the law at best offers imperfect procedural justice . There can be no absolute guarantee of material justice. So if some imperfection in the path of the law is reasonably to be expected, clients and lawyers may *reasonably* take recourse to 'improper' procedure.

This leads to the second problem, concerning the quality of the legal order, including conduct of members of the Bar and the courts. Even if lawyers are willing and able to stick to legal means in presenting their clients' cases, they are often confronted with so-called *confrères* who do not care that much about the principles of the Bar. Is 'tit for tat' an adequate reaction to unprofessional behaviour by other parties' lawyers?

This may be unavoidable at times. Further, principled lawyers' conduct may depend upon (what they regard as) the rightfulness of the claims they are representing. These is slippery ground to be sure but lawyers may still feel free to use any effective means on behalf of a mistreated child, for example, whereas they may be more careful (or less willing to act with impunity) when pleading the case for the bankruptcy of a company division whose sole and hidden motive is getting rid of employees in a cheap way.

It should be emphasised, however, that most legal orders offer real possibilities for realisation of rightful claims. Though many factors may stand in the way to this, it is surely slightly outlandish to state that the courts do not generally do justice in most jurisdictions, at least in the North. In that sense, no serious bending of the law in violation of lawyers' fidelity to the legal order is needed in order to obtain just and fair results in most cases.[15]

It is paramount that lawyers and other legal practitioners must bear in mind at all times that the human quality of the law and the legal order is in part a product of their own conduct. In an instrumentalist (and ethical subjectivist, relativist) conception, the legal order is a given set of complex facts and circumstances to be used or at least circumnavigated at will. Such a conception not only leaves out the essentially purposeful nature of law and the legal order, as explained above, but also the constitutive contribution to it by lawyers' mentality and behaviour. This implies that lawyers should also consider the costs of negative contribution when they try to bend the law when they deem it appropriate.

PROFESSION, PERSONALITY AND COMMUNITY

When asked who one is, one may answer: a lawyer, a legal professional. Such an answer implies notions of personality partly defined by roles in society. People do not just act as lawyers during working hours; they are lawyers, with all that entails, in a more than accidental sense (at least if they are worth their job).[16]

This implies that living up to professional standards is a kind of *self-realisation*, not just a realisation of professional morality. As a result of doing their job from a deeply felt and effective understanding of the meaning of their profession, legal professionals may come to a self-conception in which their personal life acquires a more profound meaning.

On the other hand, if lawyers' prerogatives are used as just so many opportunities to further what is (mistakenly) seen as self-interest, not only is a privileged position in society seriously misused but an important part of personality is neglected as well. It would appear to be a return to the lonely state of nature, away from the civic solidarity of the legal order.[17] While it may be a bit simplistic to consider that acting according to professional ethics and having professional self-respect come down to the same thing, it still may be worthwhile to consider this analogy.[18] Such a conception of one deriving meaning of self through society does not necessarily imply some form of crypto-communitarianism. On the contrary, even in a modern liberal state, there is no state and society without just and effective roles defined by the rule of law.[19]

The agenda of professional ethics in law seems clear by now. It is better to explain who lawyers and other legal professionals are than to try to teach abstract professional ethics as distinct from an adequate explanation of legal roles and their underlying principles. This may well have important implications for the academic curriculum as well. Students ought not to be bothered by philosophy like natural law theories versus positivism and similar arguments. Even a separate part of the obligatory curriculum like legal ethics, however indispensable in many circumstances, holds something suspect. This view holds true not only for studies in law but for many other studies in public administration as well. Thus, the title of this chapter, 'Against professional ethics', also implies 'Against teaching professional ethics'. It is integration that counts and a determined movement away from the separation of law, individuals and (at best) morals.

The Bar and other organisations of legal professionals, willing to contribute to justice and fairness in the legal order, should try to institute and foster principled tradition in the first place. (The importance of principled tradition is very well expressed by Kekes.) Such an approach may not only avoid any inborn professional resistance to abstract moral philosophy; it may also appeal to one's notions of professional character and even honour.[20]

These precepts apply beyond members of the Bar and other legal professionals. The analysis of a lawyer's roles offered here presupposes not only explanations of the role of the courts but also of the legislature and public administration, among which the police and the public prosecution are predominant here. Public service ethics in general may greatly profit from such considerations as well. Indeed, it is a notable that discussions of professional ethics generally steer clear from such basic issues. (Sherman, Chapter 1, refers to the linkage between personal notions of professional character.) Unless such issues are confronted explicitly, some form of instrumentalism, reducing the legal or other public sectors to mere facts, will vitiate discussion.

It is integrity that counts here. Not only integrity as integration of personality and profession but also integrity as understanding and acting upon the proper role of the profession in the legal order and in society. Within this context, Sherman's list finds its proper place. (Sherman, Chapter 1.) If left on its own, it may fall foul to the impotence of ethical abstraction. But as a canon of interpretation, it is indispensable. Without such guidelines, the legal order can be no more than the realm of instrumentalism or the lonely state of nature. With them, law in its proper light, interpreted in terms of justice and fairness, makes clear what it is good for.[21]

What matters in the end is motivation. Abstract notions of professional ethics or morals won't do that job. Such notions are at best signs of oblivion of the sense and meaning of legal and public professions. Motivation in the right direction has to do with meaning, with the meaningfulness of what one does and who one is. This presupposes insight into the constitutive character of legal institutions for legal professionals. And for society.

NOTES

1 Such discussions may acquire a less friendly character at times. Not all legal professionals take kindly to what they take to be mingling with their affairs by outsiders not 'hindered', in their opinion, by inside knowledge and experience.

2 Grahame Lock, himself a well-known publicist in political science, remarked that 'Universities are like Russian shoe factories. They produce hundreds of thousands of shoes yearly, without any regard for the market. In the same way, universities produce tens of thousands of scientific and scholarly articles each year'. Now that the Soviet Union and its shoe factories are things of the past, there may come an end to the production of pointless paperwork on professional morality as well (see Giesen, 1992).

3 In fact, David Luban's splendid essay on legal ethics in Becker and Becker (1992) is almost exclusively concerned with lawyers' ethics. Apart from a few exceptions, no differences need be made here between lawyers, attorneys, barristers, solicitors and other official representatives and/or legal aides (members of the Bar, for example in the United States). What is of concern here is the morality of professionals having prerogatives in legal procedures in which their clients are involved.

4 Dworkin's principle of 'equal concern and respect' and criticisms levelled against it are an example of this. See Kaptein, 1995a, p 88.

5 Susan Wolf expressed the problem as follows: '[I]t would be useful to reflect on a fact that contemporary moral philosophy fails generally to appreciate — namely, that the role distinctively moral thought plays in most of our lives is quite small and that much of what we most deeply value in ourselves and those around us has nothing to do with morality at all ... There are limits to the degree to which the average person tries to be a good person, and we have reasons to question the assumption that we would all be better off if the average person tried more' (Wolf, 1984). One may well wonder whether this observation holds good for considerations presented here as well. For obvious reasons, this remark is relegated to a footnote, as its appositeness to this essay may well impair any good sense the latter may make.

6 Or maybe even the perceived cost of criticism by colleagues and/or outsiders, though diehards in the field appear to be rather insensitive to that. In fact, this was explicitly maintained by a prominent criminal lawyer in The Netherlands against the unsettling results of parliamentary investigation into criminal law proceedings in The Netherlands and the role of its Bar. There were signs of serious criminal offences by lawyers, both in criminal and in civil cases. The aforementioned lawyer, himself the subject of several official investigations, tried to do away with this by stating that 'there are no criminal lawyers in The Netherlands, as no lawyer has ever been convicted (that is, as a lawyer) in criminal court'. As usual, this was wrapped in that well-known legal language luring outsiders into believing such (otherwise patently) absurd opportunism. See G Spong in *NRC Handelsblad* (1995) and my rejoinder in the same newspaper (28 September 1995).

7 It may seem that this is opting for natural law theory and/or a Dworkinian conception of law, to be defined in terms of purposes or ends and to be contrasted with an instrumentalist, factual and thus positivist conception of law. Let it suffice here to state that no general concept or conception of law is suggested here and that any plausible positivist conception of law can accommodate a conception of the purpose of the Bar as stated here.

8 In the common law system, duties of lawyers to the court officially predominates. Duties to clients follow and rights of practitioners come a long way behind both of these duties. In most civil law systems, it is the same, though couched in different legal terms. However, practice has it that relevant legal rulings are too vague to be enforced within 'partisan' legal professions.

9   Think here of lawyers impatiently interrupting clients' legally largely 'irrelevant stories' and other misunderstandings.

10   Some lawyers seem to interpret independence as putting their own interests before everything else.

11   Depending upon defendants' purses too, of course. Some criminal lawyers might suggest that defendants going free still pay their dues: to their lawyers.

12   A disheartening example of this is the ill-famed case in the United States of the Menendez brothers, teenagers charged for killing their parents for no other apparent reasons than money, cars and worse. See, for example, Hardwick (1994) for a chilling account of criminal lawyers not interested in any truth and justice at all and the extent to which modern criminal procedure accommodates for this.

13   This first objection was forcefully presented by The Hon BSJ O'Keefe, Commissioner of the Independent Commission Against Corruption, Australia (discussion at presentation of an earlier version of this chapter at the 5th International Ethics in the Public Sector Conference, Brisbane, 5-9 August 1996).

14   See Bordewijk (1956 and 1988). In the books for Bar exams in The Netherlands, the problem of informing colleagues on deadlines is noted but the possible solutions to dealing with it are left to (prospective) lawyers themselves.

15   Of course, things may be very different in countries not having politically and financially independent courts and/or legislatures. In such circumstances, lawyers may need professional ethics independent from the law in order to serve their clients' rights. And, as noted above, criminal law in particular poses its own problems.

16   The introduction to a well-known book on lawyers and justice ends with the admonition that lawyers are not only to act in morally responsible fashion but are also to do their job according to professional standards. It should be clear by now that this is a false contrast. David Luban is the culprit here, in his otherwise excellent *Lawyers and Justice: An Ethical Study* (Luban, 1988).

17   Rousseau's impressive criticism of Enlightenment philosophies of states of nature leading to civilised society culminated in turning things round: the rat race of 'civilisation' is the true state of nature.

18   There is, of course, the 'Aristotelian principle' which implies that happiness in life can be a by-product of developing personal and professional skills. On self-respect, personal development and the legal profession, see Rawls (1971).

19   One may think here of Rawls' conception of the state as a social union of social unions, as expounded in Rawls (1971).

20   And, not to forget, to shame as an important part of social control of professional conduct. Professionals may not be moved by appeal to ethical abstractions but they may well be ashamed, and reformed, by not living up to professional standards expressing parts of their personalities as well. See Dubnick, ch 5; Kekes (1987); and, again, Rawls (1971).

21   Sherman, ch 1, recognises the need for supplemental measure to support codes. Even so, adequate explanation of roles and professions in the legal order and in public administration (in the light of the list, of course) may still have to come first. Sherman's list is important in another respect. As mentioned earlier, principles of the profession alone may not solve all problems of human necessity against the law. In such circumstances, the values of Sherman's list are essential guidelines.

3

AUTHORITY, DISCRETION AND ACCOUNTABILITY
The Case of Policing

Seumas Miller

INSTITUTIONAL CULTURE, AUTONOMY AND ACCOUNTABILITY

Individuals and Institutions

Institutions consist of individual persons who occupy roles defined in terms of tasks, rules, regulations and procedures. Normatively speaking, these roles are related to one another in terms of their contribution to the function(s) or end(s) of the institution, as well as (usually) hierarchically. The relationship between these roles can be referred to as the structure of the institution.

Aside from the explicitly defined tasks, there is an important implicit and informal dimension of an institution roughly describable as 'institutional culture'. This notion comprises the attitudes, values, norms, and the ethos or 'spirit' which pervades an institution. In this sense, institutional culture determines much of the activity of the members of that institution or at least the manner in which that activity is undertaken. So while the explicitly determined rules and tasks may say nothing about being 'secretive', 'sticking by one's friends come what may' or having a hostile or negative attitude to particular social groups, these attitudes and practices may in fact be pervasive; they may be part of that culture.[1]

While the structure, function and culture of an institution provide a framework within which individuals act, they do not fully determine the actions of individuals. There are a number of reasons for this. First, rules and regulations, norms and ends cannot cover every contingency that might arise. Secondly, rules, norms and ends themselves need to be interpreted and applied. Indeed, changing circumstances and unforeseeable problems make it desirable to vest individuals with discretionary powers.

The fact is that the individuals who occupy roles are possessed of varying degrees of discretionary power in their actions. These discretionary powers are of different kinds and operate at different levels. For example, senior and middle-level public servants have discretion in the way they implement policies, in their allocations of priorities and resources and in the methods and criteria of evaluation of programs. Indeed, senior public servants often exercise discretion in relation to the formulation of policies. For example, Gordon Chase, the New York Health Services Administrator, conceived, developed and implemented the methadone program in New York City in the 1970s notwithstanding political opposition to it (Warwick, 1981, p 93). Lower echelon public servants may also have discretionary powers. Police officers have to interpret rules and regulations, customs officers have the discretionary power to stop and search one passenger rather than another and so on.

Moreover, it is more than the individual actions of institutional actors that are not fully determined by structure, function and culture. Many joint or co-operative actions that take place in institutions are not determined by these factors. For example, a senior public servant might put together a team of like-minded people and they may pursue a specific agenda which is not one determined by the prevailing institutional structure, function or culture and is even in part inconsistent with them. For example, the current initiatives within the New South Wales (NSW) Police Service in Australia to move to less hierarchical structures and to professionalise policing by having a registry of professional police practitioners is an example of such internal joint or collective discretionary activity.

Institutional Independence

Legitimate individual or collective discretionary activity undertaken within an institution is typically facilitated by a rational internal structure, including role structure, and policy and decision-making procedures, as well as by a rational institutional culture. By rational, it is here meant both internally consistent and rational in the light of the institution's purposes. Yet it is by no means always the case that such rational structures and cultures exist.[2] Accordingly, it is likely that many individual and collective discretionary judgments will be ones which do not facilitate the realisations of the institution's purposes.

Aside from the internal dimensions of an institution, there are its external relationships, including those to other institutions. In particular, there is the extent of the independence of an institution from other institutions, including government. Here it should be noted that independence is not the same thing as autonomy but is a necessary condition for it. An institution possessed of independence from other institutions might still lack autonomy if it lacked the kinds of rational structure and culture noted above. Indeed, internal conflicts can paralyse an institution to the point where it becomes incapable of pursuing its institutional purposes.

The extent to which an institution, as distinct from an individual member of an institution, ought to have independence from government turns on the nature of the function of that institution as well as the extent to which it is necessary for that institution to have independence in order to properly carry out its function(s) or end(s). For example, the judiciary needs a high level of independence from the legislature and the executive.[3]

Historically, the proper extent of independence of one public institution from another has been problematic. To what extent should the public service be independent of the government of the day? By some accounts, the public service exists to serve the public interest simply by implementing the policies of the government. In some countries, the public service is allegedly neutral with respect to different governments, with the various ministers accountable for the actions of the public servants in their departments. The legislature in turn oversees the actions of the ministers. However, there is inevitably a tension arising from the possibly disparate commitments of public servants to the policies of the government of the day and to the public interest. And there is the general practical problem of trying to make the members of large, complex bureaucratic structures ultimately accountable to one person (for discussions of public service accountability in a range of different countries, see Jabbra and Dwivedi, 1988).

As suggested above, police services provide a somewhat different kind of example (for a useful introductory discussion of this issue, see Bryett et al, 1994, pp 39–57). To what extent should a police service have operational autonomy? A police service exists to uphold the law and maintain the peace. As such, it is at times the proper instrument of government. On the other hand, it ought not to be used for narrow political purposes. Police operational autonomy has on occasion been abridged by government in order, for example, to create and preserve a manageable level of public disorder, from which the incumbent political party and their supporters may politically or materially benefit.[4]

The existence of institutional independence provides the members of an institution, and especially those occupying the upper echelons of that institution, with an important dimension of discretionary power. Indeed, if an institution has substantial independence from other institutions and if that institution has a very hierarchical structure, then those who occupy the upper echelons will have a relatively high degree of discretionary power. Military commanders, especially in time of war, are a case in point.

Accountability and Responsibility

Institutional independence stands in some tension with another highly desirable feature of institutions: accountability. (Accountability and various perceptions of it are examined in Dubnick, Chapter 5.)

The notion of accountability is not the same as, but yet should go hand in hand with, the notion of responsibility. Here we need first to distinguish some different senses of responsibility. To say that someone is responsible for an action is to say that the person reasoned or deliberated concerning some action, formed an intention to perform that action and then acted on that intention on the basis of those reasons. However, there are occasions when 'being responsible for an action' means that the person in question occupies a certain institutional role and that the occupant of that role is the person who has the institutionally determined right and duty to decide what is to be done in relation to certain matters. If the matters in question include directing the actions of other agents, then the occupant of the role is not only responsible for what transpires, he or she is a person in authority. So being in authority can be considered to be a species of being responsible.

If a person is responsible in this latter sense for some action or sphere of activity, then typically that person is, or at least ought to be, accountable for it. To say that someone is accountable in this sense is to say that he or she is able to be, or ought to be able to be, called to account for and to justify the action or actions in question. Sometimes accountability brings with it liability; an adverse judgment on the part of those to whom one is accountable can result in the infliction of punishment. For example, given the opportunity in policing for wrongdoing and the historical tendency to corruption in Australian police services in particular, accountability is obviously of great importance in this sector of the public service.

The notion of accountability is complex. There are different kinds of accountability and different persons to whom one can be accountable. Personal accountability is accountability to oneself and typically involves the provision of justifications to oneself for one's actions. With the possible exception of psychopaths, each of us has moral standards and values. Each of us can think of things we simply would not do and other things we regard as so important we would do them even if it is not in our interest. Accountability is not to be equated with liability, but it typically implies liability, including especially punishment. In relation to personal accountability, if we fall short of our own moral standards and values, we suffer shame or remorse or at the very least are disappointed with ourselves.

As members of a community or society, we are also accountable to others in a number of ways. Some of our actions are subject to legal scrutiny and judgment. Moreover, sanctions, including punishment by imprisonment, can flow from adverse legal judgments. But we are also held morally accountable by the other individuals and groups. Our actions can be judged as unfair, weak and so on by our friends, spouses and the members of the community to which we belong. Moreover, adverse judgment is typically followed by expressed attitudes and actions which signal disapproval and even contempt. Such judgment-making and expressed disapproval constitutes a process of holding individuals accountable. And while this process is informal and carries no legal sanctions, it is one that can powerfully influence our behaviour.

As members of an institution, we are not only morally and legally accountable; we are administratively accountable and there are typically an elaborate array of institutional mechanisms to ensure accountability. In recent times, the number and kinds of these mechanisms has increased markedly to the point where the costs, as well as the benefits, of accountability mechanisms are beginning to become an issue of concern. For example, the recent coming into existence of a plethora of administrative accountability mechanisms in Australian universities is a concern of many Australian academics. For example, at some Australian universities, a three-year non-renewable contract academic position involves three lengthy probationary reviews over two and one-half years before the contract is confirmed.

A particular problem for accountability procedures arises in institutional contexts. Obviously, everyone ought to be held accountable for their own actions. In institutional contexts, however, there are many actions, outcomes and spheres of activity to which many different persons contribute.

Because of the co-operative nature of activity in institutions, it is often unclear who is actually responsible for some untoward outcome and the extent of their contribution to that outcome. This issue is known in moral philosophy as the problem of many hands. An example that comes to mind in the recent history of policing in NSW is the 1989 investigation of Police Superintendent Harry Blackburn. After a lengthy police investigation, Blackburn was falsely accused of being a sex offender. However, in the course of the investigation, hypotheses were accepted without adequate testing, evidence eliminating Blackburn as a suspect was discredited, witnesses were extensively prompted and so on. The point of interest here is that these errors, acts of negligence and so on were not committed by one person but by quite a large group of individuals, each of whom was supposedly being guided by their own judgment. So the question arises as to how moral responsibility for these actions is, as it were, to be parceled out. Of course, there are also the corresponding questions as to how accountability and liability are to be ascribed to these different individuals.

AUTHORITY AND DISCRETION IN POLICING

In order to set the stage for a discussion of the authority and discretion of individual police officers, I will first present four case studies that exemplify the exercise of authority and discretion.[5]

Case Study 1

In the 1980s, a hawkish former Israeli general is invited by Australian Jewry to speak at Sydney Town Hall. The Arab community obtain a street march permit to protest his presence in Australia; a thin line of police separates the marchers and the arriving audience. The protest is passing off without incident, although National Front members are in the crowd on the footpath. Also present is 'The Screaming Skull', a well-known self-proclaimed Nazi. 'The Skull' is using offensive language.

Present also is a police sergeant with a reputation for poor judgment in public ordering situations. He peremptorily orders a constable to arrest The Skull and charge him. Operationally, this is a bad call; this action may create a 'flashpoint' for disorder and a widespread disturbance, the very situation police are posted there to prevent. The constable tells the sergeant he will assist him to make the arrest, if he is ordered to, but will not arrest or charge The Skull himself.

Case Study 2

Police are called to a liner at the overseas terminal in Sydney. A customs officer has found a small amount of marijuana in a plastic envelope, perhaps enough for half a joint, in a boarding crew member's jacket pocket . The seaman explains that he bought the marijuana for personal use at King's Cross the prior evening whilst drunk and thought he'd consumed it. At the time of boarding, he was unaware of the residue in his jacket.

Prosecution for possession of an illegal drug, including marijuana, will involve his dismissal by the shipping company; the ship will leave Sydney that afternoon, leaving him stranded in Australia. A conviction will result in the seaman's union withdrawing his membership, losing him his livelihood. He'd been flown to Australia from the UK to take the place of another crew member and will become indebted to the shipping company for the airfares. He is penniless, having spent the remainder of the travelling expenses advanced to him by the shipping company. He will become subject to detention and deportation from Australia (at some cost to the Commonwealth) as an inadvertently illegal immigrant. He is the sole support of his wife and child in the UK; they have been living on relief and this is his first ship in six months.

Case Study 3

Criminal Investigation Division (CID) officers were frequently asked to a factory to arrest and charge (as was the company policy) employees caught stealing the little cast metal scale model autos (the 50¢ Corgi/Matchbox type) the company manufactured. These arrests were, however, a source of some discussion amongst the detective constables since the value of the item was small and the crime insignificant.

On one particular occasion following such a call, the officers learned that it was alleged that one of the managers had altered the production instructions in the plant, substituting inferior materials and selling the high-quality metal specified for the casting of the cars. By so doing, he had accumulated and sold some £20,000 sterling (US$50,000) worth of metal. The company's board of directors was meeting to decide whether to file a legal charge against the manager. As the CID sifted the facts, they were convinced of his guilt. They waited outside the boardroom, were served dinner and drinks but were finally informed by the chairman of the board that the company had decided not to prosecute. The police suspected that since the manager held stock in the company, the board had decided to drop the case to avoid public embarrassment and possible financial loss.

Soon thereafter, the same company called to have an arrest made for stealing one of the 50¢ model cars and were informed they would have to proceed in the matter by private summons (Manning, 1978, pp 263–89).

Case Study 4

David Martin was a dangerous criminal being pursued by police in an underground subway in London in 1982. Cornered by armed police, Martin was persistently ordered by police to give himself up but refused to do so. However, he made no hostile movements against the police. It was a case of passive non-compliance. The police were concerned that he might have a gun and might use it against them before suiciding. Certainly his history indicated he was capable of this kind of action. On the other hand, if the police were to allow him to go free, his history indicated the lives of others would be at risk. Finally, the police decided not to shoot him but to rush and disarm him. He was found to be unarmed (Waddington, 1991, p 62).

POLICE DISCRETION

By any account, individual police officers have a significant measure of legal power (on general issues of autonomy and accountability in policing in Australia, see Moore and Wettenhall, 1994). They are legally empowered to 'intervene — including stopping, searching, detaining and apprehending without a warrant any person whom he, with reasonable cause suspects of having committed any such offence or crime' at all levels of society (*Crimes Act* 1990 (NSW) s 352(2)(a)).[6] Moreover, in exercising this authority, they interfere with the most fundamental of human rights: depriving the person of his or her liberty. Should a suspect attempt to evade or resist arrest, that person can under certain circumstances lawfully be deprived of his or her life by a police officer. For example, police officers are legally entitled to shoot fleeing suspects in many jurisdictions around the world.

These substantial legal powers are to a large extent discretionary. For example, the decision whether to arrest a suspect or merely issue them with a summons is by law a matter of police discretion. Naturally, such discretion should be exercised on the basis of a variety of considerations, such as the severity of the suspected offence or the likelihood that the suspect will abscond if merely summoned and so on. Although the police have considerable discretionary powers, they are also accountable for these actions to their superiors, to their departments of internal affairs, to the courts etc.

These discretionary powers include those discussed below.

The law has to be interpreted and applied in concrete circumstances as a part of policing. There is a need for the exercise of discretion by police in undertaking this task. But as few will deny (including lawyers and judges), the interpretation and application of the law is not always a straightforward matter.

The law does not, and cannot, exhaustively prescribe. It often grants discretionary powers or has recourse to open-ended notions such as that of the 'reasonable man' or 'reasonable suspicion'. Accordingly, a number of police responses to a situation might be possible in a given situation and all of them might be consistent with the law. Discretion is involved at most stages of police work. It is often involved in the decision to investigate a possible crime and involved in the decision to arrest or not arrest. And it is often involved in the decision to lay charges or not.

Upholding and enforcing the law is only one of the ends of policing; others include maintaining of social peace and the preservation of life. When these various ends come into conflict, there is a need for the exercise of police discretion. Consider this point with regards to case studies 1, 2 and 4.

Policing involves unforeseen situations and problems requiring an immediate, on-the-spot solution. It is therefore necessary to ensure that police have discretionary powers to enable them to provide such solutions.

Assuming the necessity for these discretionary powers of police, what further issues can be identified in relation to police discretion? One set of issues concerns the analysis of the concept of police discretion. What is police discretion? How does it differ from related concepts, including in particular the concept of so-called original authority? Another set of issues relates to the precise nature and extent of particular discretionary powers possessed by the police. Consider, for example, the discretionary power of the police to arrest or not arrest a suspect. A further set involves the correctness or incorrectness of particular exercises of police discretion. The police officer in case study 1 had the power to arrest The Skull but was it correct for him to do so in the circumstances? A final set of issues concerns the accountability of police in relation to the exercise of their discretionary powers.

It is beyond the scope of this chapter to examine each set of issues in detail. Instead, I will consider two more overarching considerations with regards to police discretion: the concept of original authority and its relation to police discretion; and the structure of some of the situations confronted by police and calling for the exercise of discretion.

ORIGINAL AUTHORITY OF THE POLICE

We need to distinguish compliance with laws from obedience to the directives of men and women (including especially one's superiors) in considering original authority. Thus, according to the law, an investigating officer must not prosecute a fellow police officer if the latter is innocent. On the other hand, he might be ordered to do so by his superior officer. Now individual police officers are held to be responsible to the law as well as their superiors in the police service. However, it is claimed that their first responsibility is to the law. So a police officer should disobey a directive from a superior officer which is clearly unlawful. However, the highly controversial doctrine of original authority evidently goes further than this. It implies that there are at least some situations in which police officers have a right to disobey a superior's lawful command, if obeying it would prevent them from discharging their own obligations to the law.[7]

Consider case study 1. According to the doctrine of original authority, there are at least some actions, including the decision to arrest or not arrest (at least in some contexts), which are ultimately matters for the decision of the individual officer and in respect of which they are individually liable. Accordingly, the police officer in case study 1 may be entitled to disobey their commanding officer to the extent of refusing to arrest The Skull, although not to the extent of refusing to assist the sergeant in the sergeant's carrying out the arrest. It is not that the sergeant has issued an obviously unlawful directive. Rather, the sergeant's authority to direct is overridden by the authority of the individual police officer in respect of the police officer's discretionary power to arrest at least in some contexts. The contexts in question are ones in which the action of arresting a given person would prevent the police officer from discharging their obligations to the law and, in this instance, their obligation to keep the peace in particular.

Now consider case study 4. Could or ought one of these police officers have been required to shoot Martin, if he had been ordered to do so? Could or ought one of these police officers been required to put his life at risk by rushing at Martin, if he had been ordered to do so? It is not clear that either of these directives would have been unlawful. What does seem evident is that, in this kind of case, the authority of a superior officer to direct is overridden by the authority of the individual police officer to choose to put their own life at risk or to shoot (and face the possibility of a murder charge).

Concomitant with their first responsibility being to the law, individual officers can be held legally liable for their actions. This liability is both criminal and civil. Hence, the police officer in case study 1 may have a real concern that he might be sued and held liable for damages in a civil court if his arrest of The Skull turned out to be unjustified in the circumstances and led to, say, damage to persons or property.

This problem is further illustrated by case study 4, in which police officers are confronted with a situation of passive non-compliance by a criminal known to be dangerous. On the one hand, if they shoot him and he turns out to be unarmed, they might be up on a murder charge. On the other hand, they put their own lives at risk by rushing him and trying to overpower him. Faced with this unpleasant dilemma, it might seem that a third option is preferable: to let him go free. Certainly this is an option open to ordinary members of the public. But matters are somewhat different for the police. They have a moral and legal duty to apprehend the suspect. Failure to try to apprehend an armed and dangerous offender would amount to serious neglect of duty on their part. Indeed, if they simply let him go and he went on to murder someone, this neglect of duty might be held by a court to be criminal negligence.

Moreover, if a senior and superior officer issued an apparently lawful directive to these subordinate officers to shoot the offender on the grounds that the evidence indicated that he was very probably concealing a dangerous weapon and highly likely to use it, the subordinate officers might well be acting within their rights to refuse to do so. They might disagree with the senior officer's judgment and hold that they might find themselves liable for wrongful killing if it turned out that the offender was unarmed.

The general moral notion underpinning this apparent legal right of individual police officers, including subordinate officers, to refuse to comply with apparently lawful directives to shoot, is the moral enormity that we attach to taking someone's life. The specific moral principle governing these actions of police dictates that if a certain police officer is to do the killing, then that very police officer (and not, for example, a superior officer) ought to be the one to decide whether or not they in fact do the killing.

45

This individual civil and criminal liability of police officers stands in some contrast with military combatants. A civilian would in general sue the military organisation itself rather than the soldier whose actions resulted in harm to the civilian. Moreover, soldiers do not reserve a general right to refuse to shoot to kill when ordered to do so by their commanding officers. In keeping with the absence of such a right, criminal liability in relation to negligence and many categories of wrongful killing is generally sheeted home to the military officer who issued the command rather than their subordinates who were their instruments.

This notion of the individual police officer's responsibility to the law, as opposed to responsibility to their superior officers, and the concomitant legal liability of individual police officers, is known as original authority in order to differentiate it from mere delegated authority. This notion of the original authority of individual police officers also needs to be distinguished from that of the quasi-judicial independence of police forces from other institutions, especially government. In Western liberal democracies, police forces have traditionally jealously guarded their independence from government on the grounds that they exist to uphold the law and not to implement the political policies of the government of the day. This notion of the institutional independence of the police from political control has obvious resonances in South Africa, for example.

At any rate, the legal situation in relation to the doctrine of original authority in those countries in which is has been claimed to exist, namely the United Kingdom and Australia, seems unclear. While there is in law the notion of the individual policeman or woman's original authority, there is also some legal support for the opposite view. For example, the right of police commissioners to order their subordinates to arrest or not arrest people is underpinned by legal constructs, irrespective of whether it is desirable or otherwise problematic for the subordinates to make those arrests (see Hogg and Hawker, 1983, p 160, and papers by Alderston, Goldring and Blazey, and Plehwe and Wettenhall in Moore and Wettenhall, 1994).

As far as the factual situation of police officer's exercise of this original authority is concerned, it can be argued that there is a contradiction between this notion of the individual police officer's independence on the one hand and the reality of the hierarchical and militaristic structure of actual police forces and the powerful strictures of police culture on the other. Notionally, individual police officers might have original authority but in practice, it is sometimes suggested, they do what their superiors tell them. Further, they conform to conservative police cultural norms, including the norm of not reporting a fellow officer's misdemeanour. However, it should be noted that there is no logical inconsistency between hierarchy on the one hand and a suitably circumscribed sphere of individual police office autonomy on the other hand.

In addition to the legal and factual questions, there is a normative or value question concerning police original authority: is it desirable for individual police officers to have and to exercise original authority?

In short, one is asking whether it is desirable for: (a) individual officers to have the legal right to make decisions on the basis of their judgment of what the law requires, and to do so, at least in some circumstances, even in contradiction to the commands of superior officers; (b) individual officers to be legally liable for the untoward outcomes of these judgments; and (c) for the administrative structures and cultural norms within the police services to be such that individual police officers in fact act on that original authority in a significant number of situations.

This is a vexed and complex issue. On the one hand, if the police officers in the lower echelons are in fact the most competent to make decisions in a variety of circumstances — possibly more competent than their superiors — then establishing original authority may be for the good. For when there is a clash between the judgments of such officers and their superiors or external authorities, it is likely that acting on the judgments of lower echelon police officers will lead to the best outcomes. Case study 1 provides backing for this line of argument. On the other hand, since authority brings with it power, giving individuals authority enables the possibility of abuses of power. It also enables the possibility of bad consequences flowing from the poor judgments by inexperienced junior officers.

The question of removing original authority needs to be distinguished from the issue of curtailing discretionary powers. In the case of original authority, officers have a legal right on occasion to override the lawful orders of their superiors in favour of complying with their obligations to the law and may be held liable for the untoward consequences of their actions, irrespective of whether these actions were performed in compliance with the directives of their officers.

Accordingly, police officers could in principle lose their original authority without their sphere of *de facto* discretionary powers being substantially curtailed. Moreover, the extent of their *de facto* discretionary powers could be limited while they retained their original authority.

On the other hand, it is probable that curtailment of discretionary powers would go hand-in-hand with the elimination of the original authority of police officers. This could be undertaken in a variety of ways, such as the authority of individual police officers being taken in law to derive from the minister of police or the enactment of more and more laws to restrict the areas of police discretionary powers.

EXERCISING POLICE DISCRETION

Case studies 2, 3 and 4 evidence the complexities inherent in the exercise of police discretion. In each case, there are competing ethical considerations. In case study 4, there is the overwhelming ethical requirement to preserve life, including not only the life of the police officers and of the dangerous criminal but also the lives of citizens that might be threatened if the suspect were to escape. On the other hand, there is the *end* of law enforcement, in the sense of the ethical requirement that the suspect be apprehended so that they can be brought before the courts and, if found guilty, punished for their serious crimes.

In case study 2, there is the illegality to consider. The structure of the ethical problem here is as follows: (1) an illegal action has taken place; (2) the police have as an obligatory moral duty the enforcement of the law; and (3) the consequence of enforcing the law in this instance is a state of affairs which is morally undesirable.

Here, an individual will be disproportionately harmed, even though, as the magistrate says, they have brought this upon themselves. Perhaps the police have a general obligation, as do ordinary citizens, to avoid contributing to bringing about an injustice, the injustice of disproportionate harm for wrongdoing. However, the particular feature of this situation is that the law is the instrument whereby the disproportionate harm will be done. Yet a fundamental aim of the law is to ensure justice and the police have a particular obligation to ensure that the law not be used to bring about an injustice. Moreover, in addition to the matter of the injustice to the seaman, there are the following consequentialist considerations. If the law is used as an instrument of injustice, this will have a criminalising effect on those unjustly penalised and will tend to undermine public support for the law.

Case study 3 seems to involve contradictory behaviour on the part of the police and the company. Initially, the police are prepared to arrest those responsible for the petty theft of 50¢ model cars but after the company refuses to press charges against the manager for a much more serious crime, the police discontinue their practice of arresting those who steal the 50¢ model cars. For their part, the board of directors of the company is prepared to pursue petty thieves, but not a manager guilty of a serious crime. The apparent inconsistency in the behaviour of the board is easy to explain. They want legal action to be taken against anyone who steals from them, unless taking legal action would go against their business interests.

By contrast, the police use their discretion in relation to time and resources invested in pursuing particular crimes and petty theft is a low priority. However, one ethical consideration in play here might be the extent to which members of the public are prepared to assist the police in achieving police ends, such as law enforcement. Perhaps when the company demonstrated that it put its business interests above enforcing the law against those who steal its property, the obligation on the part of the police to pursue those who offend in minor ways against the company was diminished. This suggests that there is a quasi-contractual relationship between the police and those they protect. This 'contract', which would seem to generate moral obligations, is one in which the police are obligated to protect the public and the public to assist the police to fight crime. However, if the protected fail to discharge their obligation, and especially if the reasons that they do not assist are self-interested ones, then they have broken the contract and can no longer expect police discretionary judgments to go in their favour.

De Facto Powers

The term police discretion is used rather loosely but it seems to typically refer to *de facto* discretionary powers, as opposed to legal discretion. *De facto* discretionary power is the power that individual police officers actually have to make decisions within delimited areas. So it might be a matter of a police officer's discretionary power whether they can detain a disorderly member of a crowd. Notice here that police discretion has not been given a legal rendering; it is simply a matter of whether the police officer is physically able to detain the person and, if so, whether they can choose on the basis of their own judgment not to do so in the light of various considerations.

If in addition to *de facto* discretionary powers police have legal discretionary power, this is because they have a legal right as individual officers to exercise certain discretionary powers. It is not simply a matter of having a *de facto* power; it is a matter of having a legal right.

Accordingly, in the case of the disorderly member of a crowd, a police officer might have the *de facto* power to detain or not the individual as well as being legally entitled to detain the person. Alternatively, they might have the legal right to do so but in fact be incapable of exercising that right.

A police officer does not exercise discretion in respect of performing or not performing an action, if they are in fact unable to perform it. Further, breaking the law, as distinct from refusing to enforce it, could thus be considered be an exercise of police discretion.

The extent of police discretion is a matter of controversy. Some argue that, in order to reduce the extent to which police abuse their powers, their discretionary powers should be significantly curtailed. Such abuse of powers in relation to the rights of suspects is well-known in many countries, such as South Africa, and of course discretionary powers have enabled or facilitated corrupt police activities in police forces throughout the world.[8]

ACCOUNTABILITY IN POLICING

This final section will briefly consider accountability in policing. We saw earlier that accountability is distinct from but ought to go hand-in-hand with responsibility and, therefore, with authority and discretion. To say that someone is accountable is to say that they are or ought to be called to account for their actions and asked to justify them. Accountability typically brings with it liability and the imposition of penalties.

There is a requirement that accountability in policing be especially stringent. This is because there is a pervasive tendency to corruption in policing. Indeed, I have argued elsewhere that moral vulnerability is a fundamental defining feature of police work, and that in the case of the profession of policing, the tendency to corruption ought to be regarded as a basic occupational hazard and treated accordingly (Miller, 1997, p 106). (See Kim, Chapter 7, for a comparative discussion of corruption in the public sector.)

There are a number of factors which contribute to the moral vulnerability of police officers. These include the necessity at times for police officers to deploy harmful methods, such as coercion and deception, which are normally regarded as immoral, as well as the high levels of discretionary authority and power exercised by police officers in circumstances in which close supervision is not possible. Further, police officers have ongoing interaction with corrupt persons who have an interest in compromising and corrupting police and often police confront morally ambiguous lose/lose situations calling for discretionary ethical judgments. Finally, many police officers operate in an environment in which there is widespread use of illegal drugs, large amounts of drug money and little evidence that the drugs problem is being adequately addressed.

Detection and deterrence of police corruption is achieved in large part by institutional mechanisms of accountability, both internal and external, and by policing techniques, such as complaints investigation, use of informants, auditing, surveillance and testing. The above-described constitutive tendency to corruption in police work can be used to justify an extensive system of accountability mechanisms — a system more extensive than may be necessary in other professions — and also used to justify the deployment of techniques of detection and deterrence that might not be acceptable in some other professions.

In most Western police services, there are an array of accountability mechanisms, including internal accountability on the part of individual members of police service to their superiors and to departments of internal affairs. Indeed, the existence of departments of internal affairs, some of which function as internal spy agencies, implies that police services realise that the tendency to corruption is a constitutive feature of policing. Typically, there are also mechanisms to ensure external accountability of a police service to government and the community.

Sometimes these mechanisms of internal accountability are less successful than they might be, due in part to the tendency for such mechanisms of accountability to come to embody and to re-inforce the 'us-them' mentality that sometimes exists between lower echelon police officers and the police hierarchy on the one hand and between police officers and departments of internal affairs on the other. Part of the solution to this problem may lie in the introduction of mechanisms of *peer accountability* to supplement existing mechanisms. Accountability mechanisms whose members include lower echelon police officers may be more successful because peers may have a more precise knowledge of what is actually going on at street level in a particular place at a particular time. More generally, such mechanisms may be more acceptable to lower echelon officers and hence successful, due to the fact that they are 'owned' by them.

Mechanisms of external accountability, such as the police boards, can suffer from the fact that their members are either senior police officers, and therefore not disinterested, or they are members of the public who do not have detailed knowledge and understanding of police matters. Part of the solution to this problem may lie in bringing ex-police officers onto these boards.

Mechanisms of accountability ought to include joint police/community institutional structures. Such structures allow communities to make problems known and to hold police to account — via ministers of police, for example — in relation to police responsiveness to these problems. It is a platitude that police/community co-operation is necessary for successful policing. An ambivalent community will shield lawbreakers, contribute to an 'us-them' mentality and lead to a secretive police force in which police corruption is more likely to flourish.

Techniques of detection and deterrence that may be appropriate for a profession with constitutive tendency for corruption include not only routine procedures, such as complaints investigation, but also techniques, such as granting indemnity to corrupt officers in order to get them to implicate others, testing for drug use and elaborate testing for corruption. If corruption is an occupational hazard in policing, then extraordinary methods may have to be used to combat it. Some of these methods raise important ethical and other problems. For example, it is not unknown for criminals who have been granted indemnity to provide evidence which turns out to be false.

CONCLUSION

I have argued that the constitutive tendency in policing to corruption justifies an elaborate system of accountability mechanisms. However, I want to close with a number of qualifications and caveats.

Systems of accountability have significant costs not only in terms of resources but also in terms of the discretionary powers of individual police officers and the institutional independence of the police service. While accountability is not the same thing as commandability, the logical endpoint of increasing accountability is a huge corpus of regulations and ongoing and intrusive investigative and regulatory activity, all of which stands in some tension with individual professional autonomy and institutional independence.

Most important, reliance on accountability mechanisms alone bypasses the issue of moral responsibility which lies at the heart of corruption. In the last analysis, the only force strong enough to resist corruption is the moral sense: the desire to do what is right and avoid doing what is wrong. If most police officers, including members of departments of internal affairs and of the police hierarchy (the ones who investigate corruption), do not for the most part have a desire to avoid doing what is illegal or otherwise immoral, no system of detection and deterrence, no matter how extensive and elaborate, can possibly suffice to control corruption.[9]

The desire amongst police officers to do what is right can be reinforced by ensuring a just system of rewards and penalties within the police organisation and an appropriate system of command and control — appropriate, that is, to the kinds of responsibilities that are attached to the role of police officer. Finally, the desire to do what is right can be reinforced by ensuring that ethical issues in police work, including the ethical ends of policing itself, are matters of ongoing discussion and reflection in initial training programs, further education programs, supervision, ethics committees and in relation to ethical codes. (See Corbett, Chapter 12, for the importance of training.)

NOTES

1   Kaptein, ch 2, addresses the notion of institutional culture and its impact on ethics in the context of the legal profession, while Taylor and Waghorne, ch 11, consider the issue within the trade union environment.

2   For example, one might argue that the current Australian police structure and culture are not rational in this sense, either in themselves or in relation to one another. In particular, a culture of secrecy and solidarity amongst street cops is inconsistent with a hierarchical organisational structure preoccupied with accountability.

3　　The issue here concerns the precise degree and form that judicial independence ought to take and not whether the judiciary ought to have substantive independence.

4　　This has regretfully occurred at most levels of government, from national (eg Hitler) to city (Richard Daley in Chicago). In Australia, this is evidently what happened in Queensland under Premier Bjelke-Petersen (see Whitton, 1989).

5　　Case studies 1 and 2 were provided by John Blackler (former police officer, NSW Police Service) through written communication with the author.

6　　Although this wording is specific to the NSW act, it is representative of statements of the scope of police power in many other jurisdictions.

7　　Two relevant legal cases here are *R v Metropolitan Police Commissioner; ex parte Blackburn* [1968] 2 QB 118, in which Lord Denning considered the Commissioner of the London Metropolitan Police 'to be answerable to the law and to the law alone' (cited in Bryett et al, 1994, p 43), and *Fisher v Oldham* [1930] 2 KB 264, in which the court found the police service was not vicariously liable in virtue of the original authority of the office of constable.

8　　Doyle suggests that investigative and peacekeeping roles could constructively sustain a fairly high degree of police discretion, whereas law enforcement involving coercion and curtailing of freedom cannot. He argues that the possibility and complete unacceptability of abuse of police power is very great in these latter areas; hence, there is a need to curb individual police discretion in these areas (Doyle, 1985).

9　　This notion of systems of accountability being useless without a desire to do right is the partner logic to that found in many other chapters here (eg Sherman, ch 1; Bernier, ch 9; Corbett, ch 12). Lists of ethics, codes of conduct etc are nothing more than theory unless there is the institutional accountability to back it up. But equally, accountability mechanisms need to interlock with ethical attitudes, especially the desire to do what is mutually right.

4

BUSINESS PRACTICES AND THE PUBLIC SERVICE ETHOS

Alan Lawton

INTRODUCTION[1]

In the ongoing debate on the applicability of business practices to the public sector, Henry Mintzberg adds his considerable voice to those who argue that government should not be treated as a business (Mintzberg, 1996, p 75).[2] Recent protagonists in the debate have been characterised as either 'genericists' or 'differentialists', depending upon their belief either that management in the public sector is essentially the same as in the private sector or that there are fundamental differences between the two. For example, Murray argues that the two sectors are converging, since a concern with efficiency or planning is now a feature of both sectors. Further, business is not just about profit and is also constrained by a political and legal context (Murray, 1975, p 364). Rainey et al (1976, p 233) and Stewart and Ranson (1988, p 13) take the opposite view, with the latter arguing that the purposes, conditions and tasks of the public sector are totally different to the private sector. Allison argues that public and private sector organisations are alike but in unimportant or superficial respects and that the content and conditions of the public sector are so different from the private sector that the transfer of generic management skills is inappropriate (Allison, 1983).

In short, the debate is usually conducted in terms of the goals or purposes of public and private sector organisations, the political, social and economic environment within which they operate, their functions, the processes and structures adopted to achieve goals, the people employed, the skills required and the techniques adopted.

However, any debate that relies upon a view that the public sector and the private sector can be treated as homogenous entities will prove, ultimately, to be sterile. The diverse purposes of the public services include the delivery of services, monitoring and regulating service delivery by organisations in the private and voluntary sectors, policy advice to politicians, collecting revenue and so on. Public services organisations will adopt different techniques and structures to carry out these functions, charging for some services but not for others. Equally diverse is the private sector, in that there will be variations in ownership and management, size, structures, functions etc. Mintzberg argues that the concept of the private sector used in the debate is too simplistic, noting that their are 'public' organisations that are privately owned, publicly owned, state owned, co-operatively owned and 'non-owned', such as quangos (Mintzberg, 1996).

It is more than sufficient to state here that there is a rich diversity of public and private sector organisations and that this diversity needs to be reflected in any debate concerning the reforms of the public sector. Unfortunately, this has not been the case in the United Kingdom in particular in recent years, where the conventional wisdom amongst Conservative Party politicians has been that the private sector is by definition good and the public sector bad. This view is neither unusual nor confined to the United Kingdom (see Goodsell (1994), who defends the government bureaucracy in the United States).

Metcalfe and Richards, however, argue that this belief is accompanied by a limited understanding of what management in the private sector is all about (Metcalfe and Richards, 1990)! At the same time, those who wish to defend the public services because of the perceived inequities of the private sector fare no better in the debate. Public officials are keen to protect the public service ethos from the possibilities of corruption or dilution by private sector values and techniques, yet there is little evidence that such a corruption occurs. Lawton argues that the notion of the public service ethos is a contested one, where 'jobs for the boys', 'don't dob on your mates' or 'stuff the customer' can be used to characterise the public service ethos (Lawton, 1995).

This chapter will first note the arguments concerning the distinctiveness or otherwise of the public services, particularly in terms of goals and functions. Secondly, it will examine the practices and values of managers in the public services and in the private sector. Thirdly, it will consider the changing nature of the relationships between internal and external stakeholders. The ethical dimensions in these areas will also be drawn out.

FROM PUBLIC TO PRIVATE: A QUESTION OF PURPOSE

That public sector reforms should reflect private sector practices has, in a number of countries, been taken for granted. The assumption is that the public sector will become more efficient if it:

- measures organisational achievements in terms of targets;
- focuses on outcomes rather than inputs or processes;
- is more responsive to what is now known as the customer;
- devolves responsibility;
- develops an entrepreneurial culture;
- weakens collectivist approaches to managing the employment relationship;

- develops performance measures;
- introduces local pay bargaining;
- develops mission statements to demonstrate organisational objectives and 'capture' commitment by employees; and
- adopts delayering, benchmarking and process re-engineering (see Cabinet Office, 1994).

There have been both hopes and fears expressed surrounding these developments. As a sceptical Peters puts it:

> All these paeans of praise were being raised to the private sector despite evidence that the private sector was not performing particularly well in many of the industrialized countries. The same governments that were telling their own employees to emulate the private sector were bailing out banks, auto manufacturers, steel makers, and a host of other financially failing enterprises. (Peters, 1991, p 426)

Fears have also been expressed concerning the alleged corrupting influence of the private sector. For example, the Silverwater Report, concerning a contracting issue involving a government minister and a private company in Australia, highlights problems with contracts and tendering in the public sector and warns public sector managers that '[t]hose in the public sector must realise that they will be taken advantage of if possible, and they must strenuously resist that happening' (ICAC, 1991, p 10).

Notwithstanding such concerns, the adoption of private sector practices has continued apace. Thus, for example, Canada's PS2000 which was intended to reform the Canadian public services sought to preserve the best of the past but apply the best of applicable private sector management practices. The reforms were intended to change a rule-oriented administrative culture characterised by a concern with process, inflexible, over-adherence to rules, risk averse, and concerned with detailed central controls to a new people-centred, results-oriented management culture characterised by a concern with outcomes, results, flexibility, innovation, accountability for results and run by public managers (rather than public servants) who view assets to be developed rather than consumed (see Caiden et al, 1995, p 85).

Critics fear that the public service ethos is being undermined as a result of these changes (see Lawton, 1995). One of the key issues here is that the fundamental purpose of the public sector is being challenged. Notwithstanding the fact that government is increasingly composed of hybrid departments and agencies that may include a commercial function, the concept of a core public service delivering health, welfare, security, transport and education is contested and efficiency and economy are promoted as key virtues. At the same time, the notion of corporate social responsibility and a concern with the ethics of corporate governance has led to commentators questioning that the only role, particularly of large corporations, is profit maximisation. Since Friedman argued that the proper responsibility of business is to create profits, an academic industry has arisen around business ethics, contesting the 'proper' role and responsibilities of business (Friedman, 1970). Sternberg argues that what constitutes ethical conduct in business depends critically on business's definitive purpose (Sternberg, 1994). She feels that business is about maximising long-term owner value through selling goods and services. It may do other things but this is its core activity and using business resources for non-business purposes constitutes theft. She argues that '[a]n organisation which pursued moral goodness simply because it was good, and regardless of the consequences for long-term owner value, would simply not be acting as a business'(Sternberg, 1994, p 96). This is an argument that Machiavelli utilised in a different context when he argued that it was irresponsible and morally wrong to apply to political action the moral standards that are appropriate to private life and personal ends. This confusion over ends can also be said to apply to the public services. In seeking to become more efficient and economical, system goals are being confused with mission goals (Mintzberg, 1983). Efficiency and economy are system goals that any organisation would endeavour to achieve but they do not define its purpose nor measure its outcomes. Mintzberg contends that system goals have become more characteristic of large organisations (Mintzberg, 1983).

It can be argued that business depends upon government for infrastructure and that business cannot exist in isolation from the community. Even markets are regulated. Hosmer builds his arguments concerning ethical business on a number of propositions which hypothesise that companies operating in a competitive global economy are dependent upon a wide range of stakeholders for co-operative activities. It is possible to build trust, commitment and effort on the part of all stakeholders by including ethical principles in the strategic decision process of companies where the interests and rights of all stakeholders are recognised (Hosmer, 1994, p 17).

Business is composed of different sets of stakeholders (owners, managers, customers, suppliers etc) and there are sets of relationships that characterise the conduct of business. The key point here is that, even though the *nature* of business is different from the core public services, managers may be involved in similar sets of relationships. This is explored below. Whatever the debate concerning the purposes of business and the public services, it is believed by many that managers with experience of, and skills in, private sector management can transform public sector organisations.

MANAGERIAL MYTHS

As indicated above, there is a belief in many OECD countries that the public sector could be run better if it adopted private sector management practices. This view is endorsed by governments in the United Kingdom and Australia, amongst others. The concept of the 'freedom to manage' is a crucial issue. In recommending changes to the structure of the UK civil service, it was indicated that '[a]t present the freedom of an individual manager to manage effectively and responsibly in the Civil Service is severely circumscribed ... [t]he culture of the Civil Service puts a premium on a "safe pair of hands", not on enterprise' (Efficiency Unit, 1988, pp 5, 29).

The reforms to the Australian Public Service (APS) were driven by similar considerations. 'A theme underlying all the key reforms in the APS has been the freeing up of bureaucratic processes to allow managers greater scope to manage'

(Public Service Commission, 1992, p 5). The reality is often different. Campbell argues that officials in line agencies are often frustrated over disjunctions between Finance Department's managerialist rhetoric and the reality that most programmes had come under severe budgetary constraints (Campbell, 1995, p 479).

Discretion has, of course, always existed in the public services. Even where tightly circumscribed job descriptions exist or within activities that seem bound by statute, there is still room for manoeuvre. (Miller, Chapter 3, examines the power of discretion.) Discretion is exercised and judgments are made; the tax inspector who vigilantly adheres to a coded checklist might have to make a judgement between sending it forward to an overworked central office where little will happen or trying to negotiate compliance on the spot within the parameters of their own powers. The police officer might make a decision not to book the perpetrator of a minor offence because the courts are already clogged. Even within those activities that appear to be driven by legislation, there is always room for the exercise of discretion. One argument against the exercise of discretion, and in the interests of justice, is that like cases may not be treated alike when discretion is exercised. However, in the examples used above, discretion is exercised by professionals in the exercise of their professional duties. By contrast, the administrator has traditionally been depicted as merely following rules.

The professional exercises discretion at the point of delivery of services, whether they be teachers, doctors, police or social workers. Professionals perform a dual role, representing the statutory authorities and their clients. Their discretion has been circumscribed by professional codes of conduct which provide a framework for their actions. Not that professional codes of conduct are always adhered to. Parker indicates that professional codes may suffer from the lack of an effective machinery for enforcing compliance, a reluctance of colleagues to disclose unethical behaviour about another's unethical conduct and a reluctance amongst members to informally restrain colleagues from ethical deviations (LD Parker, 1994, p 507). (See Kaptein, Chapter 2, for an intriguing analysis of professional codes.) Professionals have been under attack and managers have been given greater responsibilities and freedom to act.

However, there is a belief that managerialism does constitute an ideology and the freedom to manage is the fundamental cornerstone of that ideology. Pollitt argues that 'Managerialism is a set of beliefs and practices, at the core of which burns the seldom tested assumption that better management will prove an effective solvent for a wide range of economic and social ills' (Pollitt, 1993, p 1). Similarly, du Gay et al argue that the discourse of management has come to dominate the language of the public sector manager. The discourse of 'excellence' stresses the importance of individuals acquiring and exhibiting more market-oriented, pro-active, empowered and entrepreneurial capacities (du Gay et al, 1996, p 263). This necessitates the production of certain types of individuals, namely, those who are enterprising, autonomous, productive, self-regulating and responsible individuals. The belief in managers (which appears to have replaced the belief that professionals play the key role in delivering public services) means that the role of managers has been greatly enhanced. This has necessitated the adoption of new managerial attributes, skills and capacities.

The success of organisations is increasingly premised upon managers' abilities to foster 'pro-active mindsets', 'entrepreneurship', 'self-development' and other virtues. Management text books are full of prescriptions, indicating the qualities that (usually senior) managers should possess. For example, Schröder lists 11 high performance managerial competences.

1   Information search: to aid decision-making
2   Concept formation: concerned with model-building
3   Conceptual flexibility: examine the pros and cons in decision-making
4   Interpersonal search: consider other viewpoints
5   Managing interaction: team building with others
6   Development orientation: coaching and training
7   Impact: convince others
8   Self-confidence: in team tasks
9   Presentation: communication skills
10 Pro-active orientation: towards targets and progress
11 Achievement orientation: towards tasks and progress. (Schröder, 1989)

In a similar fashion the Audit Commission in the United Kingdom came up with a list of roles for chief executives in local government in 1989: strategic, co-ordinating, operational and representative (see Lawton and Rose, 1994).

The civil servant is said to possess probity, impartiality, intellectual rigour, frankness, independence, adaptability, energy, political awareness, good oral and written communication skills, negotiating abilities and a thorough knowledge of government and political processes. These skills are welcomed by ministers (Efficiency Unit, 1993, p 23). However, in light of the acceptance of managerialism, civil servants also need new skills, including strong leadership, a team-building approach, public presentation skills, a willingness to break new ground, firmness to confront poor performance, imagination and flair, listening skills and contract management skills (Efficiency Unit, 1993, p 27). (Cf Sherman's list in Chapter 1.)

Theory v Practice

In reality, however, is there any evidence that managers actually do all the things they are supposed to do? According to Mintzberg, managers are not engaged in reflection or planning. Most managers are unable to control work and have little autonomy. The manager is driven by short-term considerations, the work is fragmented and characterised by superficiality in their tasks. They are driven by what is current and tangible and so become very good at 'quick fixes', which creates a vicious circle because the problems re-occur. There is also confusion concerning the beliefs in what managers should be doing compared to what they do. Unlike the classical management theorists such as Fayol, Taylor, Gullick and

Urwick and others, Mintzberg found that not only was it difficult to find these classical principles in operation but that managers didn't even seem to be doing what they believed they were doing (Mintzberg, 1975, p 49)!

Similarly, Hales argues that most of the evidence seems to indicate that the notion of the manager as strategist, planner and thinker is a myth. He argues that even senior managers allow themselves to be diverted by interruptions and by informal personal contacts. The day-to-day dominates rather than the strategic. He suggests that between two-thirds and four-fifths of a manager's time is spent in imparting or receiving information through face-to-face contact with others (Hales, 1986, p 88).

Conway attempted a small-scale study based upon three operational managers in social services in UK local government. He found that all three managers spent 23% of their time exchanging information, 20% handling papers, 22% socialising/politicking and 18% motivating/reinforcing (Conway, 1993, p 20).

Managers spend much of their time on maintaining and establishing relationships. If management is about achieving things through others, then it should be concerned with relationships with others.

The belief in managerialism has led to, at least in the United Kingdom, exhortations to improve the quality of management both in the public and private sectors. The vehicle for this has been through the development of management competences, defined as the ability to perform a series of work activities effectively. This would include skills, knowledge, understanding and values. The Management Charter Initiative (MCI) was set up following a number of influential reports in the 1980s which argued that UK managers lacked education and training in comparison with competitors elsewhere. Part of the MCI's function is to provide standards and guidelines for management development and training. The MCI recommended that management could be improved through the development of certain key competences, these depending upon the level of management. At level 1 for front-line managers, these are constructed around the four key roles of managing operations, finance, people and information (Lawton and Rose, 1994).

In research carried out with front-line managers in the United Kingdom personal social services provided through local authorities and agencies to individuals, Lawton et al found that, in principle, the usefulness of generic competences was recognised. However, they need to be supplemented by a wide range of more specific competences, including:

- managing ambiguity;
- coping with changing legislation;
- creating and maintaining client/user involvement;
- developing anti-oppressive practices;
- managing in small units and non-formally organised settings;
- managing in a contract culture;
- managing at and across inter-disciplinary and multi-professional interfaces;
- working with networks;

- working in a multi-cultural environment;
- managing professionals;
- coping with ethical dilemmas; and
- working with politicians (Lawton et al, 1993).

In short, there is a professional and an organisational value base to all work. Where public services managers are encouraged to become more like their private sector counterparts, there may well be learning problems involving techniques and also language. New skills might include the need to write or judge a business plan, how to specify and monitor contracts or how to price outputs to match competition. The new language could include the concepts of markets, prices, contracts, competitors, customers, business units, profit centres and so on (see Mackintosh, 1995).

However, the notion that there are a set of management prescriptions that can be used to solve organisational problems is increasingly being questioned by management theorists themselves. Nohria and Berkley claim that the uncritical adoption of the latest management nostrums can be shown to have been harmful to US business over the last 30 years. They argue that the widespread adoption of 'trendy techniques' encouraged managers to rely on ready-made solutions rather than search for creative solutions. They call for a 'return to pragmatism' which recognises uncertainties in the management environment (Nohria and Berkley, 1994, p 128). There are four guiding principles, the four faces of pragmatism.

1   *Sensitivity to context*: being able to judge the parameters of a particular situation and decide what ideas and actions will work in that context

2   *Willingness to make do*: experimenting with and using available resources and material to find workable solutions

3   *Focus on outcomes*: being concerned with getting results but not being overly 'hung up' on how to get them

4   *Openness to uncertainty*: recognising the impossibility of being able to anticipate all circumstances and thereby being required to act out of ignorance (adapted from Nohria and Berkley, 1994)

The debate concerning management competences needs an organisational context. One noted participant in the debate argues that 'the simple reality is that all managerial jobs are different at a detailed level of resolution, and all managerial jobs the same at a high level of abstraction' (Burgoyne, 1989, p 58). The reality may be different. The New South Wales government in Australia has tried to bring in people from outside at senior level to act as change agents in the belief that entrepreneurial skills did not exist among its existing officials and that these skills were transferable from the private sector. Almost without exception, the appointments met with little success, primarily because the appointees could not get used to 'interfering politicians' and had difficulty in understanding the 'rules of the game' within which government is conducted (eg the prominence of political accountability and public scrutiny).

Thus, management tasks and competences should be linked to the organisational context. In arguing for the transformative skills of private sector managers, the particular character of organisational context needs to be addressed.

THE NATURE OF ORGANISATIONAL RELATIONSHIPS

The manager is at the centre of a web of relationships entailing obligations and duties which need to be balanced. The multiplicity of different stakeholders in the public services makes the managers' commitments even more numerous. However, despite this truism, little work has been done on defining the different forms and limits of these relationships. Like any employee, a civil servant plays various roles and with these roles go various loyalties, such as those to a professional body and its professional standards, as an employee expected to implement decisions taken by superiors, as a servant of the Crown/government accountable to ministers, as a public official with a duty to act impartially to all citizens and as a private individual.

The civil servant may be subject to a number of competing duties and obligations. However, the concerns of officials concerning a public sector ethos will vary greatly depending upon function, level within the department and relationships with external stakeholders. For example, senior officials in central departments are very much concerned with traditional accountability to their minister and with ensuring that advice remains impartial. Chief executives in those departments with a commercial role are concerned with 'more bang for the buck' and with ensuring that public money is not wasted. Front-line officials are concerned with acting in a proper manner when handing out contracts and are extremely sensitive to accusations of impropriety and corruption.

Much of the debate in recent times concerning the nature of organisational relationships has focused upon the principal–agent theory as the basis of relationships. This approach stresses that individuals are opportunistic; that contracts must protect the principal from the agent; that the protection of interests is costly to monitor; that the agent has an information advantage over the principal; and that the use of multiple performance criteria is essential. Entrepreneurial government shares the same discourse and affords contracts a crucial role in re-defining social relations. For example, institutional roles in schools and hospitals are re-constituted in terms of contracts or quasi-contracts. Relationships within the public service are often defined by the employer in terms of performance instead of long-term tenure in return for compliance and loyalty (the traditional exchange).[3]

The Concept of Trust

A feature of more traditional relationships has been trust. Trust manifests itself in terms of relationships and their maintenance. Trust also operates in a number of different contexts, as relationships may be personal, economic, institutional or professional in character. Different obligations and duties towards others will arise, depending upon how that relationship is perceived. Individuals may see their roles differently. One such difference may be between those who see a role as public and those who see it as private. For example, Jones argues that '[t]he more public a role is the more the role consists in a set of standard expectations fixed in advance for the role players rather than in individual expectations that emerge in the course of their mutual interactions' (Jones, 1984, p 607). Jones suggests that public roles are designed to achieve the goals of the organisation whereas private roles are non-instrumental and will vary and develop depending upon the fulfilment of individual expectations.

Performance in a public role is judged by the extent to which the goals are achieved. The attitudes of individuals are irrelevant except insofar as they affect the ability to perform well in a role. This argument is supported by the research carried out by Gabarro on how managers develop working relationships with their subordinates (Gabarro, 1978). Task accomplishment was a central criterion in developing trust, with personal liking or attraction relatively unimportant. The distinctions between public roles and private roles can be defined in terms of why they are entered into, how they develop and what they are designed to achieve.

	Public Roles	**Private Roles**
Expectations	Defined by role	Emerge in the course of mutual interactions
Characteristics	Effectiveness	Trust
	A calculating stance	Non-instrumental
	Designed to fit a role	Grow and develop
Objectives	To achieve pre-determined goals	An end in itself

The concept of a public role may be more appropriate in characterising a relationship of contract rather than sociability or personal relations. A feature of such relationships will also be one of limited commitment. A contract specifies clearly what obligations and duties are covered, whereas a personal relationship can be covered by an open-ended commitment. A further distinction is that between an economic exchange and a social exchange. Fox argues that an economic exchange is similar to that which is specified in a contract and a social exchange indicates an absence of a specifically defined obligation (Fox, 1974). However, a social exchange may be characterised by high discretion and trust, an economic exchange will be characterised by low discretion and trust.

Fox considers that high trust will characterise a non-instrumental relationship whereas low trust will characterise an instrumental one. An example of the changing nature of the trust relationship can be seen in the relationships between ministers and senior officials in the UK central government in the 1980s. Traditionally, in the Westminster model of government, the relationship had been characterised as the neutral, loyal and impartial civil servant servicing the minister to the best of their ability and secure in the knowledge that their advice will be protected from public scrutiny. The concept of trust is thus at the heart of the relationship between the minister and the civil servant, particularly those in senior positions. This view has been criticised in recent years in the United Kingdom. Instead, it has been suggested that the notion of a departmental ethos precludes neutrality, that the role of trade unions within the civil service has led to a more overt political stance or that the social and educational background of the senior civil service represents a distorted perspective on issues of government. Indeed, even if neutrality does exist, this may not necessarily be seen as a good thing. In the age of commitment politics that characterised the United Kingdom in the 1980s, ministers required more from their advisers than previously and often sought advice from alternative sources. Furthermore, while commitment may be appropriate for a personal relationship, it may not be appropriate for other kinds of relationship.

As governments introduce formal agreements and contracts between departments and their agencies specifying responsibilities and targets to be met, this may undermine the all-embracing nature of the convention of ministerial responsibility. This is a long way from the beliefs of the founder of the modern UK civil service, Sir Warren Fisher, who indicated that practical rules were as reliant upon people's instincts and perceptions as on guidelines carved in granite; further, he noted that civil servant's jealous honour was perhaps the most reliable guideline of all (Fisher, 1928).

At present, the relationship between the minister and the senior civil servant in the United Kingdom can be described as low trust with divergent goals and values. Given the different roles and length of time in office, there would appear to be short-term obligations towards each other rather than long-term commitment. The dependence upon each other would be minimised. By using the concept of trust, generations of civil servants have endorsed an image of their relationship with ministers that has all the attributes of a personal relationship but is no longer convincing. It is a contractual exchange that involves a set of standard expectations fixed in advance, where obligations and duties are specified and order and stability would be the bedrock of the minister–civil servant relationship. A code of written guidelines would have these advantages and perhaps be more appropriate.

Interestingly enough, trust has become a key concept in discussing arrangements in private sector organisations. 'Trust generates commitment. Commitment builds effort. Effort that is co-operative, innovative and strategically directed results in success whether measured by stock price, market share, or organizational development' (Hosmer, 1994, p 29).

The focus above has been on the politician–civil servant relationship but there are other relationships between different stakeholders that might also be considered. Governments will have different sets of relationships with customers, clients and citizens. Managers will also have different sets of relationships, depending upon their roles in policy advice, revenue generation, regulation, monitoring and so on.

The notion of a formal contract may not always be appropriate, particularly where the nature of the exchange is social rather than economic. Domberger and Hall, for example, make the point that in Western Australia, contracting out is not considered appropriate for policy advice to government, certain regulatory and emergency functions and judicial and parliamentary functions (Domberger and Hall, 1996, p 129). The point is that each set of relationships is different in form and content.

ETHICAL IMPLICATIONS OF GOOD MANAGEMENT

Thus far, the focus has been upon the qualities that managers are said to possess and the relationships that managers engage in and the form that these take. What other considerations are there? Is the good manager the same as the good person? Moreover, how might good or bad be defined in general? This is at the heart of ethics theorising. It is about individuals making and acting upon decisions based upon a range of perceptions about a whole range of issues concerning other individuals and themselves. As individuals with consciences who choose to engage in relations with others, the treatment of those other individuals will need to be worked out. What would the criteria for the good person consist of? One might list sensitive to the needs of others, respecter of individual rights, unselfish, honest, loyal to family, friends and community, generous, charitable etc. What are the kinds of values associated with individuals in organisations? The good manager may be expressed in terms of achieving objectives and not in the conduct of relationships, despite the fact that the evidence given above seems to indicate that most managers spend most of their time engaging in relationships. However, criteria might include loyalty, dedication, integrity, probity, entrepreneurialism, efficiency, effectiveness, professionalism, impartiality, non-arbitrariness. A good manager *qua* manager may be defined by the purposes of the organisation. Not so a good person.

Public service values are characterised as loyalty, honesty, integrity, non-partisanship, prudence, professionalism, faithfulness to fairness and impartiality and so on and are often located in the wider context of the public interest. To what extent then is the good manager in the public sector different from a good manager in the private sector? A further consideration is the extent to which public sector managers become corrupted by private sector practices. (See again the quote from the Silverwater Report, above.) However, to counter this assumption that the public sector behaves more ethically than the private, Steinberg and Austen give a list of reasons for unethical behaviour amongst public sector managers.

- good intentions (ie frustration with red-tape)
- ignorance of laws, codes, policies and procedures
- ego power trip
- greed
- 'it comes with the territory'
- friendship
- ideology

- personal or family gain
- post-employment revolving door
- financial problems and pressures
- stupidity
- exploiting the exploiters, a feeling of being hard done by
- playing games
- not making waves
- following orders
- survival at all cost (Steinberg and Austen, 1990)

Is it the opportunities that present themselves? Do the processes encourage it? Are the tasks geared to short-cuts? There appears to be little evidence to support the notion that private sector influence automatically involves corruption. For example, the UK Committee of Public Accounts found that breaches of existing rules were the most common form of corruption, together with evidence of inexperienced staff, poor monitoring, failure to pursue money owed, failure to establish clear lines of accountability, failure to take prompt action, failure to make regular reviews and possible conflicts of interests (Committee of Public Accounts, 1994). In Australia, a 1991 Independent Commission Against Corruption report reported that seven of the 19 key issues it examined involved public sector-private sector dealings (ICAC, 1991). Badaracco and Webb found that there were four powerful organisational 'commandants' that encouraged unethical behaviour (Badaracco and Webb, 1995, p 8).[4] Organisational pressures and not character flaws seemed to be the crucial factor!

- Performance is what really counts; must meet targets
- Be loyal and show that you are a team player
- Don't break the law
- Don't over-invest in ethical behaviour

The key issues to recognise here are the extent to which it is the organisational culture, the processes adopted, the expertise of staff, personal qualities and so on that form part of the ethical fabric of an organisation as much as the nature of its business. This is the case in both the public and private sectors.

CONCLUSION: RECOGNISING THE BALANCE

There are different ways of reforming the public services and not every country has endorsed the adoption of new management practices. This is understandable, given the different traditions within which the delivery of public services takes place. For example, in much of Continental Europe, administrative law has played a much greater role than in the United Kingdom. In many parts of Europe, administration is seen as the application of laws rather than the freedom to manage that is said to characterise much of the New Public Management (see Hood, 1996, p 151; and Ridley, 1996, p 16). In those countries that have adopted New Public Management, its effect on different stakeholders has been different. Caiden et al argue that the effect of PS2000 in Canada has been a double-edged sword for middle managers.

> They have experienced greater responsibilities, authority and accountability, greater accompanying stress in implementing changes they often had no part in creating, and greater morale problems resulting from simultaneous pressures to produce higher quality services while having to retrench staff. (Caiden et al, 1995, p 97)

Without doubt, there have been improvements in the management of public services but whether this has anything to do with the private sector is open to question. In any case, the reforms have had a mixed effect.

Benefits

- Public sector organisations have been forced to think about what 'business' they are in
- The issue of management competences and skills has been placed on the agenda
- The 'mind-set' of many managers has been changed
- There has been an increased focus on outcomes not inputs
- The myth of one public sector, dominated by the mandarin class, has been debunked
- The cross-fertilisation of ideas, people and techniques has raised awareness of best practice

Costs

- Focus on results rather than processes may undermine probity. In the words of one senior New South Wales manager, 'The focus on outcomes is good whereas the obsession with process is unhealthy. Process becomes the end of public service' (personal interview). A balance needs to be achieved.
- Low morale
- Painful cuts
- Informal relationships tend to replaced by formal ones
- Decline in trust
- Focus on the customer rather than the citizen
- False expectations on the part of managers
- Undermining of traditions and judgment
- A misunderstanding of the role of bureaucracy

Freedom to manage will need to be balanced by accountability; risk-taking will need to be balanced with the political intolerance of failure and the requirements of due process; responsiveness will need to be balanced with central control and economy and efficiency will need to be balanced with effectiveness. In short, a balance of the methods from the private sector with the values of the public sector seems to be the most feasible and effective way forward.

NOTES

1   This chapter is primarily conceptual insofar as it is intended clear a way through some of the 'background noise' concerning the use of business practices, and business language, advocated for managing in the public services. It will not address comparative issues. A discussion of comparative methodology can be found in Rose (1993), and comparisons of the reform process in different countries can be found in Zifcak (1994); Campbell and Wilson (1995); and Pollitt (1993).

2   Indeed, a new paradigm of managing the delivery of public services has been proposed under the title of 'New Public Management' (see OECD (1995)).

3   The notion of 'office as a vocation' seems rather dated from this perspective!

4   Admittedly based on quite limited research (ie 30 recent graduates of the Harvard MBA program), the following characterisation does ring true.

5

CLARIFYING ACCOUNTABILITY
An Ethical Theory Framework

Mel Dubnick

INTRODUCTION

From the perspective of students of public administration throughout the English-speaking world, Tom Sherman's observations regarding public sector ethics in Australia can be applied world-wide. (See Sherman, Chapter 1.) This is particularly true with regards to pressures from a growing public demand for 'openness and accountability'. Meeting the challenges of developing and maintaining mechanisms for accountability seems especially important in an era of greater discretion to non-elected personnel and the privatisation of government services. We are comfortable with such observations because the idea of accountability makes sense to us. It is as natural to us as the idea that democracy requires competition among political parties or the extension of the voting franchise to all citizens. We take the need for accountability for granted and assume that everyone understands what the concept means and why it is so important.

We may have to reconsider our casual attitude toward the concept of account-ability. In a general critique of the existing literature on the topic, John Uhr rightly concludes that 'existing frameworks for analysing public accountability are responsible for much of our inability to contribute to more effective institutions of public policy' (Uhr, 1992, p 18). His advocacy of a 'research project on accountability tensions'(Uhr, 1992, p 1) is a welcome call to scholarly action for those of us who regard the topic of accountability as a crucial yet overlooked dimension of the modern administrative state.

Uhr's objective is to develop an approach bridging (1) normative frameworks that stress the need to assess various forms of accountability with those that are (2) more descriptive and 'realist' in perspective. To accomplish this, Uhr argues that both views 'could benefit from a return to the constitutional centre and renovate their accountability frameworks by reference to emerging practices which stand in open dispute over the appropriate public duties for executive officials'(Uhr, 1992, p 10). By contrast, I will argue that the more relevant metaphor is the need to plant deeper conceptual roots for the two perspectives rather than attempt to bridge them.

Central to my view is a concern for how students of accountability — both scholars and practitioners — have been talking past each other. There is a need to deal with the ambiguous application of the term 'accountability' by those who use the term in a less than casual fashion. This task will involve a shift in the conceptual context of the analytic endeavour from that of traditional 'action theory' to a more relevant and reflexive 'ethical theory' focus. These points will be considered in the next section after addressing the surprisingly parochial nature of the accountability idea. I then offer a framework for conceptualising accountability in a range of forms covering many of the attitudes and behaviours that term signifies to those who use it in practical situations. Finally, I conclude with some thoughts about the how to assess the framework and where it might lead those of us committed to Uhr's call.

JUSTIFICATIONS FOR CONCEPTUAL AND ANALYTIC CHANGE

There are a number of preliminary steps to be taken in this effort to reconceptualise accountability. First, it is critical that we acknowledge the 'anglican'[1] nature of the accountability idea and its implications for our endeavour. Secondly, we need to acknowledge the dualistic nature of existing accountability studies. Finally, we need to consider a useful theoretical context for conducting a reconceptualisation that will help us advance the study of accountability and public administrative behaviour in general.

The Anglican Concept

Accountability is an anglican concept. I first became aware of this while on my way to give a public lecture on 'Accountability and the Burdens of Democracy' to a Brazilian university audience. Although my knowledge of Portuguese is extremely poor, I did notice that the posters advertising the talk in the hallways used the term 'Responsabilidade' in place of 'Accountability' in the title. I politely protested to my host, noting that a major theme of my talk was the distinction between responsibility and accountability. His response: there was no equivalent term, at least in Brazilian Portuguese, for accountability as I meant it.

Having survived that episode, I undertook the task of investigating just how the term is translated in other languages. As it turns out, the English concept is quite distinctive. In most of the romance languages (French, Spanish and Italian as well as Portuguese), various forms of the term 'responsibility' are used in lieu of the English 'accountability'. The issue would seem a petty one were it not for the fact that *accountability is not synonymous with responsibility.* As Uhr correctly notes, accountability is at the least complementary to responsibility and certainly not equal to it (Uhr (1992) also speaks of responsibility as derivative from accountability as well). As he describes the term, it is almost a mirror of responsibility.

Accountability constrains and fetters official discretion, while responsibility releases discretion. Accountability is compliance with authority, whereas responsibility is about empowerment and independence. Accountability is the negative end of the band in which responsibility is at the positive end. If accountability is about minimising misgovernment, responsibility is about maximising good government ... (Uhr, 1992, p 4)

In non-English speaking countries, the term 'accountability' has been adopted only out of necessity (eg Japan) or due to the close relationship of the country to anglican governance (eg Israel). For example, in Japanese, a dictionary search turned up the transliterated term *akauntabiritii*, an all too obvious reminder of the Japanese capacity to adopt useful terms from foreign sources. To highlight the point, there were 17 distinctive traditional Japanese terms associated with 'responsibility', none of which were explicitly linked to the English-language notion of accountability. Israelis are familiar with the word and concept of accountability in its British and American manifestations but government officials charged with applying it (eg the State Comptroller) are frustrated by the fact that there is no equivalent term in modern Hebrew.[2]

Even where a term seemingly similar to 'accountability' is found, the concept is typically more narrow than the anglican form. For northern European languages (eg Dutch, Danish, German), accountability is distinguishable from responsibility. None the less, translations of accountability are closer in meaning to 'duty' or 'obligation', eg an accountability is an obligation or duty to live up to terms of a trust. Typical is the way the term is treated by the Finns. Finnish translations for accountability directly relate to the term used to stress an 'obligation' (ie *velvollisuus)*. Thus, the three key terms in the Finnish dictionary for accountability are *tilivelvollisuus (tili* meaning 'pay' or 'financial tally'), *kirjanpitovelvollisuus (kirjanpito* meaning 'book-keeping') and *vastuuvelvollisuus (vastuu* meaning 'onus' or 'burden'). But as is the case with responsibility, the term we typically use in English is not synonymous with merely forms of 'obligation' or 'duty.' While one may feel an obligation or duty for being accountable, accountability itself is neither *per se.*

In Russian, accountability is a distinct term with roots in the concept of 'report', especially as it relates to financial matters. In this sense, they have developed a term that captures not the sense of 'responsibility' but what the French call *comptes à rendre* ('the rendering of accounts').

That French phrase, in fact, does serve as a clue to the anglican conceptualisation of accountability. The key to understanding the anglican nature of accountability is to see its historical and institutional terms and especially its roots in the *idea* of accountability (in contrast to the word *per se*) that takes hold under Norman rule. Etymologically, Middle English terms related to accountability (eg *acompte, aconte*) can be traced to at least to the early 14th century and there is no doubt these were derived from the Old French equivalents for *comptes à rendre*. More interestingly, a strong case can be made for a specific link between those Old French phrases and the English concept of accountability by focusing on a watershed event in British political history: the publication of the Domesday Books in 1086.

Twenty years after the Norman conquest, William I ordered a detailed enumeration of all property in England requiring every subject to provide access to royal surveyors for the listing and valuation of all holdings. The resulting census, known as the Domesday Books, is widely cited as a critical factor in the enduring power of central authority in Britain. In some respects, the survey was merely a reflection of William's immediate need to determine the tax base of his conquered lands in order to assess his holdings and make revenue collection more efficient. In a broader sense, it was for the time an exceptional accomplishment in the exercise of monarchical authority, an effort of such scope and detail that its successful implementation could not help but enhance the legitimacy of Norman rule.

The conduct of the Domesday survey sent a message to all of William's subjects that the conquest was complete and a new ruling order was in place. Completed in an amazingly short time (one year), it relied on units of measure and jurisdictional reconfigurations that best suited the survey task rather than extant arrangements. Farm oxen were counted as a 'plough-team' units and land holdings were designated (for the first time) as *maneriums* or manors. Thus, not only were property holders required to 'render a count' of what they possessed but they were to do so in the terms set by the king's agents (see Brooke, 1961, pp 91–2, 114–15; also Douglas, 1964, pp 351–4). Medieval historians have rightly been in awe of what the Domesday Books represent. 'As an administrative achievement', noted one, 'it has no parallel in medieval history.' Still another authority regards it as 'marking an epoch in the use of the written word in government' (Douglas, 1964, p 354, quoting historians F Stenton and VH Galbraith respectively).

Beyond the Domesday surveys themselves, however, William took an additional and complementary step in 1086 when, after travelling about his kingdom as the survey was being conducted, he came:

> to Salisbury at Lammas, and there his councillors came to him, and all the people occupying land who were of any account over all England whosoever's vassals they might be; and they all submitted to him, and swore oaths of allegiance to him that they would be faithful to him and against all other men. (Douglas, 1964, p 355, quoting from chroniclers of the time)

While historian David Douglas cautions against attributing too much to William's actions (eg developing a modern form of national sovereignty), 'his acts ... were exceptional in their nature, and of high importance'. Royal authority was made more effective and feudal organisation in England was strengthened (Douglas, 1964, pp 355–6). Central to these developments, I contend, was the establishment of accountability (the idea, not the term) as a foundation for governance.

Historian James Given provides additional support for this argument in his comparative study of two local societies which came under 'foreign' rule during the 13th century: Gwynedd in North Wales (ruled by the English from the late 1200s) and Languedoc in the south of France (incorporated under the French monarchy from the early 1200s). Given takes special note of the distinctive approaches used by the English and French in governing each jurisdiction. The French took a 'minimalist' approach by establishing 'a loose hegemony over the local community'. As Uhr would note, the locals in Languedoc retained 'responsibility' for much of their own governance. In contrast, the English used a 'maximalist solution' to the governing problem, involving:

> the total recasting of local political structures. Traditional mechanisms and techniques of rule would be abolished and replaced by ones modeled directly on those of the new masters. The governors who wielded these novel mechanisms of power would be either members of the outside ruling organization or local people who had been thoroughly educated in and assimilated to the outsiders' norms. (Given, 1990, p 42)

Although not referring to accountability explicitly, Given's description of the English system of local administrative governance rings familiar to anyone knowledgeable about the Anglo-Norman system of rule created under William and his successors, who most often used it to enhance the legitimacy of the royal court. As authority in England shifted from the crown to the parliament over the next few centuries, that framework, and the accountability system that underpinned it, was held in place.

In contrast, the French did not develop a similar system until several centuries later. They did so in a way that created the institutions of centralisation while undermining the potential for the establishment and legitimacy of accountability. 'The taste for centralization and the mania for regulations date back in France to the time when lawyers came into government,' noted de Tocqueville in an aside to his commentary in *Democracy in America* (de Tocqueville, 1969, pp 723–4).

What difference does it make that the political idea of accountability is rooted in British history and is conceptually anglican? Two points are in order here. First and foremost, this finding should give one pause before proceeding with a comparative analysis — descriptive or normative — into the role of accountability in political systems past or present. It is clear that we might be flirting with errors of commission or omission in such an endeavour unless care is taken not to bias our studies with preconceived (ie anglican) notions of accountability.

Secondly, it should lead us to conclude that careful conceptualisation must precede any such comparative study, even if that study is limited to equally British Westminster-style democracies (as is Uhr's call for a comparative study of accountability). For despite the relative parochialism of the accountability term, *the idea of accountable government* is an important one in comprehending the operations of the contemporary administrative state in its many and varied forms. In this sense, the British legacy to modern political systems is perhaps even greater than its form of constitutional and parliamentary government. But the notion of accountability that characterises the world of former British holdings may be too narrow, too parochial to be of relevance to the wide range of political cultures that have taken on the idea, if not the term itself.

Two Perspectives on the Issue of Accountability

The task of developing a useful conceptual framework for studying accountability starts by noting the perspectives developed thus far by two groups of scholars. The first, comprised primarily of social psychologists and ethno-methodologists, have focused attention on the *accountability of conduct* (AC); the second group, embodying political scientists with a legal or institutional orientation, have been concerned with the *conduct of accountability* (CA). Despite indifference toward each other's work, the two groups provide a common foundation for the present task.

The AC/CA approaches are quite distinct on the surface. The AC group looks to the use of excuses or rationalisations by individuals who face situations where errors or perceived failure have rendered them accountable to some other individual or group (eg, see McLaughlin et al, 1992). Theirs is an empirical endeavour concerned with describing and/or explaining a common human behaviour. When they consider an instance of accountability in government, it is merely as just another case of a generic action. While the distinctive governmental setting has an impact, it is not the focus of attention; the floor of the legislature might as well be the factory floor or the crowded elevator. What is important is how and why individuals account for their (typically erroneous) behaviour to others.

The CA group, in contrast, tends to be more institutional in its focus and normative in its purpose. Their focus tends to be on the structures and procedures through which accountability is achieved and they typically regard the context (governmental or private, legislative or executive) as crucial. As a subset of that general group, students of bureaucracy and public administration have engaged in debates over the relative value of different forms of accountability (eg the Friedrich-Finer debate),[3] oftentimes giving more attention to the normative than the empirical endeavour (however, see Gruber, 1987).

The central point for our project, however, is that both approaches require attention in a useful conceptualisation of accountability. Either perspective by itself draws the analysis of public administrative behaviour away from its accountability-core. The AC approach does highlight the role accountability plays for the individual, both psychologically as well as socially. However, applying it out without due consideration for the institutional context trivialises the significant and distinctive role played by the governmental setting. The CA perspective, however, undervalues or oversimplifies the influence of individual psychology and social dynamics in the structures and procedures of institutionalised accountability systems.

What is required for our conceptualisation of accountability, therefore, is a framework that encompasses both the individualist AC and the institutionalist CA views. This is attempted below. However, such a reconceptualisation must be accompanied by a theoretical reorientation that will focus our attention on the linkage between the two levels of analysis represented by those perspectives.

The Ethical Theory Orientation

The effort to 'reconceive' accountability, particularly if we regard it as a key to understanding public administrative behaviour (as I do), must necessarily revisit some fundamental issues of social theory for at least two reasons. First, the current reliance on social action theory diverts attention from individual-level behaviour where accountability has its most significant impact. Secondly, the present perspective minimises, or at least fails to highlight, the ethical nature of the public administrative endeavour.

Advances in the study of human social behaviour have been accomplished through the adoption of some basic assumptions about the foundation or sources of social acts. Call them paradigms or meta-theories, they often deal with the key question of social science: why do individuals behave a certain way under given circumstances. At the risk of oversimplifying, there have been four major responses to that question. One, typified by the Freudian approach, regards human action as the product of some subconscious or repressed drives. A second, more Hegelian and Marxian in form, sees human action as the product of historical forces that ultimately manifest themselves as individual choices. A third, closely associated with utilitarians and strict behaviourists (eg JB Watson and BF Skinner), sees human choices as rational selections in response to immediate situations within the context of learned expectations (see, eg, Watson, 1958; and Skinner, 1971; for critiques of behaviourism, see Matson, 1964; and also Homans, 1987). Finally and most significant among current views of public administrative behaviour, human action is regarded as ends-oriented behaviour regulated by social and cultural norms and values. This last approach of social action theory owes much to the work of Talcott Parsons, Niklas Luhmann and other social theorists whose work has been extremely influential (as well as controversial) in the post-Second World War era (eg, see Parsons, 1951; and Luhmann; 1995; for critiques, see Gouldner, 1970; and Munch, 1987).

Despite challenges from many quarters within the study of public adminis-tration, the 'social action theory' orientation has been at the heart of most studies of public administrative behaviour. Although developed initially as a means for under-standing individual-level behaviour, it has more often drawn attention toward higher action levels and led to reductionist views of individual choice behaviour. In recent years, however, at least two developments have emerged to counter that situation. One is in the general area of social theory and the other in the study of public administrative behaviour.

In social theory, the emergence of a 'reflexive action' orientation has gained increasing favour among students of human behaviour (see Giddens, 1979; compare with Coleman, 1990). The work of Pierre Bourdieu and Anthony Giddens (eg, Bourdieu, 1977; and Giddens, 1979), among others, has give a central place to the individual actor's reflections in the shaping of human behaviour; in the management arena, Chris Argyris and Donald Schön have integrated learning and reflection into the study of organisations and organisational behaviour (see Argyris, 1994; and Schön, 1983). In public administration *per se*, more attention than ever before is being given to individual perspectives, especially in the work of Robert Denhardt, John DiIulio, Carolyn Ban and others (eg Denhardt, 1993; DiIulio, 1990; and Ban, 1995).

The potential value of a reconceptualisation of accountability depends on bringing the role of individual-level reflection into the application of the framework. Without doing so, the firm division between the AC and CA perspectives will remain and little will emerge of benefit, except perhaps new labels for well-worn concepts.

To accomplish this linkage task, I turn to the work of Robert Nozick and his concept of an *ethical theory* approach. Nozick uses the label 'ethical theory' to highlight a view of human behaviour that sees action as the outcome of tensions between forces of 'moral push' and 'moral pull'. In this regard, Nozick is relying on two great traditions in the history of ethical studies. On the one side is the Greek philosophical tradition with its stress on the urge to be a 'good' and virtuous person and thus the 'moral push' to live up to one's value. On the other side is the Jewish tradition that emphasises the need to respect the value of others: the 'moral pull'. Ethical action, Nozick argues, is the result when moral push is equal to or greater than the moral pull (Nozick, 1981, ch 5).

While Nozick's specific use of the ethical theory approach is interesting, of greater significance for present purposes is its value as a means of qualifying the basic premise of social action theory. Again, social action theory regards individual actions as the product of ends-oriented behaviour that is norm-regulated. Addressing the question of normative regulation has been the principle motivation for Parsons and others to move away from the focus on individual action and toward concerns for theories of personality, social (as well as political and economic) systems and cultures. Adopting the ethical theory (moral push and pull) assumption as a working premise for what constitutes 'normative regulation' would help keep us focused on the individual level.

Put more explicitly, our ability to understand public administrative behaviour will be significantly enhanced if we begin with the ethical theory assumption that actions result from choices public administrators must make among contending values, values that create moral pushes and pulls in the broadest sense of 'moral'. Given this basic orientation toward action, the role of accountability in shaping public administrative behaviour becomes an empirical question. What is more, that behaviour is viewed as a product of ethical choices thrust upon the individual administrator.

There are, of course, a number of significant drawbacks to this approach, particularly for those bothered by the underlying assumptions regarding the ethical nature of public administrative behaviour. The defence of this position can take two forms: either an elaborate tome addressing the nature of social action and its public administrative variant, or a brief assertion that the true test of any theory or model is in its effectiveness for the purposes here (see Friedman, 1953, part I). For present purposes, the more expedient solution seems wisest.

A CONCEPTUAL FRAMEWORK FOR ACCOUNTABILITY

As an idea rather than a specific concept — and especially as an ethical idea — accountability can be perceived as a genus encompassing a variety of species. Uhr points out that responsibility is a derivative of accountability; I contend that it is one of several such derivatives, each manifesting a particular dimension of accountability in its 'idea' form. I will posit a framework intended to conceptualise accountability by categorising several of its more significant species. The reader is reminded that the goal here is not to find the essence of accountability; rather it is but to develop a potential conceptual tool that might enhance our understanding of, and ability to systematically study, the role accountability plays in government in general and public administration in particular.

Let's begin with the simple view of accountability implied in its Anglo-Norman roots. That is, accountability is the *condition of being able to render a counting of something to someone.* How such a condition gets established remains an empirical question. It can be imposed from outside through force or legal mandate; it can come from within, through feelings of guilt or a sense of loyalty. Whatever its source(s), the condition itself is a significant development in social and ethical terms.

Socially, to perceive oneself as accountable is to accept the fact that there is an external reference point — a relevant 'other' — that must be taken into consideration as one contemplates making choices or taking actions. Being accountable is thus a social relationship.

Under Nozick's 'ethical theory' orientation, the condition of accountability is inherently ethical as well. Many forms of social relationships are ethical because they allow us to value ourselves as well as others. Nozick argues that people submit to the push of moral demands because they seek to enhance their self-worth; they are more valuable people because they value others. The pull of morality is generated by the demands of others to be treated as valued individuals. Even though one might not achieve the status of being an ethical person (again, when moral push is equal to or exceeds moral pull), the condition of accountability as used here is ethically relevant because it subjects one to the tensions of moral push and pull.

The basis for this tension in public administrators lies in the very nature of public sector work. Public administration is a complex undertaking in a number of ways. In many cases, the very nature of public sector tasks, with the risks and uncertainty they entail (Kiel, 1994), generates complexity. At other times, it is the turbulence or constraining nature of the task environment that poses the challenge (JD Thompson, 1967; and Waldo, 1971). Complementing, supplementing and manifesting these conditions are multiple, diverse and often conflicting expectations (Dubnick and Romzek, 1993; for other views of the complex nature of public sector management, see Kiel, 1994) that emerge from every corner of the public administrator's world.

Dealing with that situation is important not only for the administrator(s) subjected to it (for psychological as well as political reasons; eg, see Festinger, 1957) but also to those who seek to harness or limit the authority and energy of administrative power (Gruber, 1987; Rourke, 1984). Among the various means for dealing with the complex environment of expectations is the creation and application of institutional structures and rules (March and Olsen, 1995), mechanisms that rely on the *use of accountability*.

Four Different Contexts and Four Different Institutions

In previous work (Dubnick and Romzek, 1991), Romzek and I applied the term 'accountability systems' to these general institutional forms and posited a framework that highlighted four types: legal, organisational, professional and political.[4] I will rely here on those institutional distinctions to differentiate among various forms (species) that the idea (genus) of accountability can take.

As an institutional setting, the legal context narrows and manages expectations by establishing *liabilities* for the public administrator that are enforceable through judicial or quasi-judicial actions. Law is central to the modern administrative state. In many countries, this is reflected in the fact that a law degree is essential for employment in public sector management positions. Even where this is not the case explicitly (eg the United States), the rule of law principle permeates most, if not all, public sector activities (Rosenbloom, 1983). A typical administrator in the United States, for example, is subject to criminal actions for corrupt acts, civil action for negligent or arbitrary acts and administrative sanction for violations of due process rules and procedures. Functionally, this exposure to liability is a major factor in determining how the administrator deals with the challenge of multiple, diverse and conflicting expectations. In some instances (eg the Nuremberg Principle that one should not obey an illegal order), the priority of legal expectations is made explicit. In many others, however, legal requirements comprise one among several applicable considerations.

Similarly, organisational working environments operate as institutional means for narrowing or focusing expectations, primarily through a stress on answerability. The very nature of modern bureaucratic organisations and their reliance on hierarchical structures promote this form of accountability. But even outside an explicitly hierarchical context, the bureaucratic culture stresses the desirability of and need for answerability (Hummel, 1994).

The emergence of professionalism as a major factor in the public administrative endeavour is more than a product of a growing need for expertise in dealing with increasingly difficult tasks. It also reflects the need to create an effective institutional accountability mechanism for public servants whose jobs require significant amounts of discretion. In cases where legal or organisational instruments would be counter-productive, accountability must take the form of responsibility. To hold someone responsible is not to free them from accountability but to create a form of expectations management that relies on professional and strong peer group standards.[5]

The political form of accountability — responsiveness — is also inherent in the modern administrative state, no matter how great the efforts to insulate public servants from its influence. Put in an institutional perspective, the question isn't whether there should be political accountability but rather what form it should take. Patronage has been the least favoured approach ever since the logic of meritocracy and civil service reform came to dominate the modern state (see Ingraham, 1995) and various strategies of using representation to enhance responsiveness have proven less than effective (Krislov, 1974). Oversight mechanisms (both executive and legislative) are common means used to improve responsiveness (Aberbach, 1990; also see Gruber, 1987), although their effectiveness has varied widely. Efforts to develop 'administrative presidencies' through strategic use of personnel systems have also had mixed records (Nathan, 1983). But none of these explicit attempts to deal with the 'pull' of responsiveness has been as successful as the high moral value attached to responsiveness in most democratic political cultures (on the demands that democracy makes on bureaucracy and vice versa, see Etzioni-Halevy, 1983).

As manifestations of accountability, these four 'institutions' (liability, answerability, responsibility and responsiveness) comprise the 'moral pulls' of our conceptual framework. In terms of the general literature on accountability, they are the focal points for those who study the 'conduct of accountability'; in that sense, they are merely half the picture. The other half — the 'moral pushes' typically examined as the 'accountability of conduct' — can be regarded as the internalisation of the four accountability institutions.

Liabilities, for instance, internalise as obligations. Being liable for your actions means little unless it is matched with a sense of obligation based on either a positive commitment to the law or a desire to avoid exposure to legal sanctions. In the United States, the efforts to make law enforcement agencies and agents more accountable have for the most part relied on liability pulls: the use of litigation, external review boards etc. To the extent that those mechanisms remain 'external' from the perspective of the law enforcement official, accountability is at best partial. Accountability will be more whole and effective when it becomes 'ethical', that is, when the moral push of obligation takes hold. The objective would be to have police conduct themselves in ways that reflect a sense of obligation, that is, following certain procedures and avoiding legally questionable actions because that is the 'right thing to do' rather than 'this is what I am mandated to do'. Accountability, in short, would be at the heart of 'good policing' (Skolnick and Fyfe, 1993, chs 9–11).

Answerability manifests itself internally as deference to one's superiors in the form of obedience. It is important to understand that in its deferential form, obedience is not to be regarded as merely a response to coercive acts. Rather, it is based on the perceived legitimacy of those who are being obeyed, that is, that they have the right to be obeyed given the organisational context of public administrative actions. This deference and subsequent obedience seems an unlikely basis for a 'moral push', particularly in light of the horrors of the Holocaust and similar events when obedience was clearly a form of moral bankruptcy (Goldhagen, 1996).

And yet one's sense of self-worth and value can be fulfilled by participating in the good that can be achieved through hierarchically co-ordinated collective actions. One need only watch the highly visible work of trained fire-fighters or rescuers after a disaster strikes to appreciate why an individual can find moral sustenance in obedience. That same moral push can be found playing itself out in the more mundane roles undertaken by public servants in day-to-day program operations (V Thompson, 1975).

Fidelity (an internalised sense of honour and loyalty to the peer or professional reference group) is critical to the success of responsible accountability. At first it might seem odd to associate such emotional commitments as 'fidelity' and loyalty with technical expertise and professionalism but those subjective ties are in fact critical to the professional endeavour. 'Professional status is in principle open to all,' notes William M Sullivan, 'regardless of social origins.'

> [B]y becoming professionals individuals integrate their personal identity in important ways with a collective project, and find themselves held publicly accountable for the reliable performance of service according to prescribed procedures. ...
>
> [P]rofessional freedom of opportunity is only realized through the individual's acceptance of responsibility for the purposes and standards which define the profession. *Individual initiative and collective loyalty depend mutually upon each other and yet pull in opposite directions.* (Sullivan, 1995, p 146) (emphasis added)

The ethical push of loyalty is a strong and distinct one that often runs counter to more rational and individualistic forces found in the other forms of accountability (Fletcher, 1993). Its relevance to the public sector is reflected in the census figures indicating that around 40 per cent of all people employed as professionals and technicians work for governments. Of course, the influence of fidelity depends on the specific professional setting. The individual cases surrounding Watergate and other scandals since the early 1970s imply that members of the 'traditional' professions (eg law) are expected to give priority to their profession when faced with conflicting demands from the workplace. Studies of the traditional government professions (eg military, foreign service, forest rangers) reinforce the contention that loyalty to the collective ideals and standards play powerful roles in the behaviour of these public officials (see Kaufman, 1967). The same strong moral push is developing in the newer government (what Mosher termed 'emerging') professions as well (eg tax assessors, city planners, librarians) (Mosher, 1982).

Finally, the success of establishing and maintaining responsive administrative behaviour depends on the development of an internalised *amenability*: a desire to actively pursue the interests of the public or one's clientele groups. This striving to serve the needs of the 'public' (as variously defined) has been perceived with critical eyes by many commentators of American public policy among others (for a recent example in a long and continuing line of critiques, see Rauch, 1995). It is reflected in the oft-told tale of the Department of Agriculture bureaucrat who was found shedding tears in his office because 'his farmer died'. And yet that amenability is rewarded and promoted within many administrative cultures where the emphasis is on service to the 'customer'. At times, however, the amenability is aimed elsewhere: to an influential member of the legislature or a powerful congressional subcommittee. For those who take a more normative approach to the subject, this form of amenability is the very essence of accountability at its best.

Taken individually, each of these eight species of accountability can and has been used to understand public administrative behaviour. Taken together under the genus of accountability (Figure A), they relate to each other, both within and among institutional pairings, in potentially interesting ways. The result is a conceptualisation that begs to be explored and put to use in the systematic analysis of accountability.

Figure A: Eight Species of Accountability

	Legal Setting	Organisational Setting	Professional Setting	Political Setting
Moral Pulls	Liability	Answerability	Responsibility	Responsiveness
Moral Pushes	Obligation	Obedience	Fidelity	Amenability

CONCLUDING THOUGHTS

Analysts familiar with governmental systems tied to Anglo-Norman roots are quite comfortable with the concept of accountability, just as they are comfortable with their understandings of parliamentary democracy, federalism and similar institutional notions peculiar to their shared political cultures. It comes as a shock, therefore, to discover just how anglican such terms are, even to citizens of other countries with well-established democratic traditions.

But while the term itself is not easily translated into some similar word in most languages, the *idea* of accountability as initially develop by the English seems quite evident in modern administrative states. Just what forms and functions accountability take in those systems is an empirical question worthy of greater attention. What is required for developing the answer is a focused and useful conceptualisation of accountability. I have attempted to provide such a conceptualisation here.

A conceptualisation of accountability should achieve three things. First, it must avoid as much as possible the tendency to rely on an Anglo-centric (as opposed to a merely anglican) approach to the term. I have tried to accomplish this by focusing on the idea of accountability rather than on the term *per se*. Approaching it as a genus with many species, I shifted the focus onto forms of accountability that would translate across political culture boundaries. Responsibility, as we have seen, is more likely to be comprehended than accountability, as would liability, obligation etc.

Secondly, the conceptualisation must attempt to capture the two strong research traditions relating to accountability: the accountability of conduct and the conduct of accountability. This problem was tackled by elaborating the theoretical context within which the concept will be most useful: the ethical theory form of social action theory derived from Nozick's view that human action is the product of moral pulls and pushes.

Finally, I believe accountability to be closely related to issues of ethical behaviour and thus want this conceptualisation to reflect that assumption. Here again, the ethical theory orientation serves the purpose quite well. It must be emphasised that the purpose here is not to impose a normative cast on the concept of accountability but to give this potential analytic tool an ethical dimension. The underlying argument is not that accountability ought to be ethical, but that we ought to put this ethical conceptualisation to work to see if it proves useful. If it does, then we have indication that accountability is an ethical tools in governance. If this ethics-based concept does not 'pay off' as an analytic tool, then it is back to the 'drawing board' as far as this purpose is concerned.

How will we know if this concept is useful? That depends on our standards for assessing conceptual utility. My immediate standards are rather simple and yet grandiose in the long term. First, does the framework (when appropriately applied in a research design) generate sufficient understanding and insight to warrant its continued use? Secondly, does its continued use lead to improvements in the framework and thus further advances in our understanding and insights? Thirdly, does the continuous application and improvement of the framework move use closer toward a theory of public administrative behaviour?

These three goals were implied in my earlier work with Romzek on the general concept of accountability. Others have made significant use of that initial scheme to both enhance our collective insights into specific events (eg the Challenger launch decision) (Vaughan, 1996) and to develop more elaborate accountability-based models (Kearns, 1996). I hope this ethics-based effort is at least as fruitful.

NOTES

1   The choice of word here posed a problem, for the term 'Anglican' commonly refers to things of an ecclesiastic sort. The Oxford English Dictionary does, however, note that it also represents things of an English sort in general. My solution was to apply a violation of English usage to stress the difference. Hence, I do not capitalise 'anglican' except as necessary at the start of sentences or in titles.

2   My thanks to my colleague, David H Rosenbloom, for relating this to me after his meeting with Israeli officials in October 1996: 'It turns out that there is no precise Hebrew equivalent of "accountability", which makes things hard for those whose mission is to secure it'.

3   In the early 1940s, political scientists Carl J Friedrich and Herman Finer debated the nature of bureaucratic accountability in democratic states. Friedrich took a position that allowed more discretion to administrators than would Finer. For a summary of these 'soft core' (Friedrich) and 'hard core' (Finer) position, see Harmon (1995) pp 47–51. For a general view of the issues, see Gruber (1987).

4   By their very nature, these labels imply a good deal more and less about the type of institutional setting (ie accountability system) they represent. For a better sense of the characteristics of each, see Dubnick and Romzek (1991) ch 3.

5   This is the core of what Michael Harmon terms the 'rationalist' approach to responsibility (Harmon, 1995).

PART II

IMPLEMENTING VALUES

6

ETHICS IN PUBLIC SERVICE
An Idea Whose Time Has Come

Stephen D Potts

INTRODUCTION

The great French novelist, Victor Hugo, once wrote that 'greater than the tread of mighty armies is an idea whose time has come' (Victor Hugo, quoted in Green, 1982, p 166). As we approach the beginning of both a new century and a new millennium, there are increasing signs that ethics in public service is an idea whose time has come. We now stand at a point where the environmental movement stood some 30 years ago: on the threshold of a heightened public awareness. In this case, the new awareness is that ethics in public service is crucial to the success of democratic institutions.

THE HIGH COST OF CORRUPTION

We are moving toward a global recognition of the devastating effects of public corruption.[1] Most countries of the world now acknowledge the tremendous economic, social and political cost of corruption. In economic terms, corruption misdirects resources and discourages investment by the private sector. A study by the International Monetary Fund concluded that high rates of investment by the private sector are linked to low levels of corruption (Mauro, 1996). In an increasingly competitive global economy, countries can no longer afford the cost of corruption. It simply makes them non-competitive in world markets. A study by the World Bank of countries in transition from a planned to a market economy pointed out the importance of controlling corruption in order to promote economic development (World Bank, 1996).

Corruption also has significant social costs. It creates a culture of poverty and crime and deprives the neediest element of society of the benefits of government resources. In the late 1960s and 1970s, some social scientists thought that corruption might actually serve a positive function (see, eg, JQ Wilson, 1961, p 369; Leys, 1965, p 35; Kramer, 1977, p 74; and Nye, 1967, p 417). They argued that certain practices regarded as corrupt might nevertheless allow the lowest stratum of society to gain a foothold in the economy (see, eg, Merton, 1957, pp 72–9). These theories have now been all but completely disproved or discredited. The truth is that the poor suffer the most when government is corrupt. Goods intended for them are siphoned off for illicit purposes. Funds needed for programs to provide for transportation, schools and medical care are misdirected to less socially beneficial ends. Corruption makes it virtually impossible for the poor to lift themselves out of poverty.

Furthermore, the political costs of corruption can be ruinous. Vibrant democratic institutions depend upon the consent and support of the governed. Public confidence is necessary for democratic institutions to be healthy and flourish. Corruption destroys the confidence of people in their government and undermines the very legitimacy of political institutions. In its most pervasive and entrenched forms, corruption can be a source of political instability.

PREVENTIVE SYSTEMS

One way that governments can respond to the presence of corruption is by finding out who the perpetrators are, prosecuting them and seeing that they are punished. Another governmental response is to prevent misconduct from occurring in the first place by putting systems in place that ensure the integrity of government operations and programs.

In practice, both prevention and prosecution are necessary in order to keep the threat of corruption in check. Without the presence of an effective enforcement system, preventive measures such as codes of conduct may become little more than pious statements. On the other hand, enforcement systems may be overwhelmed if there are no effective preventive measures in place to reduce the burden on investigators and prosecutors.

Strong preventive systems also have the great benefit of avoiding corruption before it occurs. Codes of behaviour not only set high standards for public officials. They also reduce the need to invoke the more drastic measures of prosecution, administrative discipline and punishment.

The basic components of any effective prevention program are likely to include the following.

- A fair and reasonable code of conduct that establishes uniform standards that public officials will be held accountable for
- A carefully crafted system of disclosure of financial interests that avoids conflicts and introduces transparency into an official's decision-making
- An imaginative education program that makes government employees aware of their responsibilities
- A regular monitoring system to assure that the quality of these preventive systems is maintained

- Open channels of communication within government to provide assistance and address deficiencies
- An effective procurement system that emphasises integrity and fairness

THE US EXPERIENCE

Both the preventive and the prosecutorial sides of government ethics have expanded dramatically in the United States since the 1970s. Much of the reform legislation of the last quarter century was spawned by the scandals of the Watergate era. One landmark piece of ethics legislation, the *Ethics in Government Act* 1978, created the US Office of Government Ethics (OGE) to provide overall leadership and policy direction for the ethics program in the executive branch of government. This same law also established for the first time a system of public financial disclosure for senior officials in all three branches of the federal government, a system that is a cornerstone of its ethics program today.

The 1978 Act also contained provisions that put in place a procedure for the appointment of an independent prosecutor whenever there is an allegation of misconduct at the highest levels of government. In 1978, another law was passed which established statutory Inspectors General in the major departments and agencies to provide for an independent investigating office within agencies to deal with misconduct, mismanagement, fraud, waste and abuse (*Inspector General Act* 1978).

In 1989, Congress enacted the *Ethics Reform Act* 1989. This Act expanded coverage of the post-employment conflict of interest law so that it applied to Members of Congress and top Congressional staff. This law also expressly authorised all three branches of government to implement a system of confidential financial disclosure.

The legislative and the judicial branches of the US federal government have their own ethics programs. Each house in Congress is responsible for administering its own ethics program. In the Senate, this responsibility resides in the Select Committee on Ethics. In the House of Representatives, it is the responsibility of the Committee on Official Standards of Conduct. In 1995, both the Senate and the House amended their respective rules of conduct to establish tighter restrictions on the acceptance of gifts.[2] The Congress also passed the *Lobbying Disclosure Act* 1995, the first complete overhaul of the lobbying law in nearly 50 years. In the federal judiciary, the Judicial Conference of the United States is responsible for the administration of the financial disclosure system for federal judges and their staffs.

At the level of State government in the United States, there are 45 state ethics commissions or committees. These state agencies have a wide range of responsibilities. In addition to administering standards of conduct and financial disclosure, many such agencies also deal with campaign finance and lobbying disclosure. At the local level, at least 12 cities have their own ethics commissions.

INTERNATIONAL INITIATIVES

The current phenomenal growth of government ethics is taking place on a world-wide scale. The consensus on the means of preventing corruption is becoming global in nature. This was certainly reflected in the International Conference on Ethics in Government that was hosted by the OGE and the US Information Agency in November 1994. The conference was a gathering of 140 delegates from 52 countries, all searching for practical ways of making preventive government ethics programs more effective. There was general recognition among the participants that codes of conduct, financial disclosure and ethics education were keys to effective prevention.

Inter-American Convention Against Corruption

There have been other extremely significant developments that have heralded a new era in government ethics. One of the most notable recent events grew out of the Miami Summit of the Americas in 1994 that was given momentum by the international conference mentioned above. This summit led to the signing of the Inter-American Convention Against Corruption. This treaty is perhaps one of the least heralded but most vital and important international developments in government ethics. The treaty was signed in Caracas, Venezuela on 29 March 1996 by 21 countries.[3] In June 1996, the United States and Guatemala signed the treaty.

The treaty reflects the virtual unanimity among the countries of the Western hemisphere that corruption must be controlled. Some might have thought that such an historic agreement would never be reached because corruption was too entrenched in the Americas. (Kim, Chapter 8, demonstrates that corruption is by no means isolated to the Americas.) But the treaty has come into being; moreover, it has teeth.

It provides for extradition of persons charged with corruption. It makes transnational bribery illegal. It mandates preventive measures including: standards of conduct, ethics education, an obligation to report corrupt acts, protection for whistleblowers, public financial disclosure systems, open and equitable systems of government hiring and procurement and denial of tax benefits for corrupt payments.

The signatory countries must provide mutual assistance to implement the actions required by the treaty.

Other Developments

Other significant international developments include the development of a code of conduct for public officials by the United Nations and the support for and encouragement of uniform ethics rules by the Organization for Economic Cooperation and Development (OECD).[4] One result of the OECD's activity has been that Germany recently agreed to stop giving business tax deductions to companies who pay bribes in other countries.

Another development is the growth of organisations that combat corruption. Two such notable bodies have been established in Latin America. The Latin

American Institute Against Corruption (ILACC) has been created to co-ordinate ethics activities among Latin countries. In Argentina, the Public Ethics Foundation has been created to monitor government ethics activities.

There are also a number of significant private sector initiatives to curb corruption both in the United States and internationally. These include the following:

- Transparency International
- Ethics Officer Association
- Conference Board
- Defense Industries Initiative

The OGE has supported this global trend by providing technical assistance in a number of countries. It has assisted in the drafting of a new legislative code of conduct in South Africa and has provided training and briefings in Cairo to the Egyptian Administrative Control Authority. It has also visited Ukraine and the Baltic countries of Estonia, Latvia and Lithuania to provide briefings for public officials as well as briefed visiting delegations from dozens of countries including Korea, Japan and Taiwan.

Finally, gatherings such as the Ethics in the Public Service-sponsored Fifth International Conference in Brisbane in 1996 are testimony to the growing dialogue on ethics in the public sector. This dialogue and exchange on public service, ethics education, values, accountability and transparency provide the analytical framework and practical experience to carry forward this global movement.

FUTURE CHALLENGES

These developments are certainly reason enough to be cautiously optimistic about the future of government ethics. But they should not lead anyone to believe that the task that lies ahead will be easy. We must do a better job of implementing, not simply writing ethics laws and codes. A key part of an implementation strategy must be to create ethics systems which go beyond mere obedience to rules.

Our ethics systems must not only establish minimal standards of conduct but they must also set forth high aspirational goals for public employees. Of course, governments must tell their employees what not to do. But they must also tell employees what they *should* do. The real challenge is to give not only guidance as to what will not be tolerated but also inspiration as to the values that should inform public service.

There should be no mistake about it. We must be ever vigilant against the threat of corruption. There will never be a day when all temptation will be removed. Nor will there ever come a time when there will be no corrupt acts by public officials. Corruption is like a cancer on the body politic. Prevention and early detection are the best ways to deal with this disease. Just as it is much better for individuals to take preventive measures in order to maintain good health and avoid more drastic measures such as surgery, so it is better to maintain sound preventive ethics programs in order to minimise the need for more drastic forms of treatment such as criminal prosecution and administrative discipline.

We must be ready to make the commitment and have the will to take the actions necessary to curb this insidious disease. The expansion of democracy will be stopped dead in its tracks if we fail in the battle against corruption. Conferences such as those mentioned above can be the means to renew our resolve to fight corruption. It is a task of high importance. The efforts that we make today are a gift to our posterity.

NOTES

1   Kim, ch 8, compares the issue of corruption in capitalist and socialist states.

2   US Senate Resolution 158, Congressional Record S10897, July 28, 1995; House Resolution 250, Congressional Record H13078, November 16, 1995.

3   The initial signatories were: Jamaica, Nicaragua, El Salvador, Dominican Republic, Paraguay, Colombia, Haiti, Panama, Brazil, Guyana, Peru, Costa Rice, Ecuador, Uruguay, Mexico, Venezuela, Suriname, Chile, Honduras, Bolivia and Argentina.

4   The Commission on Crime Prevention and Criminal Justice of the Economic and Social Council developed an International Code of Conduct for Public Officials which was adopted by the United Nations in 1996 (UN Doc GA Res 51/59, 12 December 1996). The OECD provides support for uniform ethics rules and other preventative measures related to the management of ethics and conduct in the public service through the activities and publications of its Public Management Service. See, eg, OECD (1996a).

7

CORRUPTION IN
SOCIALIST AND CAPITALIST COUNTRIES

Young Jong Kim

INTRODUCTION

Corruption is a universal yet complex phenomenon. It has been commonly recognised as a 'social disease' only in capitalistic society. Capitalist countries, especially those in developing countries, have struggled against the powerful challenge of corruption. In socialist countries, corruption has also brought significant social changes. Although corruption might be viewed by some as a necessary evil in the process of development, its cost has in fact been a serious obstacle for national development in Russia, China, North Korea and South Korea.

Orthodox socialists believed that corruption was a by-product of capitalism (Torkunov, 1992). Their argument was based on the belief that corruption cannot be created in socialist countries. However, this argument has been overthrown, along with the political system, beginning in 1989 when most of the socialist countries in the West collapsed, in part because of the prevalent corruption. This occurred even after many socialist countries radically changed from orthodox to more revised socialist or even semi-capitalist countries.

This chapter focuses on the reality of the corruption phenomenon in socialist and capitalist countries with a comparative approach. It traces the major causes and consequences of corruption in socialist countries, specifically China, Russia, and North Korea. It then compares these cases with an example of a capitalist country: South Korea. By suggesting several strategies for combating corruption, a paradigm for preventing corruption will be suggested on the basis of integrated strategies.

THEORETICAL OVERVIEW OF CORRUPTION

Corruption has frequently been a topic of public concern in any society. While many scholars have discussed the reality of corruption in terms of their own perspectives, corruption has not been clearly defined in a general sense.

- David H Bayley et al: 'general term covering misuse of authority as result of considerations of personal gain' (Heidenheimer et al, 1989, pp 8–9)

- Van Klaveren: 'a public office as a business, the income of which he will seek to maximize' (Heidenheimer et al, 1989)

- Nethaniel Leff: 'an extra-legal institution used by individuals or groups to gain influence over the actions of the bureaucracy' (Heidenheimer et al, 1989)

- RW Fredrich and LD Lasswell: 'the result of violations of public interests in the process of decision making' (Heidenheimer et al, 1989)

- Samuel Huntington: 'the result of social frustration and dissatisfaction in the process of political development and economic growth or social mobilization' (Huntington, 1968, pp 55–6)

- Michael Johnston: 'a form of influence within the political system, rather than as some sort of despoiling force' (Johnston, 1982, pp 20–1)

For the purposes of this discussion, corruption is defined as a complex politically, administratively and socially deviant behaviour resulting from violation of socio-cultural norms or political and administrative expectations.

Causes of corruption have been discussed from different perspectives as well. Such arguments have been based mainly upon particular situations, incidences, historical heritage and socio-cultural environments. Corruption phenomena are discussed at different levels: micro and macro, individual and organisational, and macro and environmental or systems' level in a given society or organisations. For example, David Gould focuses on a particular circumstances of developing countries: a rapid economic and social change, strong kinship, ethnic ties, new institutions and overlapping system would be causes of corruption. Also, he points out that a government monopoly of economic activities, conditions of political 'softness', widespread poverty, socio-economic inequalities and maladministration could be major causes of corruption, especially in developing countries (Gould, 1983, pp 1–41 *passim*). Kim Young Jong contends that corruption is recognised as a salient phenomenon that resulted from maladjustment among the bureaucrats' behaviour, systems and socio-cultural environment in a given society (YJ Kim, 1994, p 70). Ankie Hoogvelt observes that corruption phenomena in developing countries are basically caused by their earlier colonisation by developed countries (Hoogvelt, 1976, pp 128–9).

The organisational causes may be traced to a number of factors: inadequate and unrealistic compensation levels of public servants in the bureaucracy, lack of leadership in the bureaucratic system, mismanagement or maladministration of the system, poor recruitment and selection procedures and excessive red tape in administrative procedures for personnel and lack of education and discipline for public servants (YJ Kim, 1994, p 202; Carino, 1986, pp 85–6).[1] Socio-cultural causes of corruption primarily consist of providing opportunities of corruption by individuals and may include societal tolerance of corruption and lack of political will to wage a determined anti-corruption movement. In other word, corruption can occur through individuals' lack of obedience for legal norms in a given society. We can also explain other causes of corruption based on societies or cultures. For example, since the 15th century, Confucianism has strongly dominated the philosophy of the Korean society and has consequently had a tremendous influence on its government and society. Its notions of hierarchical duty can provide great opportunity (and justification) for corruption.

A value system in which public servants generally regard public office as their private property frequently results in an abuse of power and the attitude that the state is superior to the people. For example, in Ghana, gift-giving cultures have given rise to socio-cultural acceptance of bribes and corruption in the country.

> This whole society is corrupt, corruption for us is a way of life … The bribe system was very systematic: 50 per cent to the minister, 20 per cent to junior ministers, 10 per cent to go-betweens, 10 per cent to the secretary of the political party involved, and the rest to an 'open cash fund' kept by the minister for 'expenses'. Expenses include paying informers within the ministry, providing gifts for influential visitors, and maintaining attractive women around the office. (Le Vine, 1975, pp 14, 54)

In short, corruption is a multifaceted social, political and administrative phenomenon rather than a result of a single domineering factor. In attempting to understand corruption, it is thus essential to look for more than one cause; in attempting to prevent it, more than one answer.

CORRUPTION IN SOCIALIST AND CAPITALIST COUNTRIES

While functionalists argue that corruption can be created as a by-product of or necessary evil in the process of development, post-functionalists argue that corruption is universal in any developing or developed country, a development which has a self-perpetuating or spill-over effect (Werner, 1983, p 146).

According to this latter theory, the characteristics of corruption do not vary greatly from country to country. However, I would argue that there *are* some distinguishable characteristics, as well as similarities, of corruption between socialist and capitalist countries.

First, some types of corruption seem to exist only in socialist countries. For example, corruption can occur in the process of the delivery system of services in socialist countries, especially where a serious shortage of goods and housings exists. That is, there is a higher likelihood of public officials being involved in corruption in such situations than where there are no significant shortages. On the other hand, public officials in some capitalist societies are more likely to have the opportunity to be involved in bribery related to contracts with individuals in the competitive market (ie business-related corruption).

Secondly, corruption appears to be more destructive in socialist countries than in capitalistic countries. For example, many argue that the collapse of so many Western socialist countries since 1989 indicates that corruption has played or is playing a major role weakening socialist systems. This does not mean corruption is harmless in the capitalist systems. Rather, more advanced or well-established liberal democratic capitalist systems are more resistant to the effects of corruption than socialist systems because of their higher level of appropriate remedies against corruption (Holmes, 1993, pp 271–3). Of course, corrupt regimes can collapse for reasons related to corruption even in the developed or liberal democratic countries (eg the Marcos regime in the Philippines, Nixon's government in the United States, Takeshita's regime in Japan and Park's government in South Korea).

Thirdly, anti-corruption campaigns are used by political leaders for their temporary political use and are rarely sustained for a long time. (Cf Potts, Chapter 6.) Also, 'anti-corruption drives are often associated with new leadership, although new leaderships do not always mount such drives' (Holmes, 1993, p 268). For example, a major campaign was launched by former Soviet leaders Andropov or Gorbachev within weeks of taking office but neither campaign lasted long. In capitalist countries, many political leaders seem to have used the same approach. In South Korea, Park and Jun's regime had good excuses for their illegitimate take-over of the previous regime at the time, but these were not maintained for long.

Fourthly, levels of corruption between socialist and capitalist countries can be seen to be related to the economic growth. For example, the rampant corruption in China has been caused by an economic development policy that has attempted to combine capitalist motivation with some form of communist morality, together with economic modernisation (Holmes, 1993, pp 271–2). In other words, while corruption does appear to increase at the take-off stage of economic growth, it is in fact more complex than that. Kim's research of South Korea indicates that the most frequent corruption incidences since 1960s were in the beginning of 1970s (eg the take-off stage in South Korea's economic development history) (YJ Kim, 1996, pp 123–57). Furthermore, corruption in socialist countries can increase at later modernisation stages if orthodox socialist society is replaced to some extent by a more individualistic and self-regarding approach. On the other hand, corruption in capitalist countries does not appear to be declining once the countries have reached the high point of development. This could be linked to their own consumerist ideology and a parallel decline of ethical standards.

Fifthly, the role of individual subsystem in the bureaucratic system could be an important design issue in developing the most efficient and effective anti-corruption policy for a country. The top-down control mechanism for combating corruption is not successful in either socialist or capitalist countries. For example, South Korea's recent experiences of the Kim's government indicate that the top-down anti-corruption drive has not worked very well in part due to the phenomenon called *bokgibudong* ('mannerism' or 'formalism'). The officials say that while *political* regimes pursued their nominal anti-corruption policy, the *public* officials themselves were involved in corruption in the process of solving the problems or simply failed to solve the problems at all with or without involving corruption. In short, although the top political leaders emphasised the anti-corruption policy, the government did not provide appropriate resources or, perhaps more importantly, economic compensation to make up for the loss of income previously received through bribes. Both resources and incentives (eg morale or even a bonus, though the latter is problematic) should be a part of such anti-corruption policies and their implementation.

Finally, corruption in the socialist countries has until recently rarely been reported to outside world. On the other hand, corruption in capitalist countries seems to be revealed by mass media relatively easy (Burrell and Morgan, 1980). Such coverage has increased in the past 20 years, for various reasons, including Freedom of Information Acts, increasing competition between various members of the media and increasing cynicism and disgust by the public with corruption by their so-called 'servants'. However, regardless of how much is revealed, it is important to remember that corruption is not unlike an iceberg; there is much more there than what you can actually see (YJ Kim, 1996).

CORRUPTION IN A COMPARATIVE CONTEXT

China

Corruption has long been a serious problem for China. To combat it, the Chinese government has been focusing on anti-corruption strategies which comprise two major systems: Administrative Supervisory Organs and the Supreme People's Procurator.

The Administrative Supervisory Organs perform control functions within the government. They include the central administrative supervisory organ, the Ministry of Supervision (Guang, 1995, pp 1–5). This Ministry has the power to control the supervisory work of the whole country under the direct leadership of the Premier of the State Council. The basic function of supervisory organs is to examine, investigate, recommend and punish (Ministry of Supervision, PRC, 1995, pp 3–4). The functions of the Supervisory Organs are detailed below.

- To supervise and examine implementation of state laws, decrees, policies, decisions and orders by state administrative organs and their functionaries and other personnel appointed by state administrative organs
- To receive and deal with the exposures or charges against the state administrative organisations and their functionaries and other personnel appointed by state administrative organs of their acts in violation of state laws, decrees or breach of administrative disciplines
- To receive and deal with appeals from the functionaries of state administrative organs and other personnel appointed by state administrative organs
- To examine the implementation by the departments and their personnel to be supervised of state laws, policies, decisions and regular or irregular orders

- Undertaking special examination of the departments to be supervised according to the decisions of the people's governments
- Investigating cases of violations of laws and breach of disciplines

The procurators of the PRC take rather comprehensive measures in their fight against corruption, combining punishment of criminals with prevention of corruption. The Supreme People's Procurator is a special agency which plays a significant role in the public service by accepting reports of wrong doing. For example, the Chinese procurators accepted 1,144,000 cases of embezzlement and bribery and selected 217,000 from them for investigations from 1988 to 1993 (YJ Kim, 1994, pp 1–20). The Bureau for Embezzlement and Bribery of the People's Procurator is responsible for handling and preventing corruption, organised into 3563 agencies. In 1988–93, the Bureau at all levels investigated about 220,000 cases of embezzlement and bribery, and 7000 of the total cases involved more than 10,000 yuan (approximately US$1725).[2]

In China, the largest number of corruption cases was embezzlement by forging of documents and accepting bribes as well as speculation and smuggling (Holmes, 1993, p 143). Corruption in China is likely to increase gradually in response to economic growth. The following strategies have been suggested as means to minimise the corruption prevalent in China.

- Pursue strong anti-corruption policy from the grassroots level
- Innovate the socialist democratic system now in place to respond to new trends of international environment such as decentralisation, open policy, autonomy and democratisation
- Establish and implement supervisory and control mechanisms
- Establish and perfect a legal system of ethics
- Strengthen ideological and ethical education
- Punish those convicted of corruption severely, but only according to law (Guang 1995, pp 4–5)

In conclusion, in the case of China, we emphasise the importance of controlling corruption while the country is still experiencing rapid growth. In other words, the government needs to suppress corruption while modifying its own structure and procedures to provide incentives, policies and training for ethical behaviour.

Russia

It is agreed by many that corruption in the former USSR was so prevalent and serious that it resulted in the collapse of the country. Even so, corruption and the fight against it date historically and organisationally from the earliest days of the Soviet regime. During the 1921–22 purge of the Russian Communist Party (the predecessor of the Communist Party of the Soviet Union (CPSU)), some 9% of the more than 136,000 members expelled lost their membership because of bribe-taking, extortion and other forms of corruption (Holmes, 1993, p 221). At the 19th Party

Congress in 1952, the outspoken leader Malenkov complained about corruption.[3] In the early 1960s, a major anti-corruption campaign was undertaken and in 1961, an anti-corruption act was passed (*Protection of Public Order Act*), introducing the death penalty for serious cases of corruption. After Khrushchev fell from power in 1964, the anti-corruption campaign declined in relation to the growing power of Brezhnev. Since 1982, the major campaigns against corruption have been launched in both communist giants (USSR and PRC). After Brezhnev's death in 1982, his successor, Yuri Andropov, made the war against corruption a top priority as soon as he became the new General-Secretary and on 18 December 1982, legislation was passed which increased the penalties for criminal acts, including corruption. In 1983, Andropov and other leading politicians called for an even more vigorous struggle against embezzlement, abuse of office, bribe-taking and other forms of corruption; in the same year, a process of radical restructuring of the Ministry of Internal Affairs began. In 1984, Chernenko took power and declared that various forms of corruption had to end. However, he did not appear to be as wholeheartedly committed to fight against corruption as Andropov had been.

When Gorbachev succeeded Chernenko in 1985, a new anti-corruption campaign began. In 1986, the CPSU Central Committee, the USSR Councils of Ministers and the Presidium of the USSR Supreme Soviet adopted resolutions of various kinds designed to clamp down on corruption amongst officials. In particular, Gorbachev was highly critical of corruption and moral malaise of the later Brezhnev era. In 1987, the Supreme Soviet passed legislation designed to increase the rights of ordinary citizens *vis à vis* public officials to encourage more citizen whistle-blowing. The Central Committee also adopted a resolution designed to strengthen the hand of Prosecutor's Office in investigating corruption. In 1988–89, Ivanov started commenting openly in the media about officials' corruption, including officers of law, party and state officials.[4] Surprisingly, it is noted that Yuri Churbanov, Brezhnev's son-in-law, had been arrested in 1987 for involvement in corruption. In 1991, a new Chief Administration for combating 'Most Dangerous Crimes, Organized Crime, Corruption and Drug Business' was established. The strong anti-corruption campaign since 1989 helped to bring about the collapse of Soviet communism. Thus, the organisational development to fight corruption in the USSR reveals that corruption has the power to shift a country into a completely new direction and even form a new country.

Some of the causes of corruption in Russia can be traced historically. First, there are of course cultural factors. For example, many Soviets considered that bribery was a 'relic of the past' (*Pravda,* 16 January 1975). In other words, corruption was and is a way of life in Russia. It has gown in the soil of a weak tradition of the rule of law and/or a low level of respect for the law. Further, leaders' political behaviour with regards to corruption did not serve as a good example for the public to follow. A 'culture of expectation' can develop, irrespective of pre-communist traditions. In other words, officials might (and frequently did) believe certain perquisites are the norm when they reach a given level in the hierarchy. Accordingly, over time, the public comes to see corruption as normal or even beneficial. As a result, the public grows to believe that corruption exists to lubricate the bureaucratic wheels rather than acting as a burden to the political mechanism. Corruption becomes their *modus operandi*.

Secondly, the economic system was clearly a cause of corruption in the former USSR. The highly planned economic system explicitly encouraged the legal component of the second or black market economy primarily because of ambiguities in official attitudes towards private and small-scale economic activity. The lack of a well-organised economic system created innumerable opportunities for corruption.

> The Soviet Union is a country in which there are permanent shortages of consumer goods. For the Soviet shopper, buying an article of clothing is not merely a money problem — it is a problem of finding the article he needs. Naturally, under such circumstances the buyer becomes an easy victim to the department store workers, to whom he has to pay more than the official cost in order to get what he wants. But even when the buyer doesn't pay more than the official cost, he still becomes a victim of corruption. In the food stores he is cheated, in the restaurants and cafeteria he receives smaller portions than those he paid for, and in the manufactured-goods stores he is sold goods of inferior quality for superior prices. (Simis, 1982, p 211)

Aron Katsenelinboigen compares this level of corruption with that frequently found in Western countries.

> In the Western countries the producer-enterprise corrupts the consumed-enterprise to sell its products. In the Soviet Union the enterprises corrupt the government agencies to get a reduced plan for output, in the Western countries the corporations corrupt the government agencies to get larger contracts. (Katsenelinboigen, 1983, p 237)

Thirdly, the conflict between traditional values and partially capitalist values seems to be a further cause of corruption in Russia. The wide-ranging social changes in response to urbanisation and modernisation may have profound effects on traditional values. The breaking down of old values without replacing them with sufficiently strongly internalised new ones brings forth a psychological anomie which yields an 'ethical deficit' or even a decline of morality.

Finally, inequality in the society could be another reason why the Soviet Union was so corrupt (Dobel, 1978, pp 961–2). Despite theories to guarantee the world of absolutely equal society, a enormous variation of political, economic and social status developed in most socialist countries, including the former USSR.

> The average monthly wage for manual and office workers, according to official data in 1979, is 164 rubles, before taxes. At the same time the salary of the Minister of Defense or the President of the Academy of Science is 2000 rubles a month, almost thirty times the legal minimum wage of 70 rubles a month. And this does not take into consideration all the legalized perquisites given to a minister or an academy president. If these are included, a minister's monthly income — without exaggeration — will run to as much as 4000 rubles, and is thus at least fifty-five to sixty times the minimum wage paid to a manual or office worker. (Simis, 1982, p 390)

North Korea

North Korea has continued its isolation policy since the Second World War. The rest of the world knew very little about their corruption problems compared with other communist or socialist countries. Since that time, North Korea has been controlled by a strong dictator, a monopoly of mass communication and a planned economy. Only now, with increasing defections by individuals from all levels of North Korea's society, is the rest of the world learning about the astonishing levels of corruption in North Korea.

> In February 1987, 11 North Koreans arrived in Seoul. They had defected from the North in January, and had reached the South via Japan and Taiwan. Interestingly, the leader of the group, a doctor by the name of Kim Man Chul, told the journalists of how he had bribed guards at a North Koreans port with wine and cigarettes so that they could turn a blind eye while his family boarded a boat to flee the country. Also, he revealed that he had bribed an city official with medicine so that he could see the political dossier on his family. (GC Kim, 1995, p 9)

Kim Man Chul's interview gives us an important insight into the rampant corruption in North Korea. Several defectors since Kim have further testified that Kim Jung Il has an unnamed fund for himself in the Swiss Bank. They point out that bribery is used everywhere and is a common occurrence in the daily lives of North Korean people. According to the North Korean pilot defector, Kang Chul Soo, Kim Jung Il continuously used the government funds to maintain his popularity by giving away money to particular people. Kang testified that people who are in the high position, such as government officials, have wealth, apparently in part through bribery. Thus, although socialist countries are supposed to be for 'ordinary people', it seems that it is impossible to be admitted to university without bribery.

Further, it has been reported that recently several North Korean defectors, including the pilot, Kang Chul Soo, a North Korean scientist, Chung Gap Chul, and a drama writer, Chang Hae Sung, have testified that North Korea's economic situation and food shortages are not only dismantling the country's elite class (as reflected by recent succession of defections by elite North Koreans) but also the general public as well.

The cause of corruption in North Korea is a dysfunction of government institutions. These institutions are based on Kim Il Sung's ideology of a single, all powerful leader and nepotism within government for power-maintenance and so have no autonomy or ethical independence. There is no kind of 'checks and balances' control mechanism for the one-man monarchy once ruled by Kim Il Sung or now his son, Kim Jong Il. Other government agencies exist but, in reality, they do very little but accept Kim Jung Il's order. In short, the closed and undemocratic political and social environment has been fertile soil for trees of corruption to grow.

South Korea

South Korea has also struggled to eradicate corruption for a long time. Throughout its history, corruption has brought the administration of the state to the threshold of painful changes, such as the 1960 April Revolution against Lee's regime, the collapse of Park's regime in October 1979 and the illegitimate and corrupt Jun's regime in January 1988. Former Korean presidents Jun and Roh have been charged and convicted for taking bribes of many hundreds of millions of dollars.[5] Since 1993, the new administration of Kim Young Sam energetically pursued anti-corruption policy. Regretfully, however, it does not seem very successful due to the lack of an integrated strategy.[6]

The previous top leaders all promised to eradicate corruption as soon as they took over political power. Ironically, the institutional equipment to fight against corruption in South Korea is almost perfect but its actual effectiveness is far from that. There are numerous anti-corruption bodies: President's Secretary, Prime Minister's Secretary, Board of Audit and Inspection (BAI), Commission for Preventing Corruption (CPC), Inspector-General of each ministry and Public Prosecutor, with the strongest being the Public Prosecutor and the BAI. The Public Prosecutor has the power to investigate and indict cases of corruption, including criminal cases, while the BAI is the supreme audit and inspection body for governmental organisations. The BAI's remit is as follows.

- To confirm the closing accounts of revenues and expenditures of the State
- To audit the State, local autonomous bodies, government-invested organisations and other entities subject to BAI audit by relevant laws
- To inspect the administrative duties of government agencies and public officials (YJ Kim, 1994, p 218)

The characteristics of South Korea's corruption are related to its bureaucratic system, political and bureaucratic behaviours and political and socio-cultural soil. 'Bureaucratic system' refers to the lack of systems and mismanagement or maladministration of the system, resulting in corruption ('institutional corruption'). Behaviours include bureaucrats' authoritarianism, ritualism, nepotism, formalism and sectionalism arising out of traditional Confucianism, by-products of modernisation, lack of training, decreasing of moral value and psychological anomie. The political and socio-cultural soil refers to external factors that create the opportunity for corruption.

Corruption can seriously undermine both the social fabric of the society and legitimacy of the political order so that both are seriously threatened. South Korea is by no means safe from such threats unless government anti-corruption policy works and such success is far from certain. The majority of public officials are still doubtful about such anti-corruption policies because of their relatively low morale. Nor do the people of South Korea have much faith in the government, despite its proposed aims to modify public servants' behaviour and improve their pay structure, welfare system, promotion, training and education.

What is needed is an integrated policy for efficient and effective prevention and punishment of corruption. Such a policy should include promulgation of an integrated anti-corruption act, establishment of an independent anti-corruption committee, the passage and adherence to a whistleblowers' protection act and the introduction of the ombudsman system. Nevertheless, the question still remains on how to improve the level of public officials' moral and ethical conduct throughout the different levels and sectors of the bureaucratic system.

CONCLUSION

As this discussion has shown, forms of corruption can develop in either socialist or capitalist countries. Varying social, political, economic, administrative and cultural factors can alter the causes, type and level of corruption. However, it appears that neither political system is immune from serious levels of this costly problem. Thus, what is needed in either system is a pro-active, integrated and continuous anti-corruption policy working from top-down and bottom-up. Only by undertaking a preventative and strong policy can a country hope to diminish and possibly even eradicate this seemingly ubiquitous ill of mankind.

NOTES

1   See Corbett, ch 12 in this volume, for a more detailed discussion of the importance of training. Sherman, ch 1, emphasises the impact of leadership and role models upon ethics in the public sector.

2   US$1.00 = approx 5.8 yuan

3   Malenkov was the First Secretary and Premier of the USSR at the time.

4   In 1980, the Investigation Department of the USSR Procurator's Office sent a team of over 200 investigators, led by Gdlyan, to investigate the so-called Uzbek Corruption Scandal. Ivanov was Gdlyan's closest colleague in the investigation team and so was privy to the bulk of the information uncovered.

5   While Jun was originally sentence to death, his sentence was reduced to life imprisonment. Roh's life imprisonment sentence has been reduced to a 17-year term.

6   In late 1997, Kim Young Sam lost his leadership in a national election to Kim Dae Jung, a long-time opponent to the entrenched leadership. This shift in popular party support further reflects the public's desire for a cleaner, more accountable government.

8

INTEGRATING ETHICS

Colin Hicks & Gerald Scanlan

INTRODUCTION

By any standards, the New Zealand public sector reforms since the mid-1980s have
been massive. It is not uncommonly asserted that the changes, which followed a
now familiar pattern, were different from those in most other countries.[1] Their
uniqueness relates to the breadth, depth and speed of the reforms. Much has been
written about this topic. Time and space do not allow us to provide more than a few
sketches of what has happened in the last decade.

> [B]eginning in the mid-1980s, the New Zealand government has undertaken an
> ambitious and wide-ranging reform of the public sector. It has privatised many of its
> trading operations, and those that it still owns are generally run as commercial
> businesses without subsidies or legislative protection from competition. The
> government has overhauled the way it manages its core departments, contracting
> them to produce outputs and giving them authority to choose which inputs to use to
> this end. In addition, it has replaced cash-based accounting with private-sector-like
> accounts that, among other things, provide balance-sheet information for depart-
> ments and agencies, as well as the government as a whole. In health care, it has,
> among other things, separated purchasers from providers, while in education, it has
> moved to give students and parents more choice. While other countries have taken
> similar measures, New Zealand's public-sector reforms have been more radical and
> comprehensive, in particular in the area of budgeting, management and accounting.
> (OECD, 1996c, p 91)

The poor economic conditions and outlook which faced the incoming
government after the 1984 general election created the impetus and rationale for
change. The government responded by moving on a number of fronts: to de-regulate
the private sector, restructure the commercial operations of government along
business lines and de-control the state sector. No alternatives to the reform path were
seriously entertained. Elements within the government ranks which were not
convinced by the direction, or the speed, of change were outnumbered in caucus.
The reform process was driven by a core of government ministers at a speed and

with a relentlessness that made it difficult for opponents of the reforms to consolidate effective resistance or propose other courses.

In a report prepared for the State Services Commission and the Treasury, Allen Schick considers that New Zealand has boldly gone further than any other country in the world in discarding old practices and inventing new ones (Schick, 1996, p 2). No other country has aspired higher, moved faster, thought deeper or legislated more completely to achieve a government system suited to modern social and economic conditions.

Interestingly, New Zealand also has a reputation as one of the world's least corrupt countries. It could be said that New Zealand has a Triple-A integrity rating, based on a century-long tradition of a principled, professional, non-partisan and honest public service.[2] The management reforms built on that strong ethical foundation. International observers see in New Zealand a country that is both good for business and good at government, both competent and honourable.

New Zealand seems to defy the conventional wisdom that traditional public service values (virtuous government) are an inevitable casualty of managerial reform. How, then, are management reform and ethical conduct linked? Does reform of one eventually require reform (or at least rethinking) of the other? What is the best way to promote and manage public ethics in a devolved public management system? What is the right balance to strike between control and trust, so that the public service can meet the higher expectations of a more demanding public?

These are the issues explored in this chapter.

- To present an account from the inside of the main features of the public management system in New Zealand

- To take stock of the state of our public service ethics

- To discuss some lessons learned about sustaining ethical behaviour and consider their implications for the management system

- To propose some conclusions about the place of ethics reform within the on-going process of building a high-performance, high-integrity Public Service

THE NEW ZEALAND PUBLIC MANAGEMENT SYSTEM

An Impetus for Change

The framework for government in New Zealand combines management principles, system characteristics and public purpose. It has arisen out of the realisation that old ways of running government, as well as old ways of conducting business, are increasingly inappropriate to respond to the conditions facing the modern nation state. Centralised bureaucracy is too cumbersome, too slow to respond and too prone to manipulation of vital information. Equally, management by objectives is too resource-intensive, too linear and too dependent on initial conditions. The option was to plump for a decision-making model able to cope with rapid change in a large, complex organisation based on directions rather than directives and which guides decisions taken autonomously by managers close to the action. Good decisions then depend on a high-quality flow of information and a balanced set of controls, plus the ability to learn and adapt. These insights about the modern conditions for optimal performance may be captured in a slogan: *direction, autonomy and control*. The aim is to build a 'high reliability management' that simultaneously emphasises strong organisational norms, reliance on individual judgment and personal accountability for the welfare of the whole. Few viable alternatives exist in a devolved approach to public management. Easier said than done!

How Things Work

The key to understanding how the New Zealand public service works is to view it as a devolved management system. The system rests on the assumption that public sector managers work best under conditions of clear performance requirements, sufficient authority and discretion to meet those requirements, rigorous accountability for their own and agency's performance (Dubnick, Chapter 5, examines the notion of accountability in greater detail), employment arrangement and incentives linked to that performance and good information flows to keep the system in balance and to enable risks to performance to be managed as close as possible to their source. The fundamental ordering principle for the system is that government is a single enterprise, unified around a common strategy, resource allocation system and brand, all of which reinforce common ownership. Those features create the centripetal force which allows the managers of the various government businesses considerable autonomy in pursuit of high performance.

Purchase and Ownership

An important feature of New Zealand's public sector reform is the distinction drawn between the government's *purchase* and *ownership* interests. The *purchase* interest is the government's interest in receiving goods and services to the standards specified at the right price. The *ownership* interest is the government's interest in ensuring that departments share common values and standards, are properly designed, aligned, staffed, capitalised and controlled to fit them for the government's present requirements and future needs.

Shifting the Focus

After an initial emphasis on the purchase interest as a means of driving down the cost of government and focusing effort, the ownership interest is now receiving greater attention.[3] The main reason is that governments realise that they need to take a longer and broader view of departmental performance and capability than provided by annual purchase arrangements. Ministers need to feel confident the appropriate organisational conditions, investments and management systems are in place to support strategic priorities and collective requirements, to control risks and to ensure cost effective performance over time.

Managing the ownership interest is a large part of the chief executive's job. In the New Zealand context, Public Service chief executives are responsible for ensuring that their departments are in the right condition to meet requirements over time. A set of collective management standards have been developed as performance benchmarks to underpin the reliability of the government 'brand'. The ownership interest forms the bridge between good management practice and public-regarding behaviour and gives substance to the special characteristics of public sector organisations.[4] While ethics are increasingly seen as good for business in a market context, in a government context they are essential to legitimacy and public confidence.

The Modular Approach

Complementing a chief executive's responsibility for managing government ownership interests in each department is the collective responsibility of the three central agencies.[5] Their tasks call for a sophisticated approach to control which neither undermines the devolved management system nor seems to regulate out autonomy and initiative. The approach being developed is very similar to that advocated by Simons (Simons, 1995, p 80), who proposes four modes or levers of control.

Reflective/integrative

These levers of control reflect the belief systems: the articulation of values and direction of an organisation through statements, guidance material, leadership and modelling, personnel management and education and training programmes. These controls help to shape the culture or 'ethos' of the organisation, keeping it attuned to its purpose and its responsibilities. They are invariably more concerned with promoting ethical conduct and the integrity of the organisation than with preventing unethical conduct.

Pre-emptive

These controls usually tell employees what not to do, rather than what to do, and may include statute law, manuals and regulations, codes of conduct or ethics, internal procedures and employment conditions. By their nature, they specify and provide the basis for enforcement; they may also allow employees to have consid-erable autonomy within set boundaries. They set the limits of an ethics framework and are normally a mix of aspirational and preventive approaches.

Diagnostic

These controls allow managers to ensure that important goals are being achieved, including the monitoring and evaluation of performance, and clarification of targets through the use of audit committees, reviews of compliance, community consultation, customer/client/citizen feedback and so forth. In terms of ethical well-being, they should be able to indicate or measure the effectiveness of an ethics regime and how well the value system is integrated into mainstream management and the organisation as a whole.

Interactive

These controls or mechanisms are needed in larger organisations to bridge the information gaps; formal systems for monitoring and reporting need to be supplemented by open-ended dialogue among decision-makers geared to the unpredictable playing-out of the organisation's strategic agenda. For a public service organisation, this may include maintaining a dialogue at an inter-departmental and governmental level as well as developing relationships with sectoral groups, a communications strategy and strategic business planning. Interactive controls focus on constantly changing information that senior managers have identified as strategically significant. From the point of view of an ethics regime, the purpose is to open up the channels of communication at all levels of an organisation (and between the organisation and those outside it) to send and receive the right signals about the well-being and integrity of an organisation.

Of these, the second mode (pre-emptive) suggests the traditional, domain-marking role of the central agencies while the third (diagnostic) captures the essence of the results-focused exchanges around the purchase and performance arrangements. The first (reflective/integrative) and fourth (interactive) modes underline the impulse behind recent attention to strategic management in government and the ownership interest. They also represent potentially fertile ground for strengthening attention to ethical conduct in ways that do not rely wholly on rules or rote compliance.

The advantage of a modular approach to control in a devolved management system is that it allows for the mix of controls to be tailored to differing circumstances and risks. The tailored approach to control is a natural result of the search for intelligent ways of managing the government system. The more that can be achieved through informal means, such as affirmation of values and beliefs, development of relationships and opportunities for dialogue, the less reliance need be placed on formal instruments and exchanges. By shifting the balance from formal to informal and from extrinsic to intrinsic, central agencies can utilise a variety of controls as incentives and send a powerful signal about the role of trust in a well-performing system.

RATING PUBLIC SERVICE ETHICS IN
THE NEW ZEALAND CONTEXT

A Paradox

While we have made a great virtue out of the discipline and focus introduced by contracts, improved government performance will continue to rely heavily on managerial discretion, that is, reliance on the quality of individuals and their understanding of their roles and responsibilities in a public-regarding manner.

We tend to take the core principles and values that underpin our public service for granted but ethics are a rare and fragile phenomenon. All organisations benefit from a strong set of values and standards and from solid ethical leadership. This is particularly so of public service organisations because of the influence and power exerted over decisions affecting citizens. It is therefore imperative for a public service organisation to conduct itself in ways that preserve and enhance public trust and confidence in the integrity of government and its institutions.

In rating the state of ethics in the New Zealand public service, it is important to draw a distinction between the design of the management system as a whole and the opportunities that arise inevitably in a devolved system. In our view, the management reforms in New Zealand have not only tended to strengthen ethical government in a systemic sense but have also increased the possibility of failure occurring at an individual level, damaging government's reputation. Equally, though, it is more likely that ethical breaches will be noticed, which is essential if we are to sustain an environment hostile to public corruption.

The key to the apparent paradox of stronger systems alongside greater opportunity for particular incidences of unethical behaviour is to be found in the management reform model which New Zealand developed. That reform transformed the public service from an essentially 'closed' society to a more 'open' society in a cultural sense. A 'closed' society in these terms is characterised by boundaries that are difficult to cross, have a common identification, relatively rigid patterns of behaviour and controls from the centre and a strong pressure from within to conform. In the 'old' public service, entry was usually at the basic grade, there was little cross-fertilisation with the private sector, compulsory retirement and generous superannuation arrangements existed, personnel management and industrial relations were tightly controlled from the centre and the public service was seen as a career service.

An accent in the reformed public service was placed on openness. The *Official Information Act* 1982 repealed the *Official Secrets Act* 1951, reversing the presumption that official information should be withheld unless there were good reasons for its release. The present law provides for proper access by each person relating to that person so as to protect official information to the extent consistent with the public interest and the preservation of personal privacy (now covered by the *Privacy Act* 1993). It has also established procedures for the achievements of those purposes. The main purposes of the *Official Information Act* are to progressively increase the availability of official information to enable effective participation in the democratic processes (the making and administration of laws and policies) and to promote accountability of ministers of the Crown and officials. A principle of availability is written into the law. There is a tendency even now, however, for some officials to try to shelter behind secrecy; however, the overwhelming impulse is to be as open as possible, consistent with the spirit and intent of the statute. Cases of 'whistleblowing' have been few and far between and inconsequential generally. Be that as it may, there has been pressure from the public, and from within Parliament, for laws to protect legitimate 'whistleblowers' who release information in the public interest. A private members bill was introduced and the government has also prepared draft legislation. Gregory asserts these moves 'may be seen as the first major attempt to address such moral issues since the managerial reforms' (Gregory, 1995, p 25).

If 'whistleblower' protection law is enacted, it will place an onus on public servants to think more about their responsibilities, and for managers to re-evaluate the ethic of neutrality. The 'ethic of neutrality' holds that one does only what one is told to do. Duty is to one's immediate superior. There is little or no room for individual choice or discretion. In the New Zealand context, the emphasis on an undivided duty to the minister, or to the chief executive, if taken to the extreme, might amount to such an ethic. Schick hints at this effect in his assessment of the New Zealand reforms (Schick, 1996, p 20).

Good information, performance-based incentives, accountability for results and clarity of roles and responsibilities are all consistent with the maintenance and development of ethical government. Society's expectation that government will be conducted largely in the open, coupled with governments' aversion to conducting activities that are better undertaken by markets, makes it exceedingly difficult to do deals, play favourites or extract public rents on a systematic or orchestrated basis. However, the reforms have created opportunities for some individuals, who mistake managerial freedom for open licence, to subordinate the collective interest of government to their own interests. At the more senior levels of the public service, this has more commonly taken the form of disingenuous claims to autonomy in defiance of the legitimate rights of the centre to enforce certain management standards than of attempts to secure personal gain.

The Logan Review[6]

An early test of the ethical soundness of the reforms was provided by the election of the government in 1990, not long after the reform of the core public service began. The government very quickly expressed its displeasure at evidence of departments failing to support the collective interest of government and disabling the machinery for co-ordinated decision-making. The review that followed has provided a good steer toward the development of an integrated approach to public management.

Under the National Government (1990–96), devices for whole-of-government integration and strategic cohesion became progressively more sophisticated and prominent. Interest is growing in ethical guidance and renewed attention is being directed at the problem of cultivating a service-wide pool of senior managers who will carry the flame of public service values without security of tenure or guarantees of career service.

The devolved management framework creates its own set of risks. We have entered a phase where, much more than in the past, public employees have to be aware of, and be able to anticipate, the opportunities for waywardness and risks to ethical values and standards that may be inferred from the new approach. We may have already experienced some of the downside.

Issues and incidents

Several high-profile recent cases have prompted a fresh look at the soundness of our ethical foundations. They involve a public inquiry into the causes of the tragedy at Cave Creek,[7] allegations of fraud made against the former chief public watchdog on public expenditure[8] and publicity concerning two public service departments, caught up in a long-running judicial inquiry into allegations of tax fraud.

In a more general sense, issues including the use of consultants, leaking of information, public comment by officials, participation in political activities, acceptance of gifts and other benefits, frequent flyer schemes and outside employment have all arisen from time to time. Some of the issues have become public and have called into question the conduct of particular individuals or agencies. It is not possible to say whether the issues arise as a consequence of the reforms or that they are more prevalent than before or perhaps more conspicuous. What seems most important is that the immediate responses to these incidents should be consistent, thorough and decisive. Further, the accent should be more on promoting appropriate behaviour than preventing unethical or unprofessional conduct.

No Room for Complacency

It is important to consider what these issues and incidents tell us about the state of ethics in government. The first point to note is that there is clearly no room for complacency; good systems are worthless without the human commitment, character and goodwill to make them work. That said, there is no need to panic; most of the incidents signify lapses in personal judgment, common sense or honesty rather than fundamental flaws. Several of them are also potent reminders that the rub between politics and administration can cause friction and contention far beyond what the facts seem to justify.

It is a luxury, not a signal for indifference, to be able to look at refining approaches to ethics and not to have to be consumed with countering systemic or institutional corruption. When serious misconduct or breaches of professional and ethical conduct occur, it is not unnatural for organisational 'soul-searching' to follow, especially when expectations of integrity are high and breaches infrequent.

Main Areas of Concern

Although the outlook is more bright than bleak, there are three broad areas of concern.

In our devolved management system, it is difficult to gauge the adequacy of the systems and controls that chief executives put in place to avoid, or detect, breaches of ethical conduct. The State Services Commission is now putting considerable effort into establishing standards for management systems and controls and for assurance about their efficacy, as well as providing much clearer guidance about conventions, obligations and expectations in respect of public service ethics. These are appropriate roles for a central agency in a devolved system; they neatly illustrate the place of both control and trust in managing that system.

The collapse of the viewing platform at Cave Creek has prompted a searching reappraisal of what responsibility and accountability mean in the public service and it has been a reminder in no uncertain manner that the standards we must measure ourselves by are ultimately those that the public itself sets. Uhr suggests, and we agree, that:

> accountability constrains and fetters official discretion, while responsibility releases discretion. Accountability is about compliance with authority, whereas responsibility is about empowerment and independence. Accountability is the negative end of the same band in which responsibility is the positive end. If accountability is about minimising misgovernment, responsibility is about maximising good government. (Uhr, 1993, p 4)

The links between ethics and responsibility, and accountability, are critical. In exchange for giving managers broad discretion in using public resources and exercising devolved authorities, a greater accent on accountability was heralded by the reforms. The trade-off is not as evenly applied as one would like and the New Zealand version of accountability, at least in an instrumental way, may have had more to do with purchase than with ownership, more to do with producing outputs than with the overall capacity of the department, more with whether managers are meeting specified targets than whether public programmes are effective.

Being too concerned with specificity and contractual arrangements may produce the effect of managers seeming to take the view that if it is not on the list, it is not their responsibility. Of course, chief executives should comply with the agreement and produce specified outputs. But the most valuable asset that chief executives bring to their relationship with ministers is not compliance but judgment and leadership.

While the contractual character of New Zealand's reforms has brought many benefits, it may have encouraged a rather narrow and mechanistic appreciation of accountability and allowed some managers to develop a myopic view of their responsibilities: if it is not specifically stated, it is not their responsibility.

The general election of October 1996 heralded the beginning of a new era. A new multi-member proportional electoral system has had an effect on the government formation process and may change the way they operate in the future. This will undoubtedly have a knock-on effect for the public service. The key risk for the public service lies as much in the transition as it does in the change itself, while the system is still unfamiliar. Some commentators anticipate that under proportional representation, more power will accrue to public servants. If electoral change ushers in a new era of lobbying and political rent-seeking, some public servants might be tempted to trade on their influence and access to the political process. Although this is an uncertain outcome, it does highlight the need to keep updating our views on what are the ethical requirements for effective management of a government's business. A number of new or reinvigorated initiatives are in-train to help keep public service ethics current and to help deal with some of the possibilities which might arise under the new electoral system.

- The establishment of an inter-departmental public service Ethics Advisory Group
- A re-examination of post-employment conditions for chief executives in the light of the new employment environment
- The need for provisions for public servants to register their interests
- Statutory protection for disclosure of information about actions which are unlawful, unethical or dangerous
- Greater use of internal governance arrangements, notably audit committees

PROPOSALS FOR INTEGRATION: MAKING THINGS WORK

The Broad Aim

New Zealand set out in the mid-1980s to move from a centralised, tightly controlled, compliance-based system toward a devolved, integrity-based management framework. In making that change, it was inevitable that the public service would be exposed to risks to its integrity. Nevertheless, the principal concern was to create the conditions for effective government of a modern society. That task has been largely achieved. Along the way, we have learned something about managing and promoting public service ethics in a manner consistent with the core design ideas governing our public management system.

Lessons

We now recognise that the reinforcement and transmission of common cultural values need to be planned and systematic. Codes and guidance material compete with other systems of incentives and sanctions that operate within departments.

Strong departmental allegiances have developed, with some cost to horizontal relationships. If a common ethos is a necessary ingredient of a modern public service, then more attention needs to be paid to inculcating core values and standards. We have discovered that the emergence of strategic management within government is helping to broaden the perspective of departmental managers as well as strengthen business connections across government.

The way the public service responds publicly to instances of illegal, unethical or dubious conduct within its ranks can be critical to the maintenance of public trust and confidence. Sending the right signals, especially from a central agency, is an important means of reinforcing key values, and maintaining public and political confidence. (Miller, Chapter 3, discusses the strength of institutional ethics.)

Effective, pervasive change is often accompanied by a shift in language. This is particularly true in the context of the New Zealand reforms. New language and symbols have helped effect the desired cultural sea-change. But the new language is not necessarily self-explanatory; definition and contextualisation is important. We need a better, more coherent understanding of the terms we employ and we need to communicate in a language that is understood by politicians and the public alike.

The concepts of *responsibility* and *accountability* in government are examples of terms which merit further clarification and discussion.

The role of the central agencies in the new governance arrangements needs clarification. There is a tendency for departments to mis-interpret central agency motives and resent interventions. The central agencies are working towards a common understanding of the best way of managing our devolved system so as to enhance both the motivation of departments and their sense of connection to the whole of government.

Implications

The devolution of authority and responsibility makes heavy demands on agencies. Things have to happen within departments if change is to be effective. Chief executives need to be active leaders, sending the right signals to staff and able to adopt strategic-level perspectives with broader and longer horizons than their predecessors. Such demands need to be recognised in recruitment and appointment processes and in on-going senior management education and training programmes. In that respect, being clear about the right competencies and qualities of senior managers and about succession management, are important elements. It is one thing to know what the principles or values are in a given situation; it's quite another to recognise when those principles and values ought to apply and then have the judgment and courage to apply them.

Performance agreements and the system of incentives and sanctions need to be well directed. That is, senior managers should be in no doubt what is expected of them in terms of responsibility and accountability while wisely employing operational discretion and autonomy. Renewed attention to the value of a known cadre of senior managers who are developed for top positions, together with initiatives to involve existing chief executives in the wider task of public service governance, are both aimed at reinforcing the government-wide responsibilities that come with senior status.

The State Services Commissioner has a vital role in sending the right messages (to the Government, to the public and to the rest of the public service) on behalf of that collective leadership, and to act independently and assertively when that seems appropriate.[9] Key qualities are timeliness, decisiveness and credibility. The transition to government under proportional representation is likely to draw considerable attention to the Commissioner's role and test those qualities.

Applying the Integrated Approach

New Zealand is gradually developing an integrated approach to managing the ethical dimension of government. By integrated we mean the employment of a range of initiatives that, when applied, are mutually reinforcing, consistent with the design of the devolved management system, supportive of the government's priorities and reflective of the values of the wider political context.

One way of categorising the initiatives is to use the 'levers of control' model discussed earlier which demonstrates how 'ethical control' need not rest only on rules, proscriptions or prescriptions. Moreover, many of the controls could fit in more than one category. That represents a useful form of redundancy which helps ensure that wherever a manager picks into the ethical question, a wide array of issues and responses are made available for reflection and action.

CONCLUSIONS

We return to the original question: what is the best way to promote and manage public ethics in a devolved public management system? Our answer, in brief, is that the best way is an integrated approach, involving the following vital elements.

- Recognise and assert the importance of ethics to good government
- Integrate the management of ethics into the wider system
- Exercise leadership from the centre and demand similar leadership in departments
- Promote through a combination of standards, guidance, education and recognition of good practice
- Allow information to flow to inform and guide devolved decision making
- Continue to test theory and rules against experience and remain responsive to changes in the political and policy environment

Behind this approach lie some critical assumptions.

- There are enduring principles and values that are integral to public service.
- Those who enter the public service do not necessarily come equipped with those value sets.
- Therefore, we should ensure that our foundation values are made known to public servants, and reinforced, in a systematic way.

The core challenge for the New Zealand public service, and probably for most government systems, is that of integration. In a sense, it is a truism that the integrity of government and its constituent organisations depends on the integration of values into the totality of their management arrangements and into the human fabric of those organisations.

The integrated approach, outlined above, offers a way of understanding what we are doing now and where we might need to put our energies and resources in the future. It provides a framework for action and a reminder to maintain balance between the different forms of intervention possible within a devolved management system. For example, it became clear to us in surveying the range of tools at our disposal that we need to place more emphasis on *diagnostic* initiatives to remedy deficiencies in empirical information on ethics in government.

Government has an important and unique job to do and it has to be in the right shape to do it. The New Zealand reforms have been about getting into shape: becoming leaner, quicker, more productive and more strategic. But good government is about style as well as substance, quality as much as quantity. Respecting core values, behaving ethically, obeying the law and sustaining public confidence: these are cornerstones of high-performance, high-integrity government.

NOTES

1   See, for instance, OECD (1996a) for a useful analysis and discussion of the trends in nine OECD countries, including Australia and New Zealand.

2   The increasing scale of central government administration in New Zealand in the years before 1912 necessitated some innovation in the machinery of government imperative. But it took additional factors and circumstances ('jobbery', corruption, nepotism, etc.) to determine the particular nature and timing of that innovation, embodied in the *Public Service Act* 1912. That legislation established the Public Service Commission (later to become the State Services Commission) and set the framework for the public service until 1988.

3   Lawton, ch 4, reveals the dangers of applying business management ethics and structures to the public sector.

4   We assume a persistent and clear distinction between public and private sector organisations based on the assertions that public sector organisations are shaped by their functions as crucial links in the system of democratic government, the inescapable political context of the role of the public official and the trust that is reposed in all those holding public office, whether elected or appointed.

5   The Treasury, the Department of the Prime Minister and Cabinet and the State Services Commission form what might be described as a 'corporate office' role or, more accurately, the 'governance office' role. The three agencies share the task of supporting decisions by government on strategic direction, investment and the organisational and management conditions for effective government and government with enduring integrity and capability.

6   A steering group was set up under the convenorship of a businessman, Basil Logan, to review the reforms. A *Report of the Review of State Sector Reforms* was published in 1991 by the State Services Commission.

7   Cave Creek refers to a tragic incident on 28 April 1995 when a party of 17 students from Tai Poutini Polytech at Greymouth and the Department of Conservation's Punakaiki Field Centre Manager were plunged into the Cave Creek ravine from a viewing platform which collapsed. As a result, 14 young people were killed and four were injured, some seriously. Following the tragedy, a Commission of Inquiry found that while there were serious failing (to provide qualified engineering for the building of the viewing platform; to adequately manage the construction; to comply with statutory requirements; to adequately inspect the site; to provide adequate warnings; and that systemic failure existed), no individual could be held responsible. In May 1996, the Minister of Conservation resigned his portfolio; in May 1997, the Director-General of Conservation resigned from the Public Service.

8   In October 1994, the Controller and Auditor-General resigned. He was later charged with multiple fraud and theft by the Serious Fraud Office. In March 1997, he was sentenced to a total of 6 months imprisonment; in May 1997, following an application from the Crown, his sentence was increased to 18 months by the Court of Appeal.

9   The State Services Commissioner is the effective head of the New Zealand public service, chief adviser to governments on the organisation, management and development of the State sector and responsible for the selection, appointment and employment of public service chief executives.

9

CANADIAN DEFENCE ETHICS
Principles and Values

Rosalie Bernier

INTRODUCTION

The national and global environment has undergone radical change in recent years. Internationally, Canada remains committed to NATO but few Canadian troops remain in Europe. On the other hand, the Canadian Forces (CF) have been involved in an unprecedented number of very challenging peacekeeping operations, often in a multinational force environment. On the domestic scene, fiscal restraints and downsizing efforts continue. In addition, the existence of the Charter of Rights and Freedoms adds a constitutional dimension that generates in the Canadian public an increased awareness of the corresponding values. Although the mandate of the CF and the Department of National Defence (DND) has not changed, they have had to adjust to a radically new environment produced by these significant changes. There is every indication that further developments will continue to affect how the military can accomplish its mission. Some of these important changes have brought winds of renewal related to the delegation of authority, increased responsibilities and greater freedom in decision-making, which in turn impacts on how the CF carry out operations. Well-founded defence ethics will assist its military and global environment. In response to the growing need to re-emphasise ethical decision-making and integrity within government as a whole, in February 1994 Defence senior leadership endorsed the Defence Ethics Program to provide a visible and expressed ethical focus for the CF and DND.

The Defence Ethics Program is an umbrella program that provides an ethical framework to assist personnel to lead and manage ethically. The program is being implemented through the chain of command and line management. The Defence Ethics Program office offers expertise, advice and support to the Commands and National Defence Headquarters Groups. Thus, the program provides military commanders and defence managers with a number of tools and policies to assist them in meeting the challenges they face in a changing environment as well as supplying members and employees with the skills and tools they need to perform their duties ethically.

The Defence Ethics Program is a values-based program. Its primary focus is to foster the common values possessed in many democratic societies rather than a strict compliance approach that is enforced by the threat of sanctions and disciplinary measures. A fundamental assumption of the Defence Ethics Program is that any decision or action that directly or indirectly, actually or potentially affects other people has an ethical dimension and entails a duty to consider and protect their rights and interests. Thus, although the Defence Ethics Program recognises the importance of ethically managing money, time, equipment and information, it places special emphasis on the belief that leading people entails ethical obligations.[1]

The objectives of the programme are to:

- foster an ethical culture within the CF and the DND;
- cultivate an ethical mindset;
- enhance individual reasoning abilities concerning the ethics of a decision or action through training, workshops, discussions, case studies, individual learning and open dialogues;
- provide a framework and context for the ongoing administration and application of the Conflict of Interest and Post-Employment codes; and
- develop awareness of ethical risk factors and vulnerabilities through pro-active or vulnerability assessment.

The Defence Ethics Program fulfils its role and mandate by developing and providing continuous renewal of the programme's components. This chapter will provide short description of each of these components.

ETHICAL CULTURE

Statement of Defence Ethics

This Statement prescribes ethical principles and obligations governing all members of the DND and the CF in the performance of their professional roles and duties. It is intended for use as a normative guide to professional conduct and as an aid to resolving ethical questions and dilemmas which will be encountered in day-to-day work. It is being integrated into the existing range of professional development and management courses. (Corbett, Chapter 12, discusses different approaches to ethical training.)

The Statement of Defence Ethics consists of two main parts: a hierarchically ordered set of three general principles; and a list of specific ethical obligations that personnel have to society, lawful authority, third parties and subordinates. Whereas the obligations are intended as standards of conduct that all should strive to meet in the performance of professional roles and duties, the principles are intended as aids for decision and action in establishing priorities when faced with conflicting ethical obligations or dilemmas.

The Statement is enunciated as follows:

As members of the Canadian Forces, liable to the ultimate sacrifice, and as employees of the Department of National Defence having special obligations to Canada, we are dedicated to our duty and committed to:

- respect the dignity of all persons;
- serve Canada before self; and
- obey and support lawful authority.

Guided by these fundamental principles, we act in accordance with the following ethical obligations:

Loyalty
We dedicate ourselves to Canada. We are loyal to our superiors and faithful to our subordinates and colleagues.

Honesty
We honour the trust placed upon us. We value truth and candour, and act with integrity at all times.

Courage
We face challenges, whether physical or moral, with determination and strength of character.

Diligence
We undertake all tasks with dedication and perseverance. We recognize our duty to perform with competence and to strive for excellence.

Fairness
We are equitable in our dealings with others. We are just in our decisions and actions.

Responsibility
We accept our responsibilities and the consequences of our actions.[2]

Defence Ethics Centre of Excellence

The Defence Ethics Centre of Excellence is conceived as an agent of cultural change. It is composed of a matrix of professionals who are competent in providing guidance on significant ethical issues. A core of expertise is already in place and will continue to expand as the program evolves. In addition, each Command and Headquarters Group has appointed a Senior Ethics Coordinator to provide on-going communication and co-ordination with the corporate Defence Ethics Program office. The team of Ethics Coordinators also serves as a committee to provide guidance on the development of the program.

ETHICAL MINDSET

Ethics Awareness

Ethics must be reflected in everyday behaviour and actions. Ethics awareness is therefore a major component of the Defence Ethics Program. Communication opportunities and technologies are used to foster a healthy ethical environment for personnel at all levels of the organization. In addition, awareness will be expanded by creating venues for group gatherings that allow the sharing of experiences of ethical decision-making in action. In these special information and awareness-raising sessions, individual leaders and managers can communicate shared defence values and foster ethical decision-making. An example of this was the Ethics in Defence Conference, held 24 and 25 October 1996 in Ottawa. It brought together people from across the country, various backgrounds and all levels within the CF and the DND to share views on current ethical issues. Appropriately, the conference theme was *The Many Faces of Ethics in Defence*. The conference program included such subjects as: ethics and the burden of office, the ethical dilemmas of commanders in multi-national missions, the military moral character, business ethics in defence (the utilisation of business ethics and practices in the public sector is considered in Lawton, Chapter 4) and a survey of psychological views on ethical development.

Ethics Resource and Assistance Centre

The Defence Ethics Program Resource Centre provides reference and research tools as well as training aids. The resource centre already has a number of publications including books, journals, papers and articles as well as videos. The centre has an on-going program to collect important and relevant material on ethics.

Ethics assistance in the workplace responds to the need for an internal information and guidance mechanism that personnel at all levels can turn to when they seek additional knowledge for making decisions or a more focused understanding of the choices in the face of ethical dilemmas. As part of the process of designing the ethics assistance component, the Defence Ethics Program office is working in concert with Commands and National Defence Headquarters Groups. The goal is to create an ethics assistance service that supports all members of the CF and DND in ethical decision making and actions.

ETHICAL REASONING

Ethics Training

Initial developmental efforts of the ethical reasoning component of the program have centred around producing an introductory education module to be delivered throughout the CF and the DND. A flexible initial training package called *Ethics in the Workplace* has been developed and is given as a workshop. This workshop combines discussions, slides, videos and case studies to facilitate the learning and practice of basic ethical concepts and values in the ethical decision-making process. The primary objective of the workshop is to provide tools that allow participants to understand the nature of ethical issues and dilemmas and to use strategies to deal with them in interactive discussions. This initial package contains a core of ethical information and concepts that can be presented as an overview in approximately one hour to one and ½ hours. The full ethics workshop itself is structured to last between three hours and a full day, depending on the time available and the number of case studies used. It gravitates around a 25-minute video also called appropriately *Ethics in the Workplace*. In the opening scenes of the video, the Chief of the Defence Staff and the Deputy Minister of our department personally deliver their own ethical and cultural message. This is one way for them to take the lead and to demonstrate to senior military and civilian leaders and managers the need to be seen and perceived as strongly committed to the practice of ethical principles and values. (Kim, Chapter 7, reveals how influential the appearance and reality of leaders' approaches to ethics can be.)

Although the ethical concepts and the decision-making framework provided in the workshop can generally be applied to most situations in the workplace, the situations and case studies in this first introductory *Ethics in the Workplace* module are mainly focused on resource and administrative management issues. Work has already begun on designing two additional modules, at the intermediate and advanced levels, called *Ethics at Work*. These modules will deal with issues relevant to the ethics of combat and field operations and include appropriate case studies.

Ethics Learning

While ethics training is based on the acquisition of ethical concepts and the elements of ethical decision-making and actions in a structured environment with a course leader or facilitator, ethics learning will focus on individual, self-paced learning. Innovative approaches are being explored to develop case-driven modules. Maximum use of interactive learning technologies will be the focus in the development of ethical reasoning learning tools.

CONFLICT OF INTEREST AND POST-EMPLOYMENT CODE

The Defence Ethics Program is responsible for the administration of the Conflict of Interest and Post-Employment Code as well as the provision of advice and expertise with regard to this code. Members of the CF and of the DND are subject to the provisions of the Conflict of Interest and Post-employment Code issued by the federal government of Canada.

Under this code, military and civilian personnel must take the necessary measures to prevent real, potential or apparent conflicts of interest from arising. The objective of this requirement is to enhance public confidence in the integrity of the CF and DND and its personnel by establishing clear rules of conduct respecting conflict of interest for, and post-employment practices applicable to, all personnel. In addition, it seeks to minimise the possibility of conflicts arising between the private interests and public duties of personnel as well as provide for the resolution of such conflicts in the public interest should they arise. Under this code, all personnel shall conform to the following rules.

Ethical Standards

a. personnel shall act with honesty and uphold the highest ethical standards so that public confidence and trust in the integrity, objectivity and impartiality of Government and the CF and DND are conserved and enhanced;

Public Scrutiny

b. personnel have an obligation to perform their official duties and arrange their private affairs in a manner that will bear the closest public scrutiny, an obligation that is not fully discharged by simply acting within the law;

Decision-Making

c. personnel, in fulfilling their official duties and responsibilities, shall make decisions in the public interest and with regard to the merits of each case;

Private Interests

d. personnel shall not have private interests, other than those permitted pursuant to this order, that would be affected particularly or significantly by government actions in which they participate;

Public Interest

e. on enrolment or appointment and thereafter, personnel shall arrange their private affairs in a manner that will prevent real, potential or apparent conflicts of interest from arising but if such a conflict does arise between private interests and the official duties and responsibilities, the conflict shall be resolved in favour of the public interest;

Gifts and Benefits

f. personnel shall not solicit or accept transfers of economic benefit, other than incidental gifts, customary hospitality, or other benefits of nominal value, unless the transfer is pursuant to an enforceable contract or property right of the member;

Preferential Treatment

g. personnel shall not step out of their official roles to assist private entities or persons in their dealings with the government where this would result in preferential treatment to any person;

Insider Information

h. personnel shall not knowingly take advantage of, or benefit from, information that is obtained in the course of their official duties and responsibilities and that is not generally available to the public;

Government Property

i. members shall not directly or indirectly use, or allow the use of, government property of any kind, including property leased to the government, for anything other than officially approved activities; and

Post-Employment

j. personnel shall not act, after commencing retirement leave, ceasing to be employed or release from the CF or DND, as applicable, in such a manner as to take improper advantage of their previous office.[3]

A number of compliance measures further describe the duties and obligations in respect of the ten rules enunciated above and provide guidance in their interpretation.

A Senior Review Committee is planned to deal with significant ethical issues. It will also serve as the senior CF and DND review and decision authority with regard to cases of conflict of interest.

PRO-ACTIVE ETHICAL RISK ASSESSMENT

Ethical risk assessment is essential to operating in a devolved environment. Commanders and managers are best placed to identify and assess a workplace's vulnerabilities and do something about them. The Defence Ethics Program will provide an ethics risk check methodology to complement existing practices. It will make available self-assessment tools that will help commanders and managers gauge the ethical vulnerabilities and identify the areas of greatest ethical risk. Pro-active ethical risk assessment will provide commanders and managers with the skills to undertake ethical risk management checks involving the early identification of risks; access to a 'lessons learned' data base to improve ethical risk assessment and learn from mistakes and successes; and action plans to deal with or treat ethical risks in ways commensurate with the significance of the risk and the importance of the activity.

CONCLUSION

The CF and Department of National Defence personnel are proud of their ethical culture, proud of the integrity and the professionalism they have consistently demonstrated over the years. They acknowledge that they have individually and collectively an obligation, which the nation has a right to expect, to achieve their mission and mandate by adhering to sound ethical practices. The Defence Ethics Program provides a values-based ethical framework to meet this objective.

NOTES

1   The importance of leadership in promoting ethical behaviour is considered from various perspectives by Sherman, ch 1; Miller, ch 3; Kim, ch 7; and Corbett, ch 12.

2   This October 1996 Statement is a combined effort of 15 people, one from each segment of the CF and the DND.

3   *Conflict of Interest and Post-Employment Code for the Public Service* 1994 (Canada). For a discussion on the implementation of this code, see Wilson (1998).

10

ADMINISTRATIVE LAW AND GOOD GOVERNMENT

Roger Douglas

Administrative law's values reflect its origins as the creature of politicians who are sometimes torn between principle and opportunism and judges who owe their legitimacy to law and are therefore themselves constrained by it. It embodies most of the central values of good administration and contributes to their realisation, albeit in relatively subtle ways. This chapter begins with a discussion of the nature of administrative law, for this is central to the argument that follows. It follows with an analysis of the two major sources of Australian administrative law: legislation and judicial decisions. It concludes with an analysis of the ways in which administrative law, on its face and in practice, contributes to good administration.

THE NATURE OF ADMINISTRATIVE LAW

Administrative law is seen as the general body of law which regulates the relationship between the citizen and the executive branch of government. It does not concern itself with the powers of parliament: these are the province of constitutional law.[1] It neither concerns itself with the workings of the courts[2] nor with the inner workings of the bureaucracy. Indeed, this latter area of law is rarely taught in law schools and rarely discussed in administrative law textbooks; it impinges on what is conventionally defined as administrative law only when administrators are relying on the institutions of administrative law to challenge adverse employment decisions. Conventionally, administrative law is concerned with the general principles rather than with minutiae.

Australian administrative law has developed against the backdrop of a variety of somewhat ambiguous doctrines. At federal level, this development has occurred within the context of a constitutionally based separation of powers doctrine, with the crucial divide being between the intermingled executive and legislature on one hand

and the judiciary on the other. This doctrine has not always proved easy to apply, especially in the context of administrative tribunals which possess both executive and judicial elements. However, its importance is considerable, insofar as its logic implies both vigour and restraint in the area of judicial review of administrative action: vigour because of the courts' role in pronouncing authoritatively on the legality of administrative action and restraint because the legitimation of that role lies in a doctrine which implies strict limits to the role of the courts as well as to that of the other branches.

Administrative law in Australia has also developed against the backdrop of the model of government as responsible government. This model serves uneasily as a mixture of ideal and purported description. In both respects, it is somewhat unsatisfactory. While it may be reasonable to hold ministers responsible for matters over which they have or should have clear control, it is absurd to hold them responsible for all the errors of modern administrators. Moreover, while the principle of responsible government is frequently asserted, its operation is relatively subtle. It is extraordinarily rare for a minister to accept responsibility for anything and rarer still for Cabinet to treat ministers as responsible. Errors of judgment do, however, have their price. While the ritualistic calls for resignation are almost invariably defied, they can inflict political damage on both the minister and the government. Mistakes have their price.

Administrative law is traditionally seen as having evolved in response to the failure of responsible government. This teleological explanation is problematic; the difficulties with the concept of responsible government have long antedated the tightening of Australia's administrative review procedures.[3] However, administrative law can be seen as an important step towards compensating for the limits of responsible government and has developed in the shadow of this doctrine.

STATUTORY ADMINISTRATIVE LAW

Much Australian administrative law is statutory. Indeed, most of the major reforms to the Australian administrative law system have been statutory. These reforms have taken a number of forms.

The Ombudsman

The earliest and most generally adopted statutory reform was the establishment of an 'ombudsman' in each Australian jurisdiction. Like their British Commonwealth counterparts, the Australian ombudsmen possess no formal power to alter administrative decisions but they do possess considerable investigative powers, together with considerable authority (on Ombudsmen, see Anderson, 1996). Their formal power is limited to the investigation of administrative activity. The ombudsman may comment on laws which constitute the basis for administrative activity.

To a considerable extent, the jurisdiction of the ombudsmen bears a complex relationship to that of other review agencies and the courts. However, there are some respects in which their powers are narrower than those of tribunals and courts. Unlike tribunals, they are concerned with the appropriateness of a prior decision at the time it was made rather than with what is the correct or preferable decision at the time of the review decision. Their powers in relation to procedurally flawed activity are probably more limited than those of courts, since they are concerned with the correctness of the decision rather than the procedures by which it was reached. Conversely, there are some respects in which their powers are broader. They may report adversely on decisions which are based on unjust laws or which are, simply, 'wrong'. Moreover, they may make recommendations not only in relation to the particular activity but also in relation to possible changes to the practices and laws which have given rise to particular problems. They may monitor and report on compliance with recommendations in relation to both specific cases and general problems. While they usually act in response to complaints, they may unilaterally decide to investigate possible administrative irregularities.

Cross-jurisdictional variations in ombudsman legislation are relatively unimportant and certainly far less important than cross-ombudsman variations. Ombudsmen define their role in varying ways, with some taking a relatively legalistic approach, others pressing their jurisdiction to the limits, some focusing on particular cases while others are concerned with general problems. Their freedom to define their role is implicit in the relevant legislation and is probably enhanced by the fact that their decisions are recommendatory rather than binding. They are, however, constrained by the exigencies of working 'effectively' with administrators and by the need to demonstrate their worth to their funders, some of whom have seen the ombudsman's office as an appropriate target for budget cutting.

Their importance is considerable. They handle a large number of complaints (far more than the general administrative review tribunals and many times more than the courts). Their lack of a final dispositive power sometimes leads to their being dismissed as toothless but this lack of formal power probably makes them more effective. Their persuasive authority is considerable and their recommendations are overwhelmingly complied with.

Administrative Review Tribunals

Among the most important developments in Australian administrative law has been the development of relatively accessible procedures for the review of administrative decisions (for details, see Douglas and Jones, 1996, ch 7). While some areas of administrative behaviour have long been subject to internal review as well as to external review by independent tribunals (notably in the taxation and veterans' benefits areas), the past 20 years have seen a considerable expansion in the range of reviewable decisions and in the powers of the review tribunals. The most highly developed review systems are to be found at the federal level, where there are usually two or three successive review stages in the high caseload areas: internal review by 'independent' departmental officials, acting within the constraints by which the primary decision-maker is bound and review by a specialised tribunal with a less fettered discretion, from which appeal may lie to the general Administrative Appeals Tribunal (AAT).

Recent developments have included strengthening tribunal powers and increasing the range of decisions they can review.[4]

These developments are arguably more important than a third: the establishment in 1975 of an Appeals Tribunal with jurisdiction over a broad range of administrative decisions. The importance of the AAT lies to a considerable extent in its status, coupled with its broad power to make what it regards as 'the correct or preferable' decision, even if doing so means rejecting government policy (*Drake v MIEA (No 2)* (1979) 24 ALR 577). The major criticisms made of the AAT is that it is unduly formal and correspondingly less accessible.[5] However, even if this is conceded, the advent of the AAT has made review more accessible than the previous alternative: judicial review.

Freedom of Information

The third major development has been the adoption of Freedom of Information (FOI) legislation in all but one jurisdiction (Northern Territory). The nature of this legislation varies somewhat from jurisdiction to jurisdiction.[6] Broadly, it confers a general right to government information, subject to a variety of exceptions. These include such predictable exceptions as sensitive information relating to the economy, law enforcement and security; information supplied in confidence; and information whose disclosure would be inconsistent with the subject's rights of privacy.

Less easily reconciled with principle is a 'Cabinet documents' exemption, the effect of which is to restrict access to many politically sensitive documents. In the context of routine requests, FOI legislation normally ensures that people who request information are granted access to all or at least some of the requested information. About three-quarters of all requests are granted in full and another fifth are granted in part. Numerically, then, total rejection of requests is extremely rare. However, the 5 per cent of cases where requests are totally rejected include an over-representation of cases where the information requested appears to be politically sensitive.[7]

Access to Judicial Review

There has also been a general streamlining of the procedures for seeking judicial review of administrative decisions. In three jurisdictions (Commonwealth, Australia Capital Territory and Queensland), there has been a comprehensive overhaul of the procedures for seeking judicial review which is designed to avert many of the technical obstacles that once faced litigants. In a fourth jurisdiction (Victoria), the reforms were less comprehensive. Yet like the more comprehensive reforms, they have provided people directly affected by administrative decisions with a right to require reasons for those decisions. People requesting reasons need not follow any particular format and are not required to pay any fee. The relevant Acts therefore provide one of the best bargains in contemporary administrative law (apart from the ombudsman, whose services are also free). In two other jurisdictions (New South Wales (NSW) and South Australia), the procedures for seeking orders in the nature of the prerogative writs have been relaxed through changes in the relevant Supreme Court Rules. In neither, however, is there provision for a general right to reasons.

Subordinate Law-Making

Finally, in three states (NSW, Victoria and Queensland), the rules with respect to the making of delegated legislation have been tightened so as to institutionalise procedures whereby interested parties can learn of, and make submissions in relation to, proposed subordinate legislation. Bills for similar Commonwealth legislation have been introduced but have not yet been passed.

THE PARADOX OF STATUTORY ADMINISTRATIVE LAW

The last 20 years have therefore seen a considerable strengthening of statutory administrative law. In one sense, these developments should come as no surprise. They have their counterparts in other jurisdictions. However, they seem to contrast in some respects with what one would expect, given much of the gloomy rhetoric which surfaces in many discussions of executive power. For in the expansion of Australian administrative law, we apparently have a case of executive-dominated legislatures being willing to pass legislation whose effect is apparently to curb the power of the executive. An understanding of the reasons for this apparent paradox may help throw light on the more general question of the circumstances in which sometimes unethical governments might come to introduce measures to improve the ethical quality of public decision-making. It also suggests a sometimes underestimated degree of commitment on the part of hardened politicians to ideals which are not necessarily to their political advantage.

There are several explanations for this willingness. First, there are good reasons why a politically astute government should favour relatively powerful administrative review procedures. Effective review procedures can deflect responsibility for administrative error from government to more junior administrators. They can channel discontent so as to increase the likelihood of those who are upset by government decisions blaming administrators and review bodies rather than the government. They may reduce the degree to which aggrieved citizens complain to the minister. Insofar as they yield improved administration, they help ministers solve the perennial problem of how to appease an electorate which wants better services and lower taxes.

The attractiveness of effective review procedures obviously diminishes when the object of review is a relatively senior administrator's decision or where review extends to ministerial or government decisions. Consistent with this is the fact that the most widely adopted review institution is the ombudsman, an institution ideally suited to the handling of minor grievances and the arrangements which give rise to those grievances.[8] Similarly, the degree to which FOI legislation facilitates access to information tends to be inversely related to the value to the government of concealment of that information. However, in jurisdictions with relatively developed administrative review procedures, the procedures also have the potential to embarrass government. Why, then, do governments submit themselves to such systems?

One answer is that politicians are less unprincipled than their public reputation might suggest. Politicians can take pride in 'making things better'. The establishment of the Commonwealth AAT can be understood in terms of the general reformism of the 1972–75 Whitlam government (De Maria, 1992).[9] Malcolm Fraser saw the New Administrative Law as one of the major achievements of his 1975–83 Liberal-National government.[10] The 1982–90 Cain government's reforms reflected its generally reformist ideology and the Queensland reforms appear to be very much a product of the Goss government's concern to demonstrate its moral superiority to its defeated predecessor.[11]

Moreover, even unprincipled politicians may wish to appear principled; it is likely to be politically advantageous.[12] And while the public at large is likely to be relatively indifferent to the question of how administrative review procedures should be reformed, the advocates of reform can be influential. The media have an obvious interest in generous FOI legislation; lawyers constitute a powerful constituency in favour of strong review institutions; and, once established, the institutions themselves can become powerful advocates on their own behalf.

Strong administrative review procedures can also appeal to politicians for opportunistic reasons. The very fact that governments can sometimes be embarrassed by administrative review and FOI makes such procedures all the more attractive to oppositions. Oppositions are not, of course, in a position to implement such measures but they can advocate them. They may even be tempted to promise them in their election manifestoes. Moreover, they may enter government, confident that, unlike their predecessors, they will have nothing to be ashamed of, and therefore no reason to fear, open and responsible government. Inspired by a mixture of genuine reforming zeal, disinterestedness and delusion, they may proceed to implement measures which, in the long run, they may come to regret. However, by that stage, their commitment to strong review processes may be once more strengthened by the thought that it will soon be their successors who will be bearing the costs of greater openness and accountability. In any case, the realities of contemporary Australian politics are such that effective review procedures will normally be hard to repeal, once established. Minority parties, being permanently in opposition, have a vested interest in anything which can embarrass any government. Moreover, attempts to repeal effective review procedures are likely to be presented as evidence of the sinister motives of the government and may well prove more costly than the adverse effects of the relevant review procedures.

Strengthened review procedures also survive because, on the whole, they rarely embarrass governments. They are targeted at errors by administrators rather than errors by ministers; at the rectification of particular grievances rather than at government policy; and at providing access to personally relevant information rather than information which might seriously embarrass the government. Moreover, when, as is sometimes the case, review procedures yield results which seriously threaten government policy, governments are not resourceless. In such cases, they can amend the law to limit the effect of the decision in question and examples of their willingness to do so abound, especially in the areas of Social Security, Veteran's Benefits and Immigration (Carney, 1989, p 128; Creyke, 1992; Gallaghan, 1992; Rodgers and Short, 1992; and Vrachnas, 1992).

JUDICIAL ADMINISTRATIVE LAW

Courts are sometimes seen as the counterbalance to over-mighty executives, especially by judges (Mason, 1989, p 26).[13] There are good reasons why courts might be expected to perform this role. Courts do not have a stake in the outcome of administrative law litigation. While governments may be financially or morally embarrassed by a discrepancy between their behaviour and the law, courts will simply see this as an appropriate occasion for judicial intervention. Moreover, role perceptions and effective independence will mean that courts will intervene in such cases and feel free to do so. However, the norms which legitimate the exercise of judicial review also constrain it, to the point where it is arguable that the fundamental principle of judicial review is a doctrine of deference, tempered by mild individualism and a relatively keen concern for honesty.

General Principles of 'Judicial' Administrative Law

The basic principle of Australian administrative law is that decision-makers may do only that which they are permitted to do and that they may normally make their decisions only according to prescribed procedures. The courts have fleshed out these rules so that, in the absence of express provisions to the contrary, grants of power are treated as subject to a range of implied conditions. Powers are presumed not to allow decision-makers to make material errors of law. Repositories of discretions are assumed to be under an obligation to consider the particular merits of each case and not to apply policy mindlessly, regardless of its appropriateness in particular cases. Nor should they act at the dictation of others. (Both Miller, Chapter 3, and Dubnick, Chapter 5, address the issue of discretion and its power.) Powers must be exercised for the purposes for which they are conferred and not for ulterior purposes. Powers may not be exercised in a manner so unreasonable that no reasonable decision-maker acting according to law could have made the decision in question. The procedure for making decisions must be fair and it must normally involve full compliance with any prescribed procedures. The decision-maker must take account of all relevant considerations and may not take account of irrelevant considerations. Decisions made in contravention of these requirements are legal nullities, except where legislation treats the social fact of a purported decision's having been made as being of legal relevance.

Over the past 30 years, Australian courts have broadened the circumstances in which decisions may be reviewed so that there are no decision-makers or classes of decision-maker whose decisions are immune from being reviewed on the grounds of excess of powers or procedural irregularities.[14] The rules relating to procedural fairness have been refined so that the right to procedural fairness is no longer artificially confined to cases where rights (as opposed to other interests) are at stake nor to decisions by particular bodies (see Finkelstein, 1996). The government's right to object to the discovery or admission of particular kinds of evidence has been limited so that the government no longer possesses an absolute right to object to the admission of evidence, nor even a right to preclude the admissibility of evidence by certifying that it belongs to a particular category of protected material (eg *Sankey v Whitlam* (1978) 142 CLR 1). The standing rules have been broadened so that judicial review can be sought by interest groups as well as by people directly affected by the decision in question.[15]

On the whole, these innovative developments reflect a more general shift from categorical to principled reasoning. However, in the typical case, this development may well be of aesthetic rather than substantive significance. The reasons which underlay the old category-based rules still tend to be treated as being salient and decisions which might once have been justified by reference to categories are currently likely to be similar in substance but justified by reference to the rationales which underlay the old categorical distinctions.[16] Moreover, the striking developments of the last 30 years can easily conceal from the casual observer the sizeable number of cases in which the High Court turned down opportunities to expand the scope of judicial review.[17]

Nonetheless, the broad range of review grounds might seem to imply that courts are in a position to exercise a stranglehold over administrative behaviour. However, there is an obverse to these general principles: the doctrine of *intra vires* which states that as long as administrators act according to prescribed procedures and do not make errors of law, they can do more or less as they like. The breadth of judicial deference is indicated by a number of important rules.

Deference

First, the courts have traditionally afforded administrators an almost unlimited freedom when it comes to making findings of fact. So long as prescribed procedures have been complied with, findings of fact are almost review-proof. This may be the case even if there are logical flaws in the process which led to the finding of fact.[18]

Secondly, administrative law has tended to accept that 'political' decisions are subject to far more relaxed standards than administrative decisions.[19] The degree to which this is the case has, to some extent, been concealed by a series of decisions which have affirmed the potential reviewability of almost any decision. However, the gradual retreat from the position that there are non-reviewable decisions has been accompanied by a series of doctrinally superior but functionally similar approaches to political decisions. One involves the recognition that even if decisions are in theory reviewable, the discretion in relation to their making will be so broad that it will be almost impossible for anyone to be able to demonstrate that the discretion has not been exercised lawfully (see *Church of Scientology v Woodward* (1982) 154 CLR 25). A second has involved treating political decisions as largely exempt from the procedural fairness requirements.[20]

Thirdly, administrative law is sometimes willing to entertain a 'reasonable expectations' doctrine in relation to administrative decision-makers. According to this doctrine, administrative acts are to be evaluated on the basis of less exacting standards than those which might be appropriate if the decision was to be made by, say, a court.[21] The rhetoric of this sentiment is not always reflected in decisions in particular cases and is clearly a source of considerable unease to some judges. Some judges are clearly unhappy about the fact that the less exacting standards inherent in bureaucratic decision-making mean that decisions of considerable importance to individuals are based on a less thorough canvassing of all relevant evidence than would be the case if the matter were to be handled by a court.[22]

Fourthly, courts almost never claim the right to make a final administrative decision in a case where the administrator possesses a discretion. In procedural irregularity cases, the matter must simply be reconsidered and there is no guarantee that procedural regularity will mean a different decision. Even where there has been an error of law, the court will normally order reconsideration according to law rather than the making of a particular decision. Only where a court's finding means that there is only one course open to the decision-maker will the courts make a declaration that the applicant has a right to a particular outcome.

Whether one should highlight activism or deference must ultimately be a matter of judgment and will depend on the point one is trying to make and the audience to whom one is trying to make it. To those who attend too thoughtlessly to judicial rhetoric about the degree to which only the judiciary stands between Australians and tyranny, the degree of judicial deference may come as something of a surprise, just as it would to those whose images of administrative law had been formed on the basis of the contributions of Walsh or Woodward (Walsh, 1989; Woodward, 1994). To many judges and administrative lawyers, my observations may well seem banal and platitudinous. Since those covered by the last sentence have no doubt become impatient and moved on to more promising contributions, it is appropriate to address those who might be surprised and to ask: what determines why judges are as deferential/active as they are?

ADMINISTRATIVE LAW VALUES

Being both statutory and judge-made, the values of administrative law reflect its diverse origins. The political origins of much administrative law mean that administrative law will be characterised by a degree of tension between the interests shared by particular governments at particular times: the interests of governments in general and the values by which governments legitimise themselves and mobilise support. Its judicial origins mean that its values will reflect the tension between the judicial duty to leave administration to the administrators and the duty to intervene when administrators err in law. There is also the pull between the collectivism implicit in modern administration and the powerful judicial urge to treat each case as unique. Administrative law values are also likely to vary across review institutions, given the varied powers and duties of different institutions and the different backgrounds from which different reviewers are characteristically recruited. That said, it is only possible to make some generalisations about administrative law values. A convenient basis for organising these generalisations is provided by those values outlined by Tom Sherman (see Chapter 1).

Economy and Efficiency

These are not among the most highly articulated of administrative law values. However, there are nonetheless several respects in which administrative law may subtly advance those values. Once one recognises that the achievement of values other than efficiency needs to be taken into account in assessing the efficiency of particular arrangements, it becomes apparent that a reasonable case can be made for the proposition that Australia's administrative law institutions are at least moderately efficient. The ombudsman disposes of a large number of cases expeditiously and economically. The tribunals also score reasonably well on this criterion. Moreover, an accessible review system means that an otherwise unacceptable error rate among primary decision-makers becomes tolerable. This in turn means that primary decision-making procedures can be streamlined, with review serving both as an error-correction and a quality control process.

Judicial review is harder to reconcile with efficiency and even apologists for the courts would rarely list their contribution to efficiency as among their virtues. However, this reticence may be misplaced. While judicial decision-making can prove appallingly expensive, the expense needs to be interpreted in the light of the broader ramifications of judicial decisions. In one sense, litigants are providing a public good: the clarification of law and, in relation to the numbers potentially affected, the value of this may be considerable. Moreover, as interstitial law-makers, courts are considerably more efficient than parliaments. Courts also contribute to efficiency in relatively unpublicised ways. Occasionally, this occurs by their willingness to take efficiency considerations into account in their decision-making but, much more importantly, it arises by leaving administrators alone to make decisions according to their criteria of efficiency.

Respect for Persons

Such respect is implicit in both the structure of the review institutions and the individualistic thread which runs through administrative law. The institution of the ombudsman provides a means whereby those aggrieved simply at the behaviour of administrators can communicate their grievances and a means whereby pressure can be placed on departments to rectify systemic lack of respect for departmental clients. Some tribunals have an excellent reputation for going out of their way to assist appellants present their cases and the relevant law seeks to encourage this. However, respect for persons can conflict with some aspects of efficiency. Attempts to simplify decision-making processes and to make decisions more review-proof appear to be resulting in a shift towards confined discretions, with a consequent reduction in the degree to which decision-makers can take account of the unique circumstances of particular people. A paradoxical effect of enhanced reviewability can be legislative attempts to curtail administrative and thereby reviewer discretions.

Impartiality, Neutrality and Respect for Law

These three values are central to administrative law. Moreover, they values lie at the heart of judicial administrative law. Administrative law's commitment to impartiality and neutrality is reflected in its (problematic?) assumption that decisions can be objectively classed as 'correct or preferable' and in the expectation that decision-makers be unbiased, except in political contexts. Insistence on respect for law is fundamental to administrative law and while statutory ouster clauses occasionally purport to exempt decision-makers from review on the basis of error of law, administrative law's commitment to law is such that these are read down in such a way as to severely circumscribe their scope.

Responsiveness and Accountability

At first sight, responsiveness and accountability would appear to be fundamental administrative law values, with responsiveness being encouraged by institutions which encourage and facilitate accountability. However, modern administrative law still pays considerable respect to the traditional theory of responsible government, especially in those situations in which it is realistic to treat governments as politically responsible. Both statutory and judicial administrative law afford considerable respect to ministers and to 'political' decisions. In these areas, the role of administrative law is, at most, to facilitate the operation of political threats and sanctions by making administrative behaviour more visible and therefore slightly more likely to incur sanctions in the event of its being unwarranted. The accountability of lower level administrators is achieved by more direct intervention. The accessibility, powers and role of the ombudsman make that official particularly important in this respect and help ensure that administrators are accountable for the overall merits of their decisions. The review tribunals contribute less dramatically to this goal, insofar as their role is not so much to review decision-making processes as to determine the correct decision, given the material before *them*.[23] The courts' role is confined to requiring accountability for the procedures and legality of decisions. It is an important role but not a central one unless administrators would, but for the prospect of judicial review, be disinclined to take law seriously.

Honesty and Integrity

The values most deeply embedded in administrative law are, arguably, honesty and integrity. First, the concern of courts with legality requires that government-legislators be honest. The role of the courts as authoritative interpreters of statutes means that governments must take care when making laws. They must seriously address possible contingencies. They cannot bury political disagreements in ambiguous language. They cannot interfere with basic rights without making their intentions clear. If they do, they will find that they have lost control over the legislation to the courts. The threat of judicial review provides an incentive to legislators to make their meanings clear. It increases the likelihood that legislation will be drafted in such a way as to increase the likelihood that the same interpretation is placed on it by governments, by parliament and by those who might be affected by it.

Honesty is also encouraged by the courts' increasing willingness to attach legal implications to government undertakings. While courts have stopped short of binding governments to exercise discretions in accordance with prior substantive undertakings,[24] they have increasingly treated undertakings as giving rise to legitimate expectations that administrators will act in accordance with those undertakings. Legitimate expectations are not enforceable *per se* but they can give rise to an entitlement to procedural fairness that might otherwise not exist.[25] The undertakings may take the form of public statements. More recently, in *Teoh*, the High Court treated the ratification of international conventions as giving rise to a legitimate expectation that governments would act in accordance with those conventions.[26]

This insistence is at variance with the values of much contemporary political discourse. It complicates life for governments which operate in a climate in which honesty is easily dismissed as evidence of political naïveté and is likely to complicate life for governments which face demands which cannot be met from sullen electorates. However, dishonesty is at best a short-term solution to these problems. In the medium term, it is corrosive of political authority and likely to create increased sullenness, both by virtue of the contribution of civic dishonesty to mistrust and unrealistic expectations and by virtue of dishonesty being chosen in preference to the more demanding (but ultimately essential) task of convincing the electorate of the rightness of those hard choices which the electorate is expected to bear. Statutory administrative law reflects the political system's awareness that honesty is an important value; judicial administrative law rewards legislative honesty and punishes legislative fudging. Perhaps the greatest contribution administrative law is making to the modern state lies in the small but important contribution it is struggling to make to the kind of political culture needed to legitimate that state.

CONCLUSION

One could conclude on this congratulatory note, recognising the degree to which Australian administrative law, for example, is committed to the core values which one would expect of good administrators and a good administration. However, one should do so only after sounding a note of caution.

First, a minor quibble: whatever the values of administrative law, administrative law will not necessarily contribute to their achievement. Review institutions, like administrators, will make mistakes and these may produce cynicism among administrators as well as the public. The rate at which decisions are reversed at successive stages of the review process and inconsistency between tribunals may encourage a view that administrative law is, in the end, a lottery rather than a guide to sound practice. The available evidence suggests that reviewer error is not a major problem. Senior administrators generally value the contribution of administrative law to good administration (eg Conybeare, 1991, p 70; Curtis, 1989, p 65; Sassella, 1989, p 122; and Volker, 1989, p 112). However, this enthusiasm is not unanimous (see in particular Walsh, 1989; and Woodward, 1994) and we know little of how junior administrators regard the review process.

Secondly, assuming that administration is the better for its review institutions, it is also necessary to place administrative law in perspective. While the various review agencies handle a large number of cases, it is also apparent that it is rare for Australians to have any dealings with any review agency. The Commonwealth Ombudsman handles about 18,000 complaints a year (Commonwealth Ombudsman, 1995, Appendix A). The specialist tribunals process about 20,000 applications (Department of Social Security, 1995, p 340; Immigration Review Tribunal, 1995, pp 3–10; and Repatriation Commission and the Department of Veterans' Affairs, 1995, p 52). The AAT's case load is about 6,000 cases a year (Administrative Appeals Tribunal (Australia)), 1995, pp 109–21) and there were 343 judicial review applications lodged with the Federal Court in 1995 (Administrative Review Council, 1996, p 102). At least half the cases handled by the tribunals and the Federal Court result in pro-government outcomes and, as noted, many of the pro-citizen outcomes are not attributable to faulty decision-making. By these measures, administrative law is marginal to Australian administration. If the small number of successful challenges is because occasions for such challenges rarely arise, this highlights the importance of other processes as determinants of ethical behaviour among administrators. If it is because most aggrieved people are unaware of, or cannot be bothered seeking, review, this would mean that errant administrators could normally assume that they need not worry about possible review.

Administrators do worry. Departments' annual reports include references to how decisions have fared at the hands of reviewers and senior administrators and administrative lawyers believe the bureaucracy has been responsive to administrative law (see Allars, 1991, p 57; Conybeare, 1991; Curtis, 1989; Griffiths, 1989, p 34; Pidgeon, 1992; Sassella, 1989; and Volker, 1989).[27] However, this responsiveness arguably reflects a real commitment on the part of administrators to the values embodied in administrative law rather than a narrow concern with avoiding the exposure of one's errors. Adherence to administrative law values may therefore measure an administration's commitment to good administration rather than explaining it.

NOTES

1   However, executive rule-making is conventionally regarded as falling within the province of administrative law.

2   However, the law relating to the judicial review of administrative behaviour has its origins in the law developed by 'Superior' courts to review the behaviour of 'inferior' courts.

3   Belief in responsible government as descriptive may have delayed reform to the administrative review process.

4   For example, the Social Security Appeals Tribunal has been given the power to make binding as distinct from merely recommendatory decisions. The AAT now has the power to make binding decisions in criminal deportation cases. In the migration area, the establishment of the Immigration Review Tribunal and the Refugee Review Tribunal means that decisions in these controversial areas are now subject to independent external review on the merits of the case.

5   For an emphatic statement, see De Maria (1992). For a review of the relevant literature, see Douglas and Jones (1996) pp 189–94.

6   For details, see, for example, Cossins (1996). The variations are generally subtle and are probably less important than administrative practices.

7   For Commonwealth figures, see Attorney-General (Australia) (1995), and previous Annual Reports.

8   The value to governments of ombudsmen seems so self-evident that it seems odd that it was not until the 1970s that the institution came to be adopted in Australia. It also seems odd that the current Commonwealth government should be planning major cuts to its staffing levels.

9   Reforms included the ending of conscription, sharp tariff cuts, initiatives to encourage community-based decision-making in the area of welfare, the strengthening of anti-monopoly and consumer protection laws and a no-fault divorce law.

10   While regarded at the time as a 'right-wing' government, it is more accurate to describe it as conservative. It was content to leave many of the preceding Whitlam Labor government reforms in place and it even developed some of them. It cut back the rate of expansion of the government sector and dithered over health policy. However, it did not pursue the kind of agenda later carried out by the Thatcher and Reagan governments.

11   These reforms included the *Freedom of Information Act* 1992, the *Judicial Review Act* 1991 to facilitate review of government decisions and the establishment of a Criminal Justice Commission (via the *Criminal Justice Commission Act* 1989) to tackle the problem of corruption.

12   Alan Rosenthal discusses the importance of appearance in political life in Rosenthal (1998). Kim, ch 7, notes the link between campaigns and promises of ethics and reform campaigns.

13   For the perspective from the executive, see Walsh (1989) p 29.

14   See, for example, *R v Toohey; Ex parte Northern Land Council* (1981) 151 CLR 170; and *Church of Scientology v Woodward* (1982) 154 CLR 25.

15   In 1980, the High Court affirmed a relatively traditional view of the standing rules: *Australian Conservation Foundation (ACF) v Commonwealth* (1980) 146 CLR 493. However, the Federal Court has subsequently taken a far more liberal approach to this issue: *Ogle v Strickland* (1987) 71 ALR 41; *Australian Conservation Foundation v Minister for Resources* (1989) 76 LGRA 200; *North Coast Environmental Council Inc v Minister for Resources* (1994) 127 ALR 617; compare *Right to Life Association Inc v Secretary, Department of Human Services and Health* (1994) 128 ALR 238.

16   For instance, while the Church of Scientology crossed the reviewability barrier, given the generous construction placed by the High Court on the powers of ASIO, it failed to establish that ASIO had exceeded its powers (*Church of Scientology v Woodward* (1982) 154 CLR 25). In 1989, the Australian Conservation Foundation at last succeeded in establishing that it had standing to seek review of a decision with environmental implications only to lose the legal argument surrounding the legality of the Minister's behaviour (*Australian Conservation Foundation v Minister for Resources* (1989) 76 LGRA 200).

17   For example, *ACF v Commonwealth* (1980) 146 CLR 493; *Public Service Board of NSW v Osmond* (1986) 159 CLR 656 (no common law right to reasons for a decision); *South Australia v O'Shea* (1987) 163 CLR 378 (a relatively deferential approach to Cabinet decision-making); *Australian Broadcasting Tribunal v Bond* (1990) 170 CLR 321 (limited scope for judicial review); and *Attorney-General (NSW) v Quin* (1990) 170 CLR 1 (limited remedies for breach of natural justice).

18   For example, *Australian Broadcasting Tribunal v Bond* (1990) 170 CLR 321 at 355–358 per Mason CJ (with whom Brennan J agreed); cf at 367 per Deane J .

19   See, for example, *South Australia v O'Shea* (1987) 163 CLR 378 at 401 per Wilson and Toohey JJ.

20   See, for example, *Peninsula Anglican Boys' School v Ryan* (1985) 69 ALR 555; and *Minister for Arts, Heritage and Environment v Peko-Wallsend Ltd* (1987) 75 ALR 218.

21   For a strong statement to this effect, see *MIEA v Wu Shiang Lang* (1996) 70 ALJR 568 at 575–576 per Brennan CJ, Toohey, McHugh, Gummow JJ, at 586–588 per Kirby J.

22   This unhappiness emerges most strikingly in the migration area, where the clash between judicial and executive standards has been reflected in legislative attempts to curb the reviewability of migrations decisions on the grounds of denial of natural justice.

23   New material appears to be the main reason why review tribunals set aside earlier decisions. In 1994–95, the Department of Immigration and Ethnic Affairs considered that 59% of successful appeals from Internal Review Officers to the Immigration Review Tribunal were a result of new material having been presented. Only about a fifth were regarded as attributable to errors by the primary decision-maker. Department of Immigration and Ethnic Affairs (Australia) (1995).

24   *Minister for Immigration, Local Government and Ethnic Affairs v Kurtovic* (1990) 92 ALR 93.

25   See *Haoucher v Minister for Immigration* (1990) 169 CLR 648; *Minister for Immigration and Ethnic Affairs v Teoh* (1995) 183 CLR 273.

26   *Minister for Immigration and Ethnic Affairs v Teoh* (1995) 183 CLR 273. The government's subsequent response to *Teoh* (see Douglas and Jones (1996) pp 499–500) indicates that, in a paradoxical sense, administrative law has contributed to honesty. The government has frankly acknowledged that ratification of an international instrument does not necessarily mean that the government intends this to alter anyone's legal position.

27   Disney, however, notes that respect for administrative law is not always such as to produce changes to manuals following authoritative tribunal decisions (Disney, 1992). Also see Carney (1989).

11

PUBLIC SECTOR MANAGERS, PUBLIC SECTOR WORKERS AND ETHICS: A Trade Union Perspective

Adrienne Taylor and Mike Waghorne

INTRODUCTION

Many of us think that we could manage wherever we work better than those who currently do. There is nothing new about that. Of recent years, there has been an alternative myth: only managers count; the only ideas come from management; the way to make progress, however we measure it, is to give incentives to managers. 'Incentives', of course, usually mean money, although the management gurus who promote the new managerialism rarely think that offering a bit more money to ordinary workers might also raise motivation and productivity.

Because of concerns about the new commercialised public sector developing in many countries (Lawton, Chapter 4, discusses the pros and cons of utilising business practices in the public sector), the 1993 Public Services International (PSI) World Congress in Helsinki decided to call for the development of a managerial code of ethics. Our affiliates, public sector trade unions in some 129 countries, perceived a lack of organised and accepted standards to guide public sector managers. Politicians are often asking managers to work in what had almost become an amoral sphere. Such politicians are so keen on 'de-inventing' government that they simultaneously both absolve themselves of any responsibility and accountability for public services and instruct public sector case-load managers to act as if they are running a hamburger operation. It is interesting to note that in the best-seller book on entrepreneurial government, *Reinventing Government*, there is not a single reference to ethics (Osborne and Gaebler, 1993). Part of the concern was also that managers have to satisfy many legal and ethical requirements with regard to money and labour legislation, for example, but lack recognised principles, based on the ethos of the public service, to guide them in other public sector responsibilities.

When the PSI Managerial Staff Working Group started work on this issue, it quickly decided that approaching this task with a narrowly legalistic 'codification' approach might result in the language being patronising and petty. It therefore decided to look at the issues in a way which could encourage public sector trade unions and public sector managers to revise the reciprocal relationships which exist between managers and public sector workers. The real challenge is to promote positive approaches to the development of effective, efficient and fair public services. This approach could allow all of the parties involved — workers, managers, service users, taxpayers and politicians — to ensure that their legitimate interests and values were taken into account in the variety of duties, responsibilities and accountabilities of public sector managers.

BACKGROUND

Are public sector managers political opportunists who will do anything the politicians ask them to or just another group of public sector workers who happen to be at the top of the hierarchy? Neither, of course, is true of the group as a whole and there are other equally false stereotypes in between the extremes. Managers are subject to competing loyalties and pressures and respond as individuals to them — some well, some poorly.

In particular, the managerial responsibilities they have to both service users and public sector workers are poorly specified, as are their responsibilities to the political decision-makers who normally set financial or political targets. There seems every likelihood that the internationally growing practice of putting most senior managers on temporary contracts will continue, implying a succession of people who may not be familiar with the public service. A recognised code would help public sector workers and managers and their trade unions to get public acceptance of agreed good public sector managerial practice. The reason for focusing on managerial staff in this chapter is not because they are perceived to be more unethical but because of their key leadership role.[1] Many managerial staff are new to the public sector ethos and may need guidance in the many ethical considerations unique to the public sector. The Institute for Public Policy Research in the United Kingdom put it thus:

> The public service is fundamentally different (from the private sector) and cannot be reformed simply by reference to market forces … As it stands consumerism is an inadequate theoretical basis for the role of public services, failing as it does, to take account of the public interest and the need in a democracy for public accountability. (IPMS, 1996, p 20)

It is interesting to note that ethical issues and codes of conduct for public servants are reported by approximately half of OECD countries as an area of increasing importance in recent years. The reasons for this increased concern include the need for articulation of key values and standards given devolved decision-making and management and fear of corruption connected with public tasks being performed by contractors (OECD, 1996b).

Some politicians fail to understand public sector ethical issues and try to prevail on staff or managers to behave in ways which a succession of recent 'scandals' in a number of countries have shown to be out of kilter with what the public expects from a public service.[2]

Both the *content and enforceability* of such a managerial code of ethics are important. The affiliated unions of PSI often cover senior managers among their membership. In itself, this is a contentious issue for some PSI affiliates; there are some which welcome managers as members and others which exclude them. Among those affiliates with managerial members, there are some which treat them as part of the union membership in the ministry or department concerned; others which create a specific 'branch' or section for them as a group; and others which service them as individuals on individual contracts.

Members or not, there are many public sector managers who are both loyal to trade union principles and committed to the philosophies which underpin an effective, accountable and equitable public sector. Many unions also make special provision for determining how managerial staff should act if the union calls for strike activity, either exempting them or allowing for some skeleton coverage of work. This is not always easy in situations of life, death or public safety.

> The limitations which many governments place upon managerial unionism are based on assumptions which, although not entirely without foundation, are generally incorrect. Managers can handle the conflicts inherent in being both union members and employer representatives. Managerial unionism rarely leads to a significant change in the balance of power between employers and unions. Politicians and public sector employers who appoint managers who are not capable of or willing to act in this mature manner are clearly not appointing the most skilled people to these positions. From the trade union perspective, an exemplary senior civil servant is an important strategic resource for both the working conditions of all members of her/his trade union and the efficiency and productivity of public services. It is important to identify the special needs and interests of senior public servants. Trade unions must then safeguard their interests. (Kassalow, 1993, p 123)

IDEAS FOR A CODE

The role, responsibility, powers and status of senior public servants must be clearly specified. This would help with the independent shouldering of responsibility while also ensuring integrity and real responsibility for a given activity. Trade unions and employers must actively use the professional knowledge and experience of senior public servants both in the context of the strategic work of public service leadership and in trade union work.

Special attention must be paid to the working conditions and work environment of senior public servants, including their place in the organisation, their responsibilities and powers, their role *vis à vis* politicians, job security and working time. Working time is especially important because if these expectations are unrealistic, they can have consequential effects on the expectations about the hours and conditions of those they supervise, one of the reasons behind the absence of women in the higher leadership levels.[3] The ethical requirement of the public service to be a good employer should not be tossed out as commercialism enters the public sector.

Many professionals in the public services are already bound by codes of conduct, regulated by statutory or voluntary professional bodies. Public sector workers assume that managers conform to such codes which are also pro-worker and pro-union and they support managers who promote or act in accordance with such a code but who are victimised by political leaders for so doing. The integrity and professional knowledge of leading public servants must be expected, respected and safeguarded. This is particularly important for public servants at the head of administrative authorities.

It is deplorable that many professionals are increasingly experiencing ethical conflict between provisions in their professional codes of conduct and those in their employment contracts. Senior staff are or may feel pressured to show loyalty only to their employer to the exclusion of professional standards and the needs of both service users and staff.[4]

These dilemmas arise from a free-market culture. In some cases, there are specific 'gagging' clauses in contracts of employment which attempt to ensure that conscientious employees do not discredit 'hard business' attitudes and the 'rational' bottom-line administration of resources which can detrimentally affect standards of care or service.

PSI and its affiliates would wish (alongside managers and employers) to develop codes of conduct appropriate to a public sector culture or even to a specific service/agency. Such codes should respect the validity of all the loyalty relationships mentioned above. It is essential that staff can trust that their management appreciates and is free to respect such loyalties.

PUBLIC SECTOR VALUES

PSI believes that trade unions, managers and employers should incorporate the following values in the provision of public services.

- The need for the public service to be and to be seen to be politically neutral, a matter of law in some countries. Such neutrality applies not only during the 'life' of an elected administration but also during election periods and after the defeat of an administration. It is accepted in many countries that the civil service will give appropriate briefings to the officially recognised parliamentary opposition.
- Respect for human individuality, dignity and privacy of both service users and workers
- The right of a user or worker to the information held by the service on them
- The right of a user to all relevant information needed for them to make decisions in the case concerned
- Encouragement for users to make choices suited to their own needs or wishes

- The choice of options and solutions, in the social services especially, which will maximise and speed (a return to) independence and responsibility for service users or clients
- Service, treatment or care which is safe, impartial and fair for both the workers and the users
- Equity in service policy and delivery for workers and users. This would include factors which are the subject of national and international anti-discrimination laws or conventions (such as but not limited to gender, ethnic identity, age, sexual orientation or sexuality, health status/capacity, religious or political belief etc). Such an anti-discriminatory approach is not merely a formal avoidance of fault but an active commitment by public sector managers to promote equality and equity, thoroughly permeating recruitment, appointment, promotion and public information and access procedures.
- The establishment of salaries and working conditions based on free and fair collective bargaining between the employer and the trade union(s) representing the workers (Public Services International, 1994, p 1).

Public sector trade unions and their members are concerned about and committed to efficiency. It is unacceptable to make public sector workers the victims of the inefficiencies of managers or the employer. Trade unions have a vested interest in promoting our vision of the role of managers and the conduct of the public service; we *want* to argue for our ideas with the politicians and the managers. Naturally, we would therefore welcome and expect dialogue between workers' representatives and management to seek means for achieving the most effective and efficient service delivery.

In this regard, there is a matter of honesty and integrity which is a particular bane of public sector workers: privatisation, contracting out and the like. It is not the concept which is contested so much by trade unions, since that depends on ideology. Rather, it is the fact that many politicians and senior policy advisers promote such policies on the basis of free competition and a level playing field but promptly prohibit in-house bids or shackle the ability of public sector providers to compete on a level playing field with outside contractors. That is unethical. The question of truly open competition between the public and private sectors with all costs and benefits, external and internal being considered, is a matter which have taken up, with some sympathy, by PSI (through the Trade Union Advisory Committee) with the Public Management Committee of the OECD (OECD Public Management Committee, 1996, item 2.5).

PSI is not interested in ethical codes/lists which stress the obvious or are rule-based regimes which discourage ethical thinking. It is assumed that 'normal' ethical principles which are applicable to all sectors apply to the public sector workers: they should act (and be seen to act) in such a manner that they do not use their position to further any scheme or project or contract in which they have a personal interest. This includes the refusal to accept all benefits, rewards, inducements or other incentives from those involved in or seeking such schemes, projects or contracts. In a manner appropriate to the service concerned, many legal systems require managers to declare any of their assets, liabilities or interests (including secondary employment) relating to any matter under their control or influence.

PSI hears stories of managers who have been in charge of a contracting-out or asset sale proposal who leave their office on a Friday and who reappear on Monday as the director or chief executive of the successful contractor or as the owner of the new operation which they have taken over in a management buy-out. That should not be possible in an ethical organisation and there are jurisdictions where there is a legal requirement to separate the roles of those who manage the tendering/contracting operation and those who currently manage the service.

As market-oriented management encourages public officials to emulate private sector ways of doing business, the question arises as to whether public sector managers should be given a free hand to operate in the same way as their private sector counterparts; for example, offering gifts or hospitality is often normal practice in the private sector but is often disapproved of in the public sector. It is also worth noting that, while most nations have laws which say that it is illegal for anyone to try to bribe public servants in their own country, a large number of countries do not make it illegal to bribe the public servants of *another* country. Indeed, it is perfectly legal in Germany and some other OECD countries to deduct such bribes as business expenses for tax purposes! The OECD has now started work on efforts to eradicate this but it is an interesting commentary on the need for an internationally accepted agreement on a code of ethics/practice for all public services (OECD Public Management Committee, 1996). It is also noteworthy that the OECD's Development Assistance guidelines refer explicitly to the need to eradicate corruption etc in the countries being assisted by OECD member states (OECD Development Assistance Committee, 1993, pp 18–19). It is clearly possible to have such international principles.[5] In a word, the demand is for transparency.

Consistent with normally accepted principles and with modern demands for more open government, good managers should aim to provide as open and free an information system as is possible for use by politicians, workers, users and the community. Public sector workers should ensure that such systems are used in the manner intended. A PSI British affiliate, the Institution of Professionals, Managers and Specialists, has summarised this need for accountability, transparency and openness.

> Citizens are not simply customers. It is their right to be treated fairly and impartially as well as to be provided with decent levels of service; and they may wish to register a view about the criteria lying behind those services. The roles of the various bodies involved in the development of government policy and its execution, and the links between them, must be transparent and clearly accountable to Parliament and the public, both as citizens and customers of public services. (IPMS, 1996, p 54)

Whistleblowing

Many public sector workers and their trade unions have pursued a policy of promoting 'whistleblowing' legislation. This allows a worker or manager, where they suspect wrong-doing, to take appropriate steps internally. If management unreasonably ignores this internal approach,[6] the worker may bring to public notice any matters which are an infringement of law, public morality, the public interest, the political neutrality of the public service or other relevant matters. PSI and its affiliates would expect a manager to act in a manner to facilitate any such internal complaints. Managers should also defend any staff member who had complied with such internal procedures but had then been unreasonably ignored. In turn, public sector trade unions can assist a manager who, in attempting to respect any such approach, was penalised by politicians.

In respecting political neutrality, all public servants, not only managers, must conduct themselves at all times such that present politically elected officials and those who may become so can be confident in the political neutrality of the public service. It is also important for public sector unions to give full support to the concept of political neutrality; neutrality is not something to be practised when a conservative party is in power but abandoned when a worker-friendly party governs. Neutrality is neutrality.

Whistleblowing legislation or policies are not always restricted to corruption and dishonesty. The concept of wrong-doing extends to mismanagement in general and, where workers have tried unsuccessfully to bring this to the attention of their superiors, it too should be exposed. Trade unions encourage their members to use all the available, established channels to report wrong-doing, mismanagement etc and trade unions are responsible for reporting such matters. It is not uncommon for trade unions to meet with politicians and members of the senior executive service for discussions on public service management and this provides another opportunity for dealing with situations before whistleblowing becomes an issue.

ACCOUNTABILITY RELATIONSHIPS

Public sector workers have at least five sets of accountability relationships:[7] to their politically elected leadership; to taxpayers; to the users of their services; to their staff or bosses; and to other members of the management/work team. Public sector trade unions expect managers to be able to promote and take all these relationships seriously. They are the cornerstones of providing an accountable, effective, efficient and well-managed service which treats its staff fairly.

Nothing in what follows suggests that staff should denigrate or sabotage their accountability to politicians. It is the duty of public sector workers to make available to the politicians the information and expertise which has a bearing on policy decisions and not withhold relevant information from the political leadership.

The distinction between users of services and tax-payers is also an important one, especially in view of the increasing emphasis on 'user friendliness'. There are occasions when it is difficult to determine just who the 'user' is: in the prisons service, is the 'user' the inmate, society at large, the victim of the crime concerned or some amalgam of all of these? In cases where a programme serves a particular industry group, politicians may well be interested in emphasising the needs of the industrial users rather than acknowledging that the tax-payers who fund the service also have rights to information and evaluation.

Accountability for politicians is not the only serious relationship nor the one with top priority; in fact, in any clash between political accountability and adherence to democratically constituted law, the latter must always take precedence and some countries have legislation or policies in the public service which deal with this. There will be occasions when other accountabilities will require senior public sector managers to challenge the decisions of politicians. Such conflicts are not easy to handle or resolve, especially for managers who are, increasingly, on term contracts. Many unions around the world have had reason to give and have given loyalty to an ethical manager over an unscrupulous politician. Trade unions, managers and politicians can devise nationally appropriate guidelines for avoiding or handling' such clashes.

In some jurisdictions, the powers of a public accounts or audit committee acting as an adviser to a legislature or other elected body extend to being able to summons public officials to appear before them. Public sector managers must comply with such requests even if they, on the briefing of their political superior, decline to answer some questions in favour of inviting the committee to refer the matter to the politician. But in cases where an official has statutory responsibilities to ensure financial probity, it should be incumbent on such officials to report any cases to such a committee where they have reason to believe that an elected official is or is about to be in breach of the law, in spite of advice to the contrary.

Similarly, appointed public sector managers must not, even at the request/direction of elected officials, usurp the responsibility of elected officials to be accountable to the elected body responsible for legislative or financial administration of the state. So, for example, there has been concern expressed by Members of Parliament in the UK at the practice of allowing appointed Agency Chief Executives (rather than the Minister) to respond to parliamentary inquiries (*Hansard, Adjournment Debate*, 28 February 1993).

It is crucial that managers who are part of a collective managerial team show a sense of solidarity with one another. It is acceptable neither to undermine a fellow manager who has to exercise budget controls nor to ignore the legitimate concerns of a personnel manager. Trade unions do not appreciate displays of disloyalty to other managers by those who wish to establish their 'credentials' with the union. This goes for *all* managerial staff.

It is important for senior managers to insist that the political leadership respect the 'chain of command' inside the organisation as a protection to others in the management team as well as to their staff. It is unfair to both managers and staff if politicians are able to deal directly with staff under a manager's authority.

LEADERSHIP

Managers should provide leadership models for their organisation and for their staff. This leadership is not merely a matter of rhetoric but of practice. In other words, managers should not just practise what they preach, the usual aphorism, but be prepared to *preach* (and teach) *what they practise*, a much more committed approach to defending one's behaviour. The PSI affiliate SKTF (the Swedish Local

Government Officers' Trade Union) states that '[a] manager in charge of operations has to provide the professional leadership which is a necessary complement to the political leadership and must in this role be a guarantee for continuity, long-term work and stability of the operation' (SKTF, 1994, p 4). As part of this leadership role, managers have a specific responsibility to provide training and development of their staff. Such training should encourage all staff to maximise their potential personally, professionally and in ways suited to the best delivery of the service's output.

Ethics training must be provided so that all public sector workers have clear principles and guidelines to help them to recognise and deal with ethical issues.[8] Certainly, the goal of staff development should be that management can delegate work and tasks to more junior staff professionally, building trust and skills so that managers can get on with the job of managing. The principles of delegation should be respected by managers. Delegations should always *negotiate* with the staff concerned; once negotiated, they should then be honoured, such that the manager does not undermine or withdraw the delegation without discussion with the staff concerned. In turn, staff should accept that agreed delegations carry with them the ethical and other responsibilities inherent to the task.

Public sector workers expect that managers will consult them, through their trade unions if they have one, on all aspects of service planning and on major policy changes which will affect their work or conditions. Such consultation should be part of 'good-faith' bargaining, participative and allow sufficient time for collective decision-making within the union. In particular, managers should aim to be able to give service users appropriate quality assurance based on proper consultation with the workers who will be delivering the service and with the users themselves.

As a part of improving service quality, citizens or consumers' charters have been developed in some countries. They vary in quality and in the degree to which they are more committed to service quality rather than to serving the interests of ideology. Some charters reflect increased public expectations about the quality of public services and, inherently, the standards of public servants, driven in part by some governments attempting to tell the public what they should expect from public services. Charters which are genuinely aimed at service improvement and democratic accountability are to be welcomed. However, those which set service standards without allocating sufficient human and financial resources to deliver to those standards will result in failure. Anecdotal evidence from PSI-affiliated trade unions reveals some cases in which there are political steps taken to ensure that that services fail: the politicians then blame the workers and make a spurious 'case' for the privatisation of the service. One PSI affiliate, the New Zealand Public Service Association, has reported another dilemma facing public sector managers and workers:

> ... indications of frustrations with the way politicians used or abused public service agencies talking about performance and outputs and outcomes on the one hand, but not wanting to hear or have others hear when underfunding meant that departmental performance had to fall short of public expectations and political promises. (New Zealand Public Service Association, 1996)[9]

This is unacceptable to public sector workers, who expect that their managers would involve workers in the establishment of realistic and relevant standards which reflect community needs and desires. Charters based on such a process are real citizens' charters. Again, such matters are properly the subject of collective bargaining and managers have a right to expect, and will normally receive, positive inputs from trade unions and their members on these issues.

Consultants or contractors often deliver internal or external services. It should be a condition of the consultation or contract that the consultant or contractor will abide by the conditions outlined here and that public sector workers dealing with such people will behave similarly. (The concept of 'insiders' and 'outsiders' in the public sector is discussed in Lawton, Chapter 4.) There is concern among PSI affiliates about politicians preferring the advice of external consultants and think tanks to advice offered by public servants; this 'external advice' is often not published or made available.

ENFORCEABILITY

It is a basic principle for PSI and its affiliates that the kinds of issues raised here should be subject to free collective bargaining. This includes matters governing the working conditions for managerial staff as well as the matters governing relationships between the managers and their staff.

Some of the issues relating to declaring financial or other interests should be covered by law or public service regulations. Where appropriate, these should be drawn up or amended accordingly.

There are many issues mentioned above which will or should be the subject of the codes of ethics or conduct of relevant professional bodies. Managers concerned may belong to such bodies. The standards may govern the public acceptability of the work done even if the managers concerned do not belong to the professional association. Both trade unions and governments should hold discussions with these professional bodies regarding those issues where the government or union codes are. In addition, some public sector managers are also officers of the law courts or other civil authorities, including parliaments. While there may be an argument that their political superiors determine the extent of their responsibility in such areas, the fact is that where such authorities are exercising legal powers, staff must respect these.

It is interesting in this regard to read the Code of Conduct of a body such as the British Institute of Management, for example. Much of its content is compatible with the ideas discussed here. It calls on its members to apply 'expert knowledge' in the discharge of their duties, implying a need for managers and other staff to keep themselves up to date educationally — a matter which should be in the conditions of appointment or the contracts of relevant public sector workers. It cautions its members to avoid asking others to do something which offends their conscience. Rather than focusing only on technical practice, it advises members to be 'concerned with the development of quality in all management matters, including quality of life'. Strong values of environmentalism and cultural respect for the values of others are included in this code which reminds members that serious infringement could result in expulsion from the Institute.

These are high standards and sometimes difficult to implement. For example, PSI-affiliate UNISON[10] in the UK notes that there have been conflicts for responsible managers over whether following advice to take industrial action may put a solicitor working for a public authority into conflict with their professional code. (The legal professional code and conduct within are critically examined by Kaptein, Chapter 2.)

In many countries, disputes relating to public sector administration can be the subject of official investigation and jurisdiction. This could involve an ombudsman, a publicly accountable auditor or a privacy commissioner. Trade unions should, where necessary, investigate the need for and feasibility of getting the public authorities to establish such positions or structures where they are lacking. And it is essential that these positions are always politically neutral. Further, copies of any code of practice for public service managers must be available to elected officials and to the public.

WHERE TO FROM HERE?

While there can be little sympathy for public servants who profess to be surprised that there are special ethical principles which apply to the public sector, it would also be foolish to pretend that rules carved in stone in Weber's day should be immutable.

There are new expectations for and within the public services and some of the issues confronting political leaders and their employees are more complex than those of the past: bio-technology, medical dilemmas, the contest between the demands for public information versus the need to protect privacy, computer technologies. These all raise issues on which old rules may shed little light. But public sector trade unions and their members remain convinced that there are some fundamental values which do not really need the wisdom of the ages to understand and recognise. The fact that newspapers and the public all *know* that it is unacceptable to feed at the public trough when one is running the service concerned is one reason that scandal stories sell so well.[11]

PSI has been following with interest the work of the Public Management Service of the OECD in this area of ethics and has been attempting to support that work. Many of our affiliates have indicated to governments that they are keen to see high ethical standards preserved and are willing to be joint partners in that work. In the end, it is an issue on which public sector workers and their employers should be of one mind.

NOTES

1   Leadership is an important element in encouraging and ensuring public sector ethics; see Sherman, ch 1 and Corbett, ch 12.

2   The influence of appearance on ethics in the public sector is examined within the political arena in N Preston et al (eds) (1998) *Ethics and Political Practice: Perspectives on Legislative Ethics*, Routledge and Federation Press.

3   For example, the double burden of paid employment and family responsibilities.

4   The difficulties of professional codes of conduct for staff and service users are considered in Kaptein, ch 2.

5   The growing acceptance of such international codes and international involvement in developing domestic codes is covered in Potts, ch 6.

6   The difficulties and obstacles that an institutional culture may throw up in such internal inquiries is analysed in Miller, ch 3.

7   Various aspects of accountability are examined in Kaptein, ch 2; Dubnick, ch 5; and Miller, ch 3.

8   Corbett, ch 12, emphasises the importance of training and particularly sensitive ethics training for public sector staff at all levels.

9   Hicks, ch 8, provides an in-depth look at the New Zealand Public Service.

10   UNISON has more than 1 million members, the majority of whom work in the health sector, local government and public utilities.

11   Of course, there are numerous other reasons why scandals 'sell', including the public's interest in the 'personal' life of politicians.

12

TALKIN' 'BOUT HEBN

David Corbett

INTRODUCTION

This chapter is addressed to those who, like myself, conduct training sessions on ethics for public servants. My sessions are for Australians, so the material I choose is meant to be of interest to them. Even so, readers from other countries may find the general approach interesting and capable of being applied in their own way by using material drawn from their own historic and cultural heritage.

There is an American folk hymn, 'All God's Chillun', in which the following line appears: 'All dem dat's talkin bout Hebn ain't goin dere'.

Those of us who write or talk about ethics in the public sector should take warning that we are no better than those whom we presume to instruct. There is a great deal of earnest, inspirational talk about improving the ethics of public officials, but what do the authors, myself included, really know about improving ethical performance in public administration?

My practical experience is limited to having served for five years as a member of a state public service board, responsible, among other things, for enforcing discipline under the public service statutes. This entailed hearing and deciding on charges laid by department heads against officers down the line for having allegedly breached the disciplinary clauses of the Act. Those clauses reflected ethical norms, and we, as a tribunal, were conscious that we were making judgments about ethics. We could not avoid bringing our own ethical values into the interpretation of the Act. In a series of cases over the years, we tried to illustrate an ethical stance which we shared and which differed somewhat from the ethical stances of our predecessors. However, this limited experience is not enough to justify preaching ethics to others.

Not only are we no better than the trainees whom we presume to teach but we are often no clearer in the head. John Uhr points out that 'the ethics literature is crammed with elegant cop outs' (Uhr, 1996, p 2). Most of us have, at one time or another, taken easy ways out.

For example, modern managerialism and market incentives are said to expose public administration to the erosion of traditional ethical norms. (Lawton, Chapter 4, discusses the pitfalls of applying business practices and ethics to the public sector.) Then, as often as not, we say that if public officials would only recognise the fact, good ethics are good business and there need be no conflict between traditional ethical norms and the commercialisation of public sector management. Hey presto, the dilemma disappears. We can have all we want of modern managerialism and yet not lose one iota of our ethical purity. "[T]he old values of honesty, integrity and fairness are consistent with and complementary to modern management in the public service".[1] (Ives, 1996, pp 79–91)

Are they indeed?

Another cop out is to pretend that there is little or no connection between ethical behaviour in public office and ethics in daily life. Public service is a profession; therefore, a code of behaviour for public servants should only be derived from the professional roles public servants have to play in a liberal democracy. (Professional codes of conduct are critically assessed in Kaptein, Chapter 2.) We are a multicultural society; it would be arrogant to claim that norms espoused by the dominant elite are shared, or should be shared, by individuals of other cultural backgrounds or religious persuasions. Hence, public sector codes of behaviour must necessarily be minimalist, based only on the requirements of our liberal democratic constitution but avoiding any appeal to higher moral foundations or sanctions. Following this reasoning, we can leave aside, as beyond our necessary concern, the private convictions and moral attitudes of the people who occupy public offices.

Elsewhere I have argued that this is a delusion (Corbett, 1997). Good public administration requires good people, people with a highly developed moral sense. Public servants make decisions affecting the lives of others, penalising or rewarding them using powers delegated to them and exercised according to their assessment of the facts and their interpretations of policy and law. But such decisions require ethical judgment as well. A public servant's duty goes beyond mere compliance with a minimalist professional code of behaviour. It is necessary to take higher moral ground than that.

Doesn't that make it inevitable that we discriminate in favour of one group's ethical beliefs and against the ethical beliefs of other groups? No, says another of the usual cop outs, there is a common thread in all the great ethical and religious traditions: they all mean the same thing in the end. But do they?

This reminder of familiar cop outs leads to three points which are central to this discussion.

- Ethics in the public sector cannot be kept separate from the ethics prevalent in society as a whole, in segments of society and in the individual consciences of public officials.

- The limitations we have as commentators include not only our limited experience and biases but also our tendency to ignore contradictions and cop outs.

- Ethical public service means virtuous public service; two virtues needing to be remembered are courage and humility.

All dem dat's talkin bout Hebn ain't goin dere. When the saints go marching in, which of us, if any, will be of that number? For purposes of this discussion, it isn't necessary to believe in 'going to heaven' but it does serves as a useful metaphor for virtuous conduct in the time we are above ground.

If we find ourselves unable to teach ethics by confidently proclaiming universal moral principles, how are we to go about it? I would suggest that we do it by telling stories. It's an old tradition in Judaism, for example, that the rabbi, the teacher, draws moral lessons from parables and from the stories of heroes of the past. That seems to me a thoroughly good idea.

Ethics teachers often rely on hypothetical scenarios or case studies drawn from actual public service experience. Both of these are forms of storytelling and draw on ethical inferences from the story. Both have their advantages but also their drawbacks. Hypothetical scenarios tend to remain hypothetical, somewhat abstract, removed from real time and space. Case studies, 'war stories', drawn from real public service life avoid this failing but have another, rather worrisome one. Either they are widely-known horror stories drawn from the public record, in which case they may seem rather too lurid to challenge the humble, inconspicuous public servant or else they are closer to the everyday, drawn from confidential, in-house sources, in which case the identities of the persons involved will inevitably be discovered by the hearers even if the storyteller tries to disguise them.

Stories from in-house sources often rely on rumour or *ex parte* versions of the truth, sometimes slanderous. Irreparable damage can be done to the reputations of still-serving public servants in the course of such invasions of their privacy, privacy to which they have a right. If the 'war story' relies on public records of a formal disciplinary tribunal, the right to privacy is foregone. However, disciplinary authorities do most of their best work outside the range of formal, quasi-judicial proceedings and that aspect of their work ought to remain confidential. So the legitimacy of using any such material seems to me to be open to serious question. The onus should be on the user to establish that every part of the story is a matter of record and that the issues have been heard and contested in open court.

Thus, there is a case for telling rather more widely available stories. Certainly, the classic public service case studies, such as the Creighton case, have their place (RS Parker, 1965).[2] However, I suggest we can go further afield in search of new material and re-examine epic tales from a readily available cultural heritage. This heritage may or may not be shared by all members of our audiences but the stories themselves should appeal to everyone because of their dramatic content and prodigious cast of characters.

TWO STORIES AND WHERE THEY CAME FROM

The Death of Captain Cook

Captain James Cook explored a great deal of the Pacific as well as the west coast of North America in the mid-1700s. He undertook this work in part as a public servant, under the patronage of King George III. Cook's third voyage ended with his murder on 14 February 1779. It was on the west coast of the Big Island of Hawaii, at Kealakekua Bay, that he was clubbed over the head from behind, stabbed with iron daggers which the Hawaiians had got in trade from Cook's own men, then held under water until he drowned. A monument, a simple white monolith which can be seen from across the bay, stands near the spot, below the steep mountains which flank the coast.

When I was standing on the peaceful shore of Kealakekua Bay in 1996, looking across at the monument, I thought of Cook's great service to humanity and how it came to an end. Why did this happen to Captain Cook? He was a good and faithful servant of his master, George III. What did he do, or not do, that resulted in his death? How did his actions or omissions affect the outcome of the great third voyage he had undertaken at Royal command? What lessons can we learn from the event? How, in particular, does his tragedy shed light on the ethical dilemmas facing public sector managers in the modern world?

What were the reasons for Captain Cook's death?

One immediate cause was the violent behaviour of some of his men. He was about to escape and go back to his ship. He had abandoned his plan to take Chief Kalei'opu'u hostage. Just at that moment word reached the Hawaiian crowd on the beach.

> At the other end of the bay, to keep a canoe from escaping, muskets had been fired — by Rickman among others — and a man killed. The man was Kalimu, a chief of high rank. Another chief hastening to the ships in indignation to pour out the story to Cook was disregarded, and forthwith made for the beach. It was Cook he wanted, not the crowd. It was the crowd that got the news, spreading like wildfire, not Cook; and the news was enough, with the other thing, to carry them over the borderline of excitement into attack. (Beaglehole, 1974, p 671)

The 'other thing'? Cook had gone ashore because his cutter, the best of his small craft, had been stolen. He was determined to make Chief Kalei'opu'u get it back for him, even if he had to take him hostage until it was returned. Cook had no difficulty at first in persuading Kalei'opu'u to come back with him on board the *Resolution*. Kalei'opu'u had done so several times before. But this time, those who were with Kalei'opu'u were frightened. Cook had come on shore accompanied by Lieutenant Phillips and nine marines armed with muskets. The muskets were loaded with ball, not shot. Ball was for killing people; shot was for frightening them. Something in the menacing bearing of this armed party frightened the Hawaiians, though not Kalei'opu'u or his two sons, one of whom had already jumped into the pinnace, eager to go back aboard Cook's ship.

> So far all was well; but near the waterside Kalei'opu'u's wife and two lesser chiefs came up, began to argue with him, and made him sit down. There was a change in the chief: he 'appear'd dejected and frighten'd' says Phillips; apparently he was being told he would be killed. A great crowd had now gathered, quite clearly not well-disposed. So many muskets, and the obvious lack of friendliness, had caused alarm. (Beaglehole, 1974, p 670)

So the chain of causes goes father back. Why had Cook decided to go on shore with such an unusual show of force? According to Beaglehole, his biographer, Cook had become exasperated by the thefts carried out by the Hawaiians (Beaglehole, 1974, p 669). Some of his officers had all along urged him to take a stand, punish the thieves, if necessary shoot a few, to discourage the others from continuing with their thievery.

Cook had hitherto shown himself to be patient, tolerant and opposed to all forms of violence. Only when he or his men appeared to be in immediate danger had he, so far, allowed force to be used. There had been one exception, at Moorea in the Society Islands, when Cook had led a party which burned houses and war canoes to punish the islanders for stealing two goats and to set an example to others not to steal in future. The islanders' losses would take them months or years to recover from. Even on that occasion, Cook was less violent than some of his advisers recommended: '[T]hey without hesitation, advised me to go with a party of men into the Country, and shoot every Soul I met with. This bloody advice I could not follow' (Journals III, p 229, as quoted in Beaglehole, 1974, p 559).

Cook 'wished he had never started the miserable business' (Beaglehole, 1974, p 668) over the two goats. So why did he let his temper flare this time at Kealakekua Bay? Beaglehole concludes that at last Cook's 'patience had been tried beyond its limits' (Beaglehole, 1974, p 669), he had lost control, worn down by the fatigue of the three-year long voyage and the exhausting responsibilities of his command.

The chain of causes goes still farther back. Part of it was bad luck. The foremast of Cook's ship, the *Resolution*, gave way in a storm just after the expedition had left Kealakekua Bay ten days earlier. They had left, intending not to come back but to proceed to one of the other islands. The damage to the mast forced Cook to make a difficult decision. Should he try to find some other sheltered spot where the ship could be safely anchored while repairs were carried out or should he go back to Kealakekua where he knew the anchorage was safe? He decided on the latter course, though he knew there was a risk.[3]

When the expedition had left Kealakekua on 4 February, it was evident that the Hawaiians wanted them to go and were glad to be rid of them. They had treated Cook as a god but even gods can outwear their welcome. It was not, perhaps, that they had grown tired of Cook himself but some of his rough crew had become a nuisance. The constant giving of gifts, feathered robes, pigs, fruit and vegetables had become a drain on resources and the bits of iron, nails, knives and daggers which they got in return had begun to seem less attractive.

Also, there may have been ill-feeling about the women with whom the sailors made free. Women stayed on board the *Resolution* and the *Discovery*. The sailors had become used to this as one of their rewards for the risks of the voyage; women had been on board at Tahiti and at other islands. Apparently some of the women were happy enough with whatever gifts they got in return for their favours, but were the men on shore equally content? Cook wished he could prevent these contacts between his crew and the local women because of venereal disease.[4] Some of the Hawaiian men forced their women into prostitution and took from them whatever gifts or trade goods they earned. Cook heard no complaints from the chiefs about these goings on; but was the rest of the population, male and female, equally complaisant? This may have been one of the reasons for the Hawaiians' resentment when Cook and his ships returned.

Cook knew that there was a risk in returning to Kealakekua but decided that it was his best option. It turned out to be a fatal decision.

What can we learn from Captain Cook's fate?

Captain James Cook was a loyal servant of George III. King George took a personal interest in his voyages. The king was an amateur scientist and geographer and patron of the Royal Society which sponsored Cook's voyage.

The voyage had a mixture of objectives. From Cook's point of view, it was primarily meant to define the latitude and longitude of bodies of land in the Pacific, the Antarctic and the Arctic, using the new chronometer which had been commissioned for the purpose. Cook had charted many uncharted waters and coasts before.

But the voyage had several other objectives: to assert British dominion over undiscovered islands; to find out what trade was available to British merchantmen; to head off the Spanish, French, Dutch and Russians who were already trading with the islands and on the west coast of North America; to search for a northwest passage by which ships might go from Hudson's Bay to the Pacific Ocean; to report on the customs and beliefs of Pacific island peoples; to collect specimens of plants and bring home descriptions and drawings of plants and animals; to display the sophistication of British science and technology to the rest of the world; to demonstrate to the Pacific islanders that Britain and the British king would be a worthy, generous protector, one to be venerated, even loved, as well as feared; and, finally, to bring the ships, himself and his crew back home with as little loss of life as possible.

In other words, Cook was in a position not dissimilar to that of a public servant in charge of a program, the objectives of which may be confused, multiple, vague, even mutually contradictory. There is therefore a need to set priorities, to choose how resources will be apportioned among competing ends. In making those choices, a public servant makes ethical judgments. The outcomes will be in favour of some stakeholders more than others. Value judgments have to be made.

Cook made choices like that. He especially wanted the scientific and cartographic purposes of his voyages to be achieved. On the scientific and cartographic fronts, his expeditions were a huge success and the public benefits were substantial. Sailors of many nations have been saved from shipwreck because better charts resulted from the pioneering work of Cook and his officers.

Was Cook to blame?

Now comes the difficult task of judging Cook's performance in his capacity as a public servant. Standards of our own day are often inappropriate to be used in judging the performance of public officials in a different age and in circumstances we can hardly even imagine. An effort is made in what follows to make allowance for these differences.

Let us imagine for a moment that Cook has been brought before a modern public service disciplinary tribunal on the following charges.

- Failure to guard and protect government property
- Conflict of interest in allowing himself to be treated as a deity when this could cause risk to the expedition and its purposes
- Inadequate enforcement of authority. The use of firearms, contrary to Cook's orders, and the crew's conduct with Island women, ignoring Cook's orders, put the expedition and its objectives at risk.
- Rash and ill-considered resort to force on the last day at Kealakekua; in the event, a fatal mistake

To all of these charges, a possibly persuasive defence could be mounted.

- The cutter was stolen. It should have been guarded. But Cook had to rely on his officers to obey his orders that guards be kept on duty. They let him down.
- Cook let the Hawaiians treat him like a god because it was their desire to do so. They seemed to identify him with some deity well known in their mythology and there was not much he could do but go along with their beliefs if he was not to cause offence.
- Cook tried to prevent his men from having sexual intercourse with the Hawaiian women but realised that he could not control them. As for the unauthorised use of firearms, on one occasion when an officer shot a man dead, Cook was deliberately not told (Beaglehole, 1974, p 575).
- The amount of force to be used in a dangerous situation is a matter best judged by the person on the spot. On the last day at Kealakekua, Cook may have thought that the lives of his crew were threatened. Loading the muskets with ball and taking a party of armed marines on shore may have seemed to him a necessary precaution. The killing of a chief by the party at the other end of the bay may have been in response to real danger. Cook and his officers should be given the benefit of the doubt.
- Cook's expedition achieved the principal purposes for which it was undertaken. The means were indispensable to the achievement of these ends.

If that is the case for the defence, what would a prosecutor say?

- Discipline had become too lax. There were threats of mutiny (Beaglehole, 1974, p 641–2). The crew behaved as though they were their own masters. They were allowed to keep women on board, despite orders not to. Cook was not in sufficient control of his officers and crew. This amounts to neglect of duty.
- Letting himself be treated as a god and willingly accepting the homage and gifts that came with it put Cook into a compromised position, a conflict of interest. It is the duty of a public servant to obey orders without being deflected by considerations of private gain or self-aggrandisement. Could

Cook be sure the Hawaiians were sincere and not merely toying with him? Captain Clerke, the commander of the accompanying ship, the *Discovery*, followed the proper course of rejecting the attempts of the Hawaiians to treat him as though he were a deity.[5] Cook should have done the same.

- Cook's resort to force may have been excessive. Though he had previously forbidden shore parties to carry arms, during the last visit to Kealakekua Bay, muskets were carried and used with fatal effect not only by Cook's own party but by the other shore party as well. Cook himself fired one barrel of his musket at a man who threatened him with a dagger and a stone. Whether the threat had been made 'seriously or in mere bravado we cannot tell' (Beaglehole, 1974, p 671). This man, protected by a heavy garment, was unharmed, as the first barrel was loaded only with shot. Cook's second shot killed a man. His second shot was apparently meant to stop one of the Hawaiian chiefs from stabbing Lieutenant Phillips but, moments later, Cook and four of his marines were dead.
- Ends cannot justify means.

Ethical inferences

For present-day public servants, what are the ethical lessons of the tragedy?

- Keep your temper. If you can't, get someone else to take your place for the time being. (This is an option Cook himself could hardly have adopted. He was in command and beyond reach of relief.)
- If you exhaust yourself by staying at your post too long, your judgment may waver, putting yourself and others at risk.
- Guard government property entrusted to you.
- Reject temptation to accept favours or even praise and flattery from those with whom you have to do official business. You run the risk of putting yourself under an obligation to your flatterers or at the very least reducing your office's authority with persons who may have an interest in weakening that authority. Flattery is more insidious than bribery.
- Keep a close eye on the behaviour of subordinates to make sure they do not undermine the purposes of your project or program. Use the authority given to you to discipline them and keep them in line.
- However, you must be careful about using the sanctions which your office entitles you to use. Use the ultimate sanction only if others have been tried and found wanting or if you are morally certain that milder sanctions would be ineffective. Only then, resort to the final sanction.
- If you break these guidelines,[6] expect to pay the price.

Civilian public servants don't find themselves in situations like those which faced Captain Cook but they do face the moral equivalent of his predicament every day. They have to decide what means are necessary and morally permissible to achieve the ends which policy prescribes, choose the priorities to be given to the multiple aims of policy as well as choose which of the available sanctions is appropriate to the circumstances of each particular case.

Captain Cook served a nation which thought it had, by divine right, dominion over palm and pine. Cook was a brave, modest, able, dedicated, good man. He avoided arrogance throughout his career but, in the end, either a fatal hubris, submission to flattery, distorted judgment due to exhaustion or exasperation and loss of self-control led to his death.

This story tells us that courage, steadfastness and humility can come undone in a moment of stress or emotional turmoil. Public officials can act ethically if they can keep their self-control. Easy to say; difficult to do.

The challenge for good government is not just how to make it efficient or even accountable but how to make it virtuous. It is a goal worth aspiring to, even though 'All dem dat's talkin bout Hebn ain't goin dere'.

Daniel and Belshazzar[7]

Daniel was one of the sons of Judah taken into captivity in Babylon when the king of Babylon besieged and captured Jerusalem. The Babylonian king not only took home as captives the rulers and prophets of Israel but also carried off sacred vessels from the temple at Jerusalem.

Nebuchadnezzar, the king of Babylon, became mighty and proud but was troubled by dreams which only Daniel could interpret to him. He dreamed of a great tree which gave fruit and shelter to man and beast but was suddenly cut down by a messenger from on high. Daniel told him the tree was himself, Nebuchadnezzar, and that he would be sent out among the beasts of the field to forage on grass. It all came to pass as Daniel had foretold. However, Nebuchadnezzar repented of his pride and was restored to authority in his kingdom, a wiser, less arrogant man than he had been before.

Belshazzar, the son of Nebuchadnezzar, forgot the lesson of his father's experience. When he became king, he too became haughty and proud. He and some thousands of his followers, together with his wives and his concubines, held a feast at which they drank from the sacred vessels stolen from the temple at Jerusalem. Nor was this their only sacrilege; they also worshipped gods made of gold, silver, brass, iron, wood and stone.

While the feast was going on, Belshazzar suddenly became weak with fear when he saw fingers of a man's hand writing words on the wall of the palace. None of his wise men could read the words which were in the language of the sons of Judah. So the king called for Daniel to decipher the message. Daniel reminded Belshazzar of the pride and downfall of his father, Nebuchadnezzar.

The words were MENE, MENE, TEKEL, UPHARSIN. Daniel translated their message:

> God hath numbered thy kingdom, and finished it. Thou are weighed in the balances, and art found wanting. Thy kingdom is divided, and given to the Medes and Persians. (Dan 5:23–28)

That night, Belshazzar was killed and Darius, the ruler of the Medes and Persians, captured the kingdom of Babylon.

Darius appointed Daniel as his principal adviser. The 120 princes to whom Darius gave lesser powers were jealous of Daniel and conspired against him. They persuaded Darius to sign a decree that 'whosoever shall ask a petition of any God or man for thirty days, save of thee, O king, he shall be cast into the den of lions' (Dan 6:7).

Daniel continued to pray to the God of Judah. So he was cast into the den of lions and the mouth of the den was sealed up with the king's seal. After Daniel's imprisonment, King Darius could not sleep and very early the next morning went to the lions' den.

> And when he came to the den, he cried with a lamentable voice unto Daniel: and the king spake and said to Daniel, O Daniel, servant of the living God, is thy God, whom thou servest continually, able to deliver thee from the lions?
>
> Then said Daniel unto the king, O king, live for ever. My God hath sent his angel, and hath shut the lions' mouths, that they have not hurt me: forasmuch as before him innocency was found in me; and also before thee, O king, have I done no hurt. (Dan 6:20–2)

Darius relented, adopted Jehovah as his god and told his followers to stop punishing the captive Jews for practising their religion.

Those are three of the main stories of the Book of Daniel. I quote scripture not in piety but because it tells stories which some have learned, one way or another, which form part of the cultural heritage of many countries and which can be made interesting to others because of their epic scale and heroic dimensions.

What can we learn from Daniel?

What has all this to do with ethical issues faced by present-day staff of government agencies? Here are some tentative suggestions.

- Daniel was a servant of the king, not because he chose to be but because he had no choice. He was a captive. Public servants can leave the service if they choose but how free are they in reality? It is all very well to speak of public servants as managers and of management as a discipline which knows no boundaries between the public and private sectors. But the fact is that many a good public servant is not free to find employment of equal significance and satisfaction outside the service. If they have to 'hang in there' even though they would rather be somewhere else, how can they continually give good, courageous service to their clients and masters? Did Daniel manage to do this; if so, how and why? Does one have to have a creed or faith larger than self-interest in order to stay the distance and do the job well?

- Daniel was unlucky enough to be on a hit list after a change of government. It wasn't the king himself who overthrew him, it was the 120 jealous hangers-on. There are six ex-heads of Commonwealth government departments who may have felt betrayed in a similar way in March 1996 following the change in government from Labor to Coalition.

- Daniel gave advice without fear or favour, at great risk to his safety. Public servants today are not sealed up in lions' dens; being forced to take a redundancy package when still at the height of one's powers may seem hardly less dreadful a prospect. Yet the public servant's duty is to offer fearless advice. As one booklet on ethical standards states:

  > [The public servant] should be responsible to government, and serve ministers and government loyally and impartially ... [they] should provide frank, honest, comprehensive and accurate advice. (Management Advisory Board/ Management Improvement Advisory Committee, 1996, p 60)

- Daniel was saved from the lions by an angel of the Lord. That is an unlikely form of rescue for present-day public servants. To whom can they look for help when their luck runs out and their principles bring them into conflict with their superiors? Are there mentors in the service who are up to the required standard of philosophic probity? If not and if confidentiality rules preclude turning to outsiders, ought there to be a sort of 'chaplaincy' within the service, subject to its rules?

- Daniel remained steadfast in his faith and, by so doing, helped his fellow captives survive their captivity. The ethical duty implied here is that members of the profession should support their brothers and sisters who are in good professional standing and who have been victimised. 'Stand by your (deserving) friends and colleagues.'

- Nebuchadnezzar and Belshazzar were also public officials, though of very high rank. What happened to them has a lesson in it for less highly placed public servants. These two kings had become arrogant and were brought down because of it.

- Belshazzar's fate was worse than his father's because he should have learned from his father's experience but stubbornly pursued his reckless course. Study administrative history!

- In the Book of Daniel's account, God had a hand in bringing Nebuchadnezzar down. But it is equally plausible to see Nebuchadnezzar as having suffered a nervous breakdown and Belshazzar as being the victim of the fortunes of war. Their downfall serves as a warning that, no matter what office of public trust we may occupy, pride goeth before a fall, hubris is overtaken by nemesis, arrogance may lead to humiliation.

- Nebuchadnezzar and Belshazzar got their just deserts but many others do not. Failing divine intervention, investigative journalism or a royal commission may bring arrogance to justice. Of course, we cannot be sure. In the world as we know it, unethical people sometimes prosper mightily.

- The authors of the Book of Daniel told their stories in the hope of persuading readers that humility, steadfastness and courage are their best hope for survival. Public sector ethics trainers do their trainees a service if they teach the same things.

- Daniel teaches a lesson in courage. It takes guts to be a public official. Government and public servants sometimes have to do nasty things and there is usually someone who hates you for what you have to do.

- Finally, who can shut out the words written on the wall? 'You have been weighed in the balances and found wanting.' Belshazzar no doubt imagined he saw the writing, which perhaps goes to show that even a king far gone in arrogance has a conscience that can unman him. Public officials, like the rest of us, have need to fear the still, small voice that comes in the night.

CONCLUSION

This has been an attempt to make use of two legendary stories as case studies to stimulate awareness of ethical issues facing public servants. In other work, I have used stories drawn from contemporary politics and sought to draw ethical inferences from them (see Corbett, 1991, pp 103–13).[8] On reading that work six or more years later, I find that the stories have become dated and may no longer be useful for training people in ethical awareness.

The present discussion tries a different tack. It uses stories which should last longer in the public consciousness. They are stories on an epic scale, worthy of constant retelling. So far, so good; the next question is whether these stories can, indeed, be presented so as to provoke awareness and discussion of contemporary ethical issues in the public sector. That is a question which readers must decide for themselves.

One respected commentator, after reading an earlier version of this chapter, said that he could never win over his public sector audiences with material such as this; only actual events from within their own organisations will serve the purpose. When asked whether he changes names to spare the reputations or preserve the privacy of persons involved, he replied that it was usually unnecessary to do so; identities are usually known to their peers in any case. I must say I find that a shocking dismissal of the moral issue. I prefer the rabbinical method — ethical truths taught by telling epic, public stories.

Another shrewd commentator points out that I, too, am guilty of a cop out. I left open the question whether all creeds and cultures have similar ethical norms. I plead guilty but if pressed to give an answer, I tend to see more differences than universal similarities. We have had too many religious and civil wars caused by cultural division to be easily persuaded that humanity is really a single family with a common set of core values. Does the emphasis on difference imply that some beliefs and standards are better than others? It does. Then, which are better? This is where I cop out again. To answer questions and defend propositions such as these is beyond the task of this chapter and beyond my capacity.

Another wise, if somewhat cynical, commentator suggests that the lesson of Captain Cook's fate is this: 'When in the public service, guard your back!'

NOTES

1 I too have made the same illogical leap in lectures; I shall avoid doing it in future.

2 Creighton was Chairman of the Land Administration Board of Queensland. He suspected his Minister, TA Foley, of corruption and disclosed the reasons for his suspicion to a prominent trade union official who then made the case public through a union newspaper. A 1956 Royal Commission later found Foley to have acted in a corrupt manner; however, in the meantime, Creighton was dismissed from office.

3 On the options which Cook could have considered, see Beaglehole, 1974, p 661: 'If he went back he might have to abandon all prospect of seeing the other islands. He might find something better to leeward, but he could not depend upon it; Waimea Bay, which he knew, was too exposed. He decided to go back'.

4 Cook wrote in his journal on 2 January 1778, at the time of his first visit to Hawaii:

> As there were some venereal complaints on board both the Ships, in order to prevent its being communicated to these people, I gave orders that no Women, on any account whatever were to be admited [sic] on board the Ships, I also forbid all manner of connection with them, and ordered that none who had the veneral [sic] upon them should go out of the Ships. But whether these regulations had the desired effect or no time can only discover. It is no more than what I did when I first visited the Friendly Islands yet I afterwards found it did not succeed, and I am much afraid this will always be the case where it is necessary to have a number of people on shore. (Grenfell Price, 1969, p 217)

5 Clerke's journal, as quoted in Beaglehole, 1974, p 653:

> At my first landing they got me to their Morai and with a vast deal of ceremony, singing and fuss, sacrificed a small Pig to me with as much respect as though I had been a being of a superior Nature; this they very frequently did to Captain Cook and afterwards would often have done to me but I always avoided it as a very disagreeable kind of amusement ...

6 These guidelines go further than the Public Service Commission (1995). The Canberra guidelines call for politeness and respect when dealing with clients, the general public and colleagues, but they do not deal with losing one's temper, the most common human cause of insolent or rash behaviour. When dealing with government property, the Canberra guidelines warn against using it for private purposes but do not mention guarding it from loss or theft. On conflict of interest, the Canberra guidelines mention gifts, entertainment and promises of future employment but neglect flattery, an equally or even more insidious temptation. These same guidelines say nothing about the severity of sanctions to be chosen by public servants from the range of sanctions within their authority. The guidelines are very good as far as they go and are an improvement on their 1987 precursors. They do, however, avoid addressing ethical issues other than those applicable in common public service situations. This avoidance, while praised by some commentators, leads, in my opinion, to a loss of strength and vigour in the messages conveyed and neglects the connection between ethics in general and the ethical standards required of public servants.

7 There is actually an interesting link with the story of Captain Cook and that of Daniel and Belshazzar. Close to Kealakekua Bay, down a winding mountain road, is the painted wooden church of St Benedict at Honaunau, only a few kilometres from the site of Cook's death. Honaunau was a traditional place of refuge for defeated warriors, outlaws and breakers of taboo, a place where they could rest in safety, purify themselves and then return to their people. It still has an atmosphere of sanctuary and

healing, a feeling enhanced by the simple dignity of the church built there by Catholic missionaries. A Belgian priest is credited with the murals, vivid paintings presenting biblical stories. One of the most striking is of Belshazzar's Feast and the writing on the wall.

8   The stories in question were those of the collapse of the Pyramid Building Society and the downfall of Premier John Cain of Victoria.

REFERENCES

Aberbach JD (1990) *Keeping a Watchful Eye: The Politics of Congressional Oversight*, Brookings Institute.

Administrative Appeals Tribunal (Australia) (1995) *Annual Report 1994–95*, Australian Government Publishing Service.

Administrative Review Council (1996) *Twentieth Annual Report 1995–1996*, Administrative Review Council

Allars M, 'Managerialism and Administrative Law' (1991) 66 *Canberra Bulletin of Public Administration* 57.

Allison GT (1983) 'Public and Private Management: Are They Fundamentally Alike in All Unimportant Respects?' in JL Perry and KL Kraemer (eds) *Public Management: Public and Private Perspectives*, Mayfield.

Anderson J (1996) 'The Ombudsman — some nuts and bolts' in R Douglas and M Jones (eds) *Administrative Law: Cases and Commentary*, 2nd edn, Federation Press.

Argyris C (1994) *On Organizational Learning*, Blackwell.

Attorney-General (Australia) (1995) *Freedom of Information Act 1982: Annual Report by the Attorney-General into the Operation of the Act, 1994–95*, Australian Government Publishing Service.

Attorney-General (Australia) *Annual Reports*, Australian Government Publishing Service.

Attorney-General (NSW) v Quin (1990) 170 CLR 1.

Australian Broadcasting Tribunal v Bond (1990) 170 CLR 321.

Australian Conservation Foundation v Commonwealth (1980) 146 CLR 493.

Australian Conservation Foundation v Minister for Resources (1989) 76 LGRA 200.

Badaracco JL, Jr and AP Webb, 'Business Ethics: A View from the Trenches' (1995) 37(2) *California Management Review* 8.

Ban C (1995) *How Do Public Managers Manage? Bureaucratic Constraints, Organizational Culture, And The Potential For Reform*, Jossey-Bass.

Beaglehole JC (1974) *The Life of Captain James Cook*, Adam & Charles Black.

The Book of Daniel (King James version).

Bordewijk F (1956) *Geachte Confrère: splendeurs en misères van het bedrijf van advocaat*, Scheltema & Holkema.

Bordewijk F (1988) *Verzameld Werk*, Nijgh & van Ditmar.

Bourdieu P (1977) *Outline of a Theory of Practice*, Cambridge University Press.

Bowen N (1979) *Public Duty and Private Interest*, report of the Committee of Inquiry established by the Prime Minister, Australian Government Publishing Service.

Brooke C (1961) *From Alfred to Henry III, 871–1272*, WW Norton.

163

Bryett K et al (1994) 'Police and Government in a Democracy' in *An Introduction to Policing,* vol 2, Butterworths.

Burgoyne J, 'Creating the Managerial Portfolio: Building on Competency Approaches to Management Development' (1989) 20(1) *Management Education and Development* 56.

Burrell G and G Morgan (1979) *Sociological Paradigms and Organizational Analysis: Elements of the Sociology of Corporate Life,* Heineman.

Cabinet Office (1994) *The Civil Service: Continuity and Change,* Cm 2627, HMSO.

Caiden GE et al, 'Results and Lessons from Canada's PS2000' (1995) 15 *Public Administration and Development* 85.

Cain J (ed) (1954) *Les Gens de Justice,* Sauret.

Campbell C, 'Does Reinvention Need Reinvention? Lessons from Truncated Managerialism in Britain' (1995) 8(4) *Governance* 479.

Campbell C and GK Wilson (1995) *The End of Whitehall: Death of a Paradigm?,* Blackwell.

Carino LV (ed) (1986) *Bureaucratic Corruption in Asia: Causes, Consequences, and Controls,* JMC Press.

Carney T, 'Cloaking the Bureaucratic Dagger? Administrative law in the welfare state' (1989) 58 *Canberra Bulletin of Public Administration* 128.

Church of Scientology v Woodward (1982) 154 CLR 25.

Codd MH (1995) *Report of Inquiry into the Conduct of a Minister,* Department of Prime Minister and Cabinet.

Code of Conduct for Members of Parliament (1996) (UK).

Coleman JS (1990) *Foundations of Social Theory,* Harvard University Press.

Committee of Public Accounts (1994) *The Proper Conduct of Public Business,* 8th report, HMSO.

Committee on Standards in Public Life (1995) *First Report of the Committee on Standards in Public Life,* CM 2850, HMSO.

Commonwealth Ombudsman (1995) *Annual Report 1994–95,* Australian Government Publishing Service.

Conflict of Interest and Post-Employment Code of Public Office Holders 1994 (Canada).

Conway D, 'The Day of the Manager' (1993) *Community Care* 19 August, 20.

Conybeare C, 'Commentary' (1991) 66 *Canberra Bulletin of Public Administration* 70.

Corbett DC (1991) 'Ethics in Business and Government' in K Wistshire (ed) *Do Unto Others: Ethics in the Public Sector,* Royal Australian Institute of Public Administration.

Corbett DC (1997) 'Serving the Public: Six Issues to Consider' in G Clark and E Prior Jonson (eds) *Accountability and Corruption,* Allen & Unwin.

Cossins A (1996) 'Freedom of Information and Open Government' in R Douglas and M Jones (eds) *Administrative Law: Cases and Commentary,* 2nd edn, Federation Press.

Creyke R (1992) 'Interpreting Veterans' Legislation: Lore or law?' in J McMillan (ed) *Administrative Law: Does the Public Benefit?,* Australian Institute of Administrative Law.

Crimes Act 1990 (NSW).

Criminal Justice Commission Act 1989 (Qld).

Curtis L, 'Crossing the Line Between Law and Administration' (1989) 58 *Canberra Bulletin of Public Administration* 65.

De Maria W (1992) 'The Administrative Appeals Tribunal in Review: On remaining seated during the standing ovation' in J McMillan (ed) *Administrative Law: Does the Public Benefit?,* Australian Institute of Administrative Law.

de Tocqueville A (1969) *Democracy in America,* trans JP Mayer, Anchor Books.

Denhardt RB (1993) *The Pursuit of Significance: Strategies for Managerial Success in Public Organizations*, Wadsworth.

Department of Social Security (Australia) (1995) *Annual Report 1994–95*, Australian Government Publishing Service.

DiIulio JJ (1990) *Governing Prisons: A Comparative Study of Correctional Management*, Free Press.

Disney J (1992) 'Access, Equity and the Dominant Paradigm' in J McMillan (ed) *Administrative Law: Does the Public Benefit?*, Australian Institute of Administrative Law.

Disney J and JR Nethercote (eds) (1996) *The House on Capital Hill*, Federation Press.

Dobel J, 'The Corruption of A State' (1978) 72 *American Political Science Review* 958.

Domberger S and C Hall, 'Contracting For Public Services: A Review of Antipodean Experience' (1996) 74 *Public Administration* 129.

Douglas DC (1964) *William The Conqueror: The Norman Impact Upon England*, University of California Press.

Douglas R and M Jones (eds) (1996) *Administrative Law: Cases and Commentary*, 2nd edn, Federation Press.

Doyle J (1985) 'Police Discretion, Legality and Morality' in WL Hefferman and T Stroup (1985) (eds) *Police Ethics*, John Jay.

Drake v MIEA (No 2) (1979) 24 ALR 577.

du Gay P et al, 'The Conduct of Management and the Management of Conduct: Contemporary Managerial Discourse and the Constitution of the "Competent" Manager' (1996) 33(3) *Journal of Management Studies* 263.

Dubnick MJ and BS Romzek (1991) *American Public Administration*, Macmillan.

Dubnick MJ and BS Romzek (1993) 'Accountability and the Centrality of Expectations in American Public Administration' in JL Perry (ed) *Research in Public Administration*, vol 2, JAI Press.

Efficiency Unit (1988) *Improving Management in Government: The Next Steps*, HMSO.

Efficiency Unit (1993) *Career Management and Succession Planning Study* (Oughton report), HMSO.

Ethics in Government Act 1978 (US).

Ethics Reform Act 1989 (US).

Etzioni-Halevy E (1983) *Bureaucracy and Democracy: A Political Dilemma*, rev edn, Routledge & Kegan Paul.

Festinger L (1957) *A Theory of Cognitive Dissonance*, Stanford University Press.

Finkelstein RA (1996) 'Procedural Fairness' in C Saunders (ed) *Courts of Final Jurisdiction: The Mason Court in Australia*, Federation Press.

Fisher Sir W (1928) 'Report of the Board of Enquiry Appointed by the Prime Minister to Investigate Certain Statements Affecting Civil Servants', Cm 3037, HMSO.

Fisher v Oldham [1930] 2 KB 264.

Fitzgerald V (1996) 'Advice on Public Policy The Changing Balance Between the Public Service and Political Advisers' in J Disney and JR Nethercote (eds) *The House on Capital Hill*, Federation Press.

Fletcher GP (1993) *Loyalty: An Essay on the Morality of Relationships*, Oxford University Press.

Fox A (1974) *Beyond Contract: Work, Power and Trust Relations*, Faber.

Freedom of Information Act 1992 (Qld).

Friedman M (1953) *Essays in Positive Economics*, University of Chicago Press.

Friedman M (1970) 'The Social Responsibility of Business is to Increase its Profits', *New York Times Magazine*, September 13.

Fuller LL (1969) *The Morality of Law*, Yale University Press.

Gabarro JJ (1978) 'The Development of Trust, Influence and Expectations' in AG Athos and JJ Gabarro (eds) *Interpersonal Behaviour: Communication and Understanding in Relationships,* Prentice-Hall.

Gallagher J (1992) 'Administrative Law Review in Veterans' Affairs: The impact of the veterans' review board' in J McMillan (ed) *Administrative Law: Does the Public Benefit?*, Australian Institute of Administrative Law.

Giddens A (1979) *Central Problems in Social Theory: Action, Structure and Contradiction in Social Analysis*, University of California Press.

Giesen P (1992) 'De veiligheid van het academisch conformisme', *de Volkskrant*, 21 November.

Given J (1990) *State and Society in Medieval Europe: Gwynedd and Languedoc under Outside Rule*, Cornell University Press.

Goldhagen DJ (1996) *Hitler's Willing Executioners: Ordinary Germans and the Holocaust*, Knopf.

Goodsell CT (1994) *The Case for Bureaucracy: A Public Administration Polemic*, 3rd edn, Chatham House.

Gould DJ (1983) *The Effects of Corruption Administrative Performance: Illustration for Developing Countries*, World Bank.

Gouldner AW (1970) *The Coming Crisis of Western Sociology*, Equinox Books.

Green J (comp) (1982) *The Book of Political Quotes*, 1st edn, McGraw-Hill.

Gregory RJ, 'Bureaucratic "Psychopathology" and Technocratic Governance: Whither Responsibility' (1995) 4(1) *Hong Kong Public Administration* 17.

Grenfell Price A (ed) (1969) *The Explorations of Captain James Cook in the Pacific as told by Selections of his own Journals 1768–1779*, Angus & Robertson.

Griffiths J, 'The Price of Administrative Justice' (1989) 58 *Canberra Bulletin of Public Administration* 34.

Gruber J (1987) *Controlling Bureaucracies: Dilemmas in Democratic Governance*, University of California Press.

Guang W (1995) 'China's Reform and its Anti-Corruption', paper presented at the 3rd International Jerusalem Conference on Public Ethics, Jerusalem, 25–29 June.

Hales CP, 'What Do Managers Do? A Critical Review of the Evidence' (1986) 23(1) *Journal of Management Studies* 88.

Hansard, Adjournment Debate, 28 February 1993.

Haoucher v Minister for Immigration (1990) 169 CLR 648.

Hardwick E, 'The Menendez Show' (1994) *New York Review of Books*, 17 February.

Harman E, 'Accountability and Challenges for Australian Governments' (1994) 29 *Australian Journal of Political Science* 8.

Harmon M (1995) *Responsibility as Paradox: A Critique of Rational Discourse on Governance*, Sage.

Hasluck P (1968) *The Public Servant and Politics*, reprinted in the (1995) 78 *Canberra Bulletin of Public Administration* 91.

Heidenheimer AJ et al (eds) (1989) *Political Corruption*, Transaction Books.

Hogg R and B Hawker, 'The Politics of Police Independence' (1983) 8 *Legal Service Bulletin* 160.

Holmes L (1993) *The End of Communist Power: Anti-corruption Campaigns and Legitimation Crisis*, Oxford University Press.

Homans GC (1987) 'Behaviourism and After' in A Giddens and J Turner (eds) *Social Theory Today*, Stanford University Press.

Hood C, 'Beyond "Progressivism": A New "Global Paradigm" in Public Management?' (1996) 19(2) *International Journal of Public Administration* 151.

Hoogvelt AM (1976) *The Sociology of Developing Countries,* Macmillan.

Hosmer LT, 'Strategic Planning as if Ethics Mattered' (1994) 15 *Strategic Management Journal* 17.

House Resolution 250, Congressional Record H13078, November 16, 1995.

http://strategis.ic.gc.ca/sc_mrksv/engdoc/homepage.html (Canadian Lobbyists Code of Conduct).

Hummel RP (1994) *The Bureaucratic Experience: A Critique of Life in the Modern Organization,* 4th edn, St Martin's Press.

Huntington S (1968) *Political Order in Changing Societies,* Yale University Press.

Immigration Review Tribunal (1995) *Annual Report 1994–95*, Australian Government Publishing Service.

Independent Commission Against Corruption (ICAC) (1991) *The First Two Years: 19 Key Issues*, ICAC.

Ingraham PW (1995) *The Foundation of Merit: Public Service in American Democracy*, Johns Hopkins University Press.

Inspector General Act 1978 (US).

Institution of Professionals, Managers and Specialists (IPMS) (1996) *Civil Service 2000*, Institution of Professional, Managers and Specialists.

Ives D (1996) 'Ethics and Accountability in the Australian Public Service: The New Professionalism' in J Uhr (ed) (1996) *Ethical Practice in Government: Improving Organisational Management*, Federalism Research Centre, Australian National University.

Jabbra JG and OP Dwivedi (1988) *Public Service Accountability: A Comparative Perspective*, Kumarian Press.

Jackson M and R Smith, 'Inside Moves and Outside Views: An Australian Case Study of Elite and Public Perceptions of Political Corruption' (1996) 9 *Governance* 23.

Johnston M (1982) *Political Corruption and Public Policy in America,* Brooks/Cole.

Jones WT, 'Public Roles, Private Roles and Differential Moral Assessments of Role Performance' (1984) 94 *Ethics* 603.

Judicial Review Act 1991 (Qld).

Kaptein H, 'Local Heroes in Law's Empire, or The Importance of Integrity and Its Redundancy in Dworkin's *Law's Empire*' (1995a) 60 *Archiv für Rechts- und Sozialphilosophie* 88.

Kaptein H (1995b) *NRC Handelsblad*, 28 September.

Kaptein H (1996) 'Virtues of the Bar Unearthed, by Stretching Lawyers' Oaths To Their Proper Limits' in *Facing the Challenge: The Ethical Stretch*, Proceedings of the Seventh Annual National Conference on Applied Ethics, California State University Press.

Kassalow E (1993) *White-Collar Unionism in Selected European Countries: Issues and Prospects*, ILO Sectoral Activities Programme working paper, ILO.

Katsenelinboigen A (1983) 'Corruption in the USSR: Some Methodological Notes' in M Clarke (ed) *Corruption: Causes, Consequences, and Control,* Pinter.

Kaufman H (1967) *The Forest Ranger: A Study in Administrative Behavior*, Johns Hopkins University Press.

Kearns KP (1996) *Managing for Accountability: Preserving the Public Trust in Public and Nonprofit Organizations*, Jossey-Bass.

Kekes J (1987) 'Moral Tradition' in O Hanfling (ed) *Life and Meaning: A Reader*, Blackwell.

Kerhaghan K (1996) *The Ethics Era in Canadian Public Administration*, Canadian Centre for Management Development.

Kernot C (1998) 'Codes and Their Enforcement' in N Preston et al (eds) *Ethics and Political Practice: Perspectives on Legislative Ethics*, Routledge and Federation Press.

Kiel LD (1994) *Managing Chaos and Complexity in Government: A New Paradigm for Managing Change, Innovation, and Organizational Renewal*, Jossey-Bass.

Kim GC, 'A Model for a Reunified Korea: Political Unification and National Reintegration' (1995) 26 *Korea Observer* 21.

Kim YJ (1994) *Bureaucratic Corruption*, 4th edn, Chomyung Press.

Kim YJ (1996) *Korean Public Administration and Corruption Studies*, Hak Mun.

Kramer JM, 'Political Corruption in the USSR' (1977) 30 *Western Political Quarterly* 74.

Krislov S (1974) *Representative Bureaucracy*, Prentice-Hall.

Lawton A (1995) 'The Impact of Management Reforms on the Public Service Ethos: A Comparative Study of Australia and the UK', presented at the 3rd International Jerusalem Conference on Ethics in the Public Service, Jerusalem, 25–29 June.

Lawton A and A Rose (1994) *Organisation and Management in the Public Sector*, 2nd edn, Pitman.

Lawton A et al (1993) *Open and Distance Learning Materials for Front-Line Managers in Personal Social Services*, report for Social Services Inspectorate, Department of Health, Open University.

Le Vine VT (1975) *Political Corruption: The Ghana Case*, Hoover Institution Press.

Leys C, 'What is the Problem About Corruption?' (1965) 13 *Journal of Modern African Studies* 35.

Lobbying Disclosure Act 1995 (US).

Luban D (1988) *Lawyers and Justice: An Ethical Study*, Princeton University Press.

Luban D (1992) 'Legal ethics' in LC Becker and CB Becker (eds) *Encyclopedia of Ethics*, Garland.

Luhmann N (1995) *Social Systems (Writing Science)*, Stanford University Press.

Mackintosh M (1995) 'Putting Words into People's Mouths? Economic Culture and Its Implications for Local Governance', Open Discussion Paper in Economics no 9, Faculty of Social Sciences, Open University.

Management Advisory Board (1996) *Ethical Standards and Values in the Australian Public Service*, Australian Government Publishing Service.

Management Advisory Board/Management Improvement Advisory Committee (1996*) Ethical Standards and Values in the Australian Public Service,* Australian Government Publishing Service.

Mancuso M (1995) *The Ethical World of British MPs*, McGill-Queen's University Press.

Mancuso M (1998) 'Politicising Ethics' in N Preston et al (eds) *Ethics and Political Practice: Perspectives on Legislative Ethics*, Routledge and Federation Press.

Manning PK (1978) 'Rules, Colleagues and Situationally Justified Actions' in R Blakenship (ed) *Colleagues in Organisations,* John Wiley.

March JG and JP Olsen (1995) *Democratic Governance*, Free Press.

Mason Sir Anthony, 'That Twentieth-century Growth Industry: Judicial or tribunal review' (1989) 58 *Canberra Bulletin of Public Administration* 26.

Matson FW (1964) *The Broken Image: Man, Science and Society*, Doubleday Anchor.

Mauro P (1996) *The Effects of Corruption on Growth, Investment, and Government Expenditure*, Working Paper Series WP/96/98, International Monetary Fund.

McLaughlin ML et al (eds) (1992) *Explaining One's Self to Others: Reason-Giving in a Social Context*, Erlbaum Associates.

Merton RK (1957) *Social Theory and Social Structure*, Free Press.

168

Metcalfe L and S Richards (1990) *Improving Public Management*, 2nd edn, Sage.

MIEA v Wu Shiang Lang (1996) 70 ALJR 568.

Miller S (1997) *Police Ethics*, Allen & Unwin.

Minister for Arts, Heritage and Environment v Peko-Wallsend Ltd (1987) 75 ALR 218.

Minister for Immigration and Ethnic Affairs v Teoh (1995) 183 CLR 273.

Minister for Immigration, Local Government and Ethnic Affairs v Kurtovic (1990) 92 ALR 93.

Ministry of Supervision, PRC (1995) 'Administrative Supervision in China: Its Systems and Functions', submitted for the 3rd International Jerusalem Conference on Public Ethics, Jerusalem, 25–29 June.

Mintzberg H, 'The Manager's Job: Folklore and Fact' (1975) 53(4) *Harvard Business Review* 49.

Mintzberg H (1983) *Structure in Fives: Designing Effective Organisations,* Prentice-Hall.

Mintzberg H, 'Managing Government, Governing Management' (1996) 74(3) *Harvard Business Review* 75.

Moore D and R Wettenhall (eds) (1994) *Keeping the Peace: Police Accountability and Oversight*, University of Canberra.

Mosher FC (1982) *Democracy and the Public Service*, 2nd edn, Oxford University Press.

Munch R (1987) 'Parsonian Theory Today' in A Giddens and J Turner (eds) *Social Theory Today*, Stanford University Press.

Murray MA, 'Comparing Public and Private Management: An Exploratory Essay' (1975) 35(4) *Public Administration Review* 364.

Nathan RP (1983) *The Administrative Presidency*, John Wiley.

New Zealand Public Service Association (1996) *'The Workers' Audit: Downsizing the State Sector — Views and Experiences*, Report and Recommendations, New Zealand Public Service Association.

Nohria N and JD Berkley, 'Whatever Happened to the Take-Charge Manager?' (1994) 72(1) *Harvard Business Review* 128.

North Coast Environmental Council Inc v Minister for Resources (1994) 127 ALR 617.

Nozick R (1981) *Philosophical Explanations*, Harvard University Press.

Nye JS, 'Corruption and Political Development: A Cost Benefit Analysis' (1967) 61(2) *American Political Science Review* 417.

OECD (1995) *Governance in Transition: Public Management Reforms in OECD Countries*, OECD.

OECD (1996a) *Ethics in the Public Service: Current Issues and Practice,* PUMA(96)13, OECD.

OECD (1996b) *Integrating People Management into Public Service Reform*, OECD.

OECD (1996c) *OECD Economic Surveys 1995–6: New Zealand*, OECD.

OECD Development Assistance Committee (1993) *Orientations on Participatory Development and Good Governance*, OECD.

OECD Public Management Committee (1996) *Draft Programme of Work for 1997-1998*, OECD.

Office of the Prime Minister and Cabinet (1996) *Guide on Key Elements of Ministerial Responsibility*, Office of the Prime Minister and Cabinet.

Official Information Act 1982 (NZ).

Official Secrets Act 1951 (NZ).

Ogle v Strickland (1987) 71 ALR 41.

Osborne D and T Gaebler (1993) *Reinventing Government*, Plume.

Parker LD, 'Professional Accounting Body Ethics: In Search of the Public Interest' (1994) 19(6) *Accounting, Organisations and Society* 507.

Parker RS, 'Public Service Neutrality: A Moral Problem. The Creighton case' in BB Schaffer and DC Corbett (eds) (1965) *Decisions: Case Studies in Australian Administration*, FW Cheshire.

Parsons T (1951) *The Social System*, Free Press.

Peninsula Anglican Boys' School v Ryan (1985) 69 ALR 555.

Peters BG, 'Morale in the Public Service: A Comparative Inquiry' (1991) 57 *International Review of Administrative Sciences* 421.

Pidgeon S (1992) 'The Ombudsman and the Protection of Individual Rights' in J McMillan (ed) *Administrative Law: Does the Public Benefit?*, Australian Institute of Administrative Law.

Pollitt C (1993) *Managerialism and the Public Services: Cuts or Cultural Change in the 1990s?*, 2nd edn, Blackwell.

Pravda, 16 January 1975.

Preston N (ed) (1994) *Ethics for the Public Sector: Education and Training*, Federation Press.

Preston N et al (eds) (1998) *Ethics and Political Practice: Perspectives on Legislative Ethics*, Routledge and Federation Press.

Privacy Act 1993 (NZ).

Protection of Public Order Act 1961 (USSR).

Public Sector Ethics Act 1994 (Qld).

Public Service Act 1912 (NZ).

Public Service Board of NSW v Osmond (1986) 159 CLR 656.

Public Service Commission (1992) *A Framework for Human Resource Management in the Australian Public Service,* Public Service Commission.

Public Service Commission (1995) *Guidelines on Official Conduct of Commonwealth Public Servants*, Public Service Commission.

Public Services International (1994) *Managers and Public Sector Trade Unions*, Public Services International.

R v David Norman Jones (unreported, South Australia Supreme Court, 26 August 1992).

R v Hakopian (unreported, County Court of Vic, 8 August 1991).

R v Metropolitan Police Commissioner; ex parte Blackburn [1968] 2 QB 118.

R v Stanbrook (unreported, Vic Supreme Court, 16 March 1993).

R v Toohey; Ex parte Northern Land Council (1981) 151 CLR 170.

Rainey HG et al, 'Comparing Public and Private Organisations' (1976) 36(2) *Public Administration Review* 233.

Rauch J (1995) *Demosclerosis: The Silent Killer of American Government*, Times Books.

Rawls J (1971) *A Theory of Justice*, Harvard University Press.

Repatriation Commission and the Department of Veterans' Affairs (1995) *Annual Report 1994–95*, Australian Government Publishing Service.

Ridley FF, 'The New Public Management in Europe: Comparative Perspectives' (1996) 11(1) *Public Policy and Administration* 16.

Right to Life Association Inc v Secretary, Department of Human Services and Health (1994) 128 ALR 238.

Rodgers T and G Short (1992) 'The Impact of Administrative Law: Immigration and the Immigration Review Tribunal – I' in J McMillan (ed) *Administrative Law: Does the Public Benefit?*, Australian Institute of Administrative Law.

Rose R (1993) *Lesson-Drawing in Public* Policy, Chatham House.

Rosenbloom DH (1983) *Public Administration and Law: Bench v Bureau in the United States*, Marcel Dekker.

Rosenthal A (1996) *Drawing the Line: Legislative Ethics in the States*, University of Nebraska Press.

Rosenthal A (1998) ' "Appearance" as an Ethical Standard' in N Preston et al (eds) *Ethics and Political Practice: Perspectives on Legislative Ethics*, Routledge and Federation Press.

Rourke FE (1984) *Bureaucracy, Politics and Public Policy*, Little Brown.

Sampford C (1994) 'Institutionalising Public Sector Ethics' in N Preston (ed) *Ethics for the Public Sector: Education and Training*, Federation Press.

Sampford C and N Preston (forthcoming) *Institutionalising Public Sector Ethics*, Federation Press.

Sankey v Whitlam (1978) 142 CLR 1.

Sassella M, 'Administrative Law in the Welfare State. Impact on the Department of Social Security' (1989) 58 *Canberra Bulletin of Public Administration* 122.

Schick A (1996) *The Spirit of Reform: Managing the New Zealand State Sector in a Time of Change,* State Services Commission.

Schön D (1983) *The Reflective Practitioner: How Professionals Think In Action*, Basic Books.

Schröder HM (1989) *Managerial Competence: The Key to Excellence,* Kendall-Hunt.

Senate [US] Resolution 158, Congressional Record S10897, July 28, 1995.

Shaman JM et al, 'The 1990 Code of Judicial Conduct: An Overview' (1990) 74 *Judicature* 16.

Simis KM (1982) *The Corrupt Society: The Secret World of Soviet Capitalism,* Simon and Schuster.

Simons R, 'Control in an Age of Chaos' (1995) 73(2) *Harvard Business Review* 80.

Skinner BF (1971) *Beyond Freedom and Dignity*, Knopf.

Skolnick JH and JJ Fyfe (1993) *Above the Law: Police and the Excessive Use of Force*, Free Press.

SKTF (Swedish Union of Local Government Officers) (1994) *Code of Conduct for Public Services Managerial Staff,* SKTF.

South Australia v O'Shea (1987) 163 CLR 378.

Spong G (1995) *NRC Handelsblad*, 16 September .

State Services Commission (1991) *Report of the Review of State Sector Reforms*, State Services Commission.

Steinberg SS and DT Austen (1990) *Government, Ethics and Managers: A Guide to Solving Ethical Dilemmas in the Public Sector,* Quorum Books

Sternberg E (1994) *Just Business: Business Ethics in Action,* Warner Books.

Stewart J and S Ranson, 'Management in the Public Domain' (1988) 8(1–2) *Public Money & Management* 13.

Sturgess G, 'The Australian Public Sector: Another View' (1993) 75 *Canberra Bulletin of Public Administration* 84.

Sullivan WM (1995) *Work and Integrity: The Crisis and Promise of Professionalism in America*, Harper-Business.

Thompson DF (1995) *Ethics in Congress: From Individual to Institutional Corruption*, Brookings Institute.

Thompson JD (1967) *Organizations in Action: Social Science Bases of Administrative Theory*, McGraw-Hill.

Thompson V (1975) *Without Sympathy or Enthusiasm*, University of Alabama Press.

Torkunov A (1992) 'Bureaucracy and Policy in the Socialist Countries' in *Proceedings of the International Conference of Bureaucracy and Policy: A Comparative Perspective*, KAPA.

Uhr J (1992) 'Public Accountabilities and Private Responsibilities: The Westminster World at the Crossroads', presented at Annual Meeting of the American Political Science Association, Chicago, IL, 3–6 September.

Uhr J, 'Redesigning Accountability: From Muddles to Maps' (1993) 63(2) *Australian Quarterly* 1.

Uhr J (ed) (1996) *Ethical Practice in Government: Improving Organisational Management*, Federalism Research Centre, Australian National University.

UN Doc GA Res 51/59, 12 December 1996.

Vaughan D (1996) *The Challenger Launch Decision: Risky Technology, Culture, and Deviance at NASA*, University of Chicago Press.

Volker D, 'The Effect of Administrative Law Reform on Primary Level Decision-making' (1989) 58 *Canberra Bulletin of Public Administration* 112.

Vrachnas J (1992) 'The Impact of Administrative Law: Immigration and the Immigration Review Tribunal – II' in J McMillan (ed) *Administrative Law: Does the Public Benefit?*, Australian Institute of Administrative Law.

Waddington PAJ (1991) *The Strong Arm of the Law*, Clarendon Press.

Waldo D (1971) *Public Administration in a Time of Turbulence*, Chandler Press.

Walsh P (1989) 'Equities and Inequities in Administrative Law' (1989) 58 *Canberra Bulletin of Public Administration* 29.

Warwick DP (1981) 'Ethics of Administrative Discretion' in JL Fleishman et al (eds) *Public Duties: The Moral Obligations of Public Officials*, Harvard University Press.

Watson JB (1958) *Behaviorism*, University of Chicago Press.

Werner SB, 'New Direction in the Study of Administrative Corruption' (1983) 43(2) *Public Administration Review* 146.

Whitton E (1989) *The Hillbilly Dictator*, ABC Books.

Wilson H (1998) 'Ethics Counsellor to the Government: The Canadian Experience' in N Preston et al (eds) *Ethics and Political Practice: Perspectives on Legislative Ethics*, Routledge and Federation Press.

Wilson JQ, 'The Economy of Patronage' (1961) 69(4) *Journal of Political Economy* 369.

Wolf S (1984), 'Ethics, Legal Ethics, and the Ethics of Law' in D Luban (ed) *The Good Lawyer: Lawyers' Roles and Lawyers' Ethics*, Rowman & Allanheld.

Wood D (1996) *Judicial Ethics: A Discussion Paper*, Australian Institute of Judicial Administration

Woodward L (1994) 'Does Administrative Law Expect Too Much of "The Administration"' in S Argument (ed) *Administrative Law & Public Administration: Happily married or living together under the same roof?*, Australian Institute of Administrative Law.

World Bank (1996) 'Legal Institutions and the Rule of Law' in *World Development Report 1996: From Plan to Market*, World Bank.

Zifcak S (1994) *New Managerialism: Administrative Reform in Whitehall and Canberra*, Open University Press.

Index

(NB: All cases and statutes are listed under their respective jurisdictions)

Organisation for Economic Cooperation and Development
 anti-corruption policies, 142
 encouragement of uniform ethics rules, 88
 Public Management Service, 147
Parsons, Talcott, 74
Police
 accountability of, 49
 authority of police, 41, 44ff
 civil and criminal liability of officers, 46
 corruption *see* Corruption
 discretion in policing, 41, 43
  de facto powers, 48
  exercising discretion, 47ff
 harmful methods, deployment of, 49
 individual officer's responsibility, 44ff
 joint police/community institutional structures, 50
 original authority, doctrine of, 46
 structural reform in NSW, 38
Political sphere, ethics in, 13, 18
 ethics as essential part, 19
 Inter-American Convention Against Corruption, 88
 international initiatives, 88
 politicisation of public service, 18, 20
 public cynicism regarding politicians, 19
 undertaking by governments, attitude of courts, 133
 US experience, 87
Principles of public life in Nolan Report (UK), 16
Privacy concerns in training, 151, 160
Privatisation and commercialisation
 challenge to ethical standards, 18, 21
 need for open competition, 141
Professional ethics
 autonomous ethics, criticism of, 27
 legal profession, in the *see* Legal professional ethics
Public role, concept of, 62
Public sector managers
 see also Business practices in the public sector; Managerialism
 accountability of, 143
 codes
  enforceability, 146
  importance, 138ff
 competing loyalties, 138
 consultation with staff and unions, 145
 'gagging' clauses in employment contracts, 140
 leadership, 144
 politicians, relationship with, 143
 private sector practices, 142
 privatisation, contracting out, etc, 141
 public sector values, incorporation of, 140ff
 trade union perspective, 137ff
 training in ethics, 145 *see also* Training in ethics
 transparency, demand for, 142